Praise for
Adrenaline Junkie

"*Adrenaline Junkie* is a raw and harrowing memoir that brilliantly combines great sensitivity with brutal honesty. Les Edgerton is never afraid to reveal his vulnerability—and culpability—as he takes us on a head-spinning ride through the bizarre and terrifying experiences in a life that was often defined by violence. The result is a breathtaking page-turner that will keep readers hooked from page one and will never let them go."
—Lisa Lieberman Doctor, former Warner Bros. prodco president, president of Robin Williams prodco, Blue Wolf Productions

"Filled with stories of knifings, armed robberies, brutal prison fights, and Charles Manson (yes, that Charles Manson!), Edgerton proves that life can be stranger (and certainly more violent) than fiction. But Edgerton isn't just a guy with a tough story to tell. He's a poet who startles you with sentences both stark and darkly beautiful. An astonishing accomplishment."
—Jon Bassoff, author of *Corrosion*

"*Adrenaline Junkie* is the compelling, beautifully written story of an extraordinary man who has lived on both sides of the tracks. Les Edgerton achieves a sort of sainthood among sinners, an apotheosis of rebellion and force, much like Harcamone at Fontevrault, or a hero in a Johnny Cash song, a huge, Promethean work of major significance and scale."
—Richard Godwin, critically acclaimed author

"A Hillbilly Elegy with a deep, pulsing heart, *Adrenaline Junkie* makes sense of one man's life while showing us all new aspects of our own."
—Jenny Milchman, *USA Today* bestselling and Mary Higgins Clark Award-winning author

"No one can accuse Les of being a 'crime tourist.' He's lived the life, done the bird, and now he's written the book. *Adrenaline Junkie* should be on any prospective (or established) crime writer's list. An entertaining, darkly-rendered tale of one man's adventures in the very belly of the beast."
—Tony Black, author of *Her Cold Eyes*

"*Adrenaline Junkie* will be required reading for crime writers one day, a bible for future authors to study rebellion and the human spirit, that smart-ass spark inside us all that doesn't like taking orders from parents, teachers, and even the law. Author of *The Rapist* and *The Bitch*, two of the most profound noir novels published, an ex-criminal and former prison inmate, Edgerton knows what makes all of us tick, and how, with not much of a shove, any one of us could end up behind bars. One of the most fascinating autobiographies you will ever read: from professional thief and pimp to award-winning author and teacher."
—Jack Getze, author of the award-winning Austin Carr Mysteries

"Sometimes shocking, often poignant, occasionally distasteful, frequently funny, and always brutally honest, *Adrenaline Junkie* tells the story of one man's harrowing yet ultimately successful quest for redemption. Written with razor-sharp clarity, Edgerton's memoir is a triumph."
—Robert Rotstein, author of *We, the Jury*

"*Adrenaline Junkie* is at once heartbreaking as it is funny, and just plain sick. A masterful work that will be lauded by both writers and the general reading public alike."
—Vincent Zandri, *New York Times* and *USA Today* bestselling and Thriller Award-winning author

"Edgerton is a back-alley Kerouac. Walk away from this knowing that your life-defining moments were his slow Tuesdays."
—Liam Sweeny, author of
Presiding Over the Damned

"In a way, Edgerton already wrote *Adrenaline Junkie* in his crime novels. With the veneer of fiction removed, his always entertaining, often enlightening, sometimes infuriating and unapologetic stories hit even harder. Without any doubt, Edgerton is one of the great storytellers of fiction—and now non-fiction."
—Benjamin Sobieck, author of
The Writer's Digest Guide to Firearms and Knives

"Having survived an American Gothic horror story of a childhood, unrepentant former thief, dope dealer, hedonist, Navy hellraiser, and porn actor, Les Edgerton—now a writer and teacher—tells a tale of many tales: If Scheherazade were an old pirate who got away with the gold, this would be his opus."
—Earl Javorsky, author of *Down to No Good*

"Les Edgerton's expertly told memoir is in turns tragic, thrilling, funny and heart-breaking. *Adrenaline Junkie* is a powerful blend of coming-of-age story, family drama and low-life crime thriller."
—Paul D. Brazill, author of *Last Year's Man*

"Edgerton has lived a life most of us only write about. That he's actually lived it and has the chops to deliver such a vividly drawn memoir gives me a raging case of writer's envy."
—Maegan Beaumont, award-winning author

"How often is a memoir genuinely astounding? A reformed outlaw takes us through his harsh rural childhood, working harder before he was twelve than most of us ever will. There follows armed robbery, pimping, drug dealing, rape in prison, narrowly avoiding a hellcat's castration attempt, suicide foiled by the rope breaking, a walk on part for Charles Manson and his creepy serial killer mate—who got short shrift from our host. And so much more…So many startling sentences: 'She was going to be his last fuck before the operation and I was going to be his first after he became a woman.' 'It was then Charles Manson started to contact me…' There's a satisfying twist late on after he becomes a family man so this fascinating book has just the right ending. Essential reading. Makes Bukowski seem like Donny Osmond."

—Mark Ramsden, author of
The Dark Magus and the Sacred Whore

"A tryst with Brit Ecklund, a shoot-out in a deserted high school, robbing a laundromat in front of a patrol car. Those are just a few moments is Les Edgerton's checkered past. He went from a Huck Finn-like childhood in Texas, the swinging sixties as a criminal, time in Indiana's Pendleton prison, and eighties excess in New Orleans, with little slowing him down until a good woman found a way. Funny, harrowing, and poignant in spots, reading *Adrenaline Junkie* is like being lucky enough to sit at the bar next to that guy who has lived a lot of stories and knows how to tell them. Yes, Les Edgerton was an adrenaline junkie and he always knew where to get a fix."

—Scott Montgomery,
MysteryPeople Crime Fiction Coordinator

ADRENALINE JUNKIE
A Memoir

ALSO BY LES EDGERTON

The Genuine, Imitation, Plastic Kidnapping
The Rapist
The Bitch
Just Like That
Bomb! (formerly The Perfect Crime)
Mirror, Mirror (*)
The Death of Tarpons

Short Story Collections
Monday's Meal
Lagniappe

Writer's How-to Craft Books
Finding Your Voice
Hooked

Sports Books
Surviving Little League (co-authored with son Mike when he was twelve)
Perfect Game USA and the Future of Baseball

Other books on business, hairstyling, etc.

(*) - forthcoming

LES EDGERTON

ADRENALINE JUNKIE
A Memoir

Copyright © 2018 by Les Edgerton

All rights reserved. No part of the book may be reproduced in any form or by any electronic or mechanical means, including information storage and retrieval systems, without permission in writing from the publisher, except by a reviewer who may quote brief passages in a review.

This is a work of creative nonfiction. The events are portrayed to the best of the author's memory. While all the stories in this book are true, some names and identifying details have been changed to protect the privacy of the people involved.

Down & Out Books
3959 Van Dyke Rd, Ste. 265
Lutz, FL 33558
www.DownAndOutBooks.com

Photo taken by Mary Edgerton
Cover design by Lance Wright

ISBN: 1-948235-41-2
ISBN-13: 978-1-948235-41-9

Artists are here to disturb the peace.
—James Baldwin

Ugliness is beauty at rest.
—Jean Genet

FOREWORD

I first came across Les Edgerton through his how-to craft books, *Hooked* and *Finding Your Voice*. Those books offered a wealth of writing advice. So, when I heard the author would be a staff member at the Writer's Retreat Workshop (WRW), I signed up. No one told me I should bring my seat belt.

Les shared his tremendous knowledge of the craft with a passion that declared: This is how I see it; you can take what I say and let it benefit you, or you can ignore it and face the consequences. Yet, through his bluntness, a kindness and gentleness of heart shined through—he's not as good at hiding this side of him as he thinks.

When I found out WRW would be in my hometown and Les would again be a faculty member, I spoke with a local writer's group and suggested they take advantage of the opportunity to host him. An adjacent workshop would allow the group's members to learn from Les without investing the time and money required for WRW.

The group refused to host him.

The reason was simple: Les was a convicted criminal.

Les shrugged off the rejection, but not me. I invited him to lead a private workshop for twenty colleagues in my home and to stay with me and my family. Les made two unsolicited pledges.

"I promise not to smoke in your house." A gracious gesture for a chain smoker. And, with his typical self-deprecating humor, he said, "I promise not to steal anything—big."

Les does tend to flaunt his checkered past.

Adrenaline Junkie, however, is infinitely more than a renowned, multi-award-winning author entertaining with his life history. Les understands that backstory matters. It influences the present. So, he journeyed through his past seeking answers for why he was the way he was. Seeking answers for his thrill-seeking, devil-may-care, often self-destructive, behaviors. Seeking a sense of personal peace.

Les once asked me why I thought he felt compelled to be the best he could be in all his endeavors—legal or otherwise. He said he lost interest after he achieved the acme, became bored and moved on to something else. What drove him to excel, then flee success, only to strive for supremacy in another field?

Adrenaline Junkie holds the answers. With nothing held back. With his life-saving humor, an indomitable spirit, and a fierce courage to expose the ugly and painful. Like the tough, raw, vulnerable characters Les writes about in his short stories and novels, he exposes us to a man fighting against family, society, and his own sense of injustice. Fighting for a moment—regardless of how fleeting—to feel in control of his life. And, as uncomfortable at times, as Les's life adventure may be for us to witness, we come away grateful he took us with him.

So settle back. Turn the page. Meet a real-life, twenty-first-century Renaissance man. A real-life Adrenalin Junkie.

—Marjorie Brody,
Author of Twisted

A BIT OF A PROLOGUE...

When I was incarcerated in Pendleton, we didn't have TVs in our cells, only a pair of headphones and a jack to plug them into. We had an inmate DJ who had a prison music show that was just for us. Every night at exactly midnight, he'd play the same song and all of D Cellblock would get quiet while everyone listened to it and our own private thoughts. At the same time, a train would pass by and blow its whistle. Every night. The only other sound was some guy who always sobbed on the tier above me. Usually, when someone starts bawling like that, all kinds of catcalls ring out, cursing the guy or making fun of him. Not this guy, not at this particular time of night. Everyone respected his pain.

The song? Porter Wagoner's "The Green, Green Grass of Home."

I listened to this for my first six months in the joint. Never missed a night. Midnight. Wagoner singing. Train whistle blowing. This guy weeping loudly.

And then, one night, we didn't hear the guy sobbing. In the morning, after we got back from chow, here came a bunch of hacks, carrying a body down the tier walk wrapped in a bloody sheet. It was this guy. He'd cut his wrists the night before.

Postscript: A couple of years later, I'd just gotten my driver's license and bought a clunker. I was driving down the road and the song came on the radio. All of a sudden, I was blinded by uncontrollable tears and had to pull off the road before I ran into somebody.

Isn't it funny that at the time of your misery you don't feel the emotion, but later, when you're in a good place, you do?

And, that's what this book is about. A lot of moments in my life—some good and some bad—and how they formed me. I've had a chaotic life and that's been on purpose. I've consciously sought out as many experiences as I was able to and I tended toward seeking out dangerous experiences—that's what triggers the adrenaline and adrenaline is my drug of choice. This covers my existence up until about the age of forty. I've lowered the volume across the board, but even so I've run across a couple of early readers who told me they found parts hard to believe. Well, I promise you this isn't an account such as James Frey might write—it's all true. I've discovered that people often tend to judge others' lives by their own. If they didn't do it or couldn't imagine doing it, they just can't accept that some of these things happened to another. But…they did. I had a good friend, the now-deceased author Bob Stewart, who read this just before he passed away. Bob said he bought everything in it except the time where I went to bed with three different girls. Well, he was right. There'd been more than three that day. I'd cut a couple of them out for just that reason. I knew most guys hadn't experienced anything like that and might think I was exaggerating. When Bob told me he didn't buy that event, I went back and wrote it the way it actually happened. I knew then that there would be those who wouldn't believe some of the things I'd done. So I might as well get down what actually happened. Sometimes you just can't win. And the fact is, I've left an awful lot out. And, what I included I've made it a point to lower the volume, not raise it.

One of my wives, after we went our separate ways, said to me one day: "You just married me for material, didn't you?"

Guilty as charged. That's kind of what I've been doing all my life. On purpose.

Hope you enjoy the read.

I
GROWING UP

When I was eleven, my father walked into his bedroom and caught me stuffing several of the coins he collected into my pockets. Most of them were foreign ones he'd picked up overseas during World War II. I have no idea how I planned to spend English half-pence or German Reichspfennig coins or if I even planned to spend them at all. I just wanted them because I thought I could take them without getting caught. After he put his belt away, and I pulled my pants back up, my father made me take four of the smallest coins and swallow them.

"You want them, you've got them," he said. "You need to remember this. An Edgerton doesn't steal. None of the Edgertons have ever been thieves."

My mother came up while I choked them down and stood there, tears dripping quietly down her cheeks. She didn't say a word. My father was the king of his castle and she was just a slightly-higher-placed vassal than my sister and me.

She cried...but not *this* tough, eleven-year-old *criminal*. I came close, but I choked down my tears along with the coins once I saw her begin to weep. I knew in that instant if I were to begin bawling that I'd become as weak as her and what that would promise for my future. That I didn't break down made my father more angry than my theft.

"I ought to make you eat them all," he said.

"I'd like some salt then," I said. "And a glass of water." I knew what his reaction would be. Instead of being fearful, I felt a power surge through me. I also slipped into a calm I had never felt before. Fear disappeared, just plain vanished. He could hurt my flesh but he could never dominate me as he had the other members of my family. The knowledge I gained in that instant was my earliest reward for being a thief. It was also the beginning of a new-found ability to disassociate and go to a place where emotions vanished into vapor. My breathing became measured and even, my heart rate slowed.

He cursed and undid his belt again.

The calmer I became, the more enraged he became.

I was in control, not only of myself, but of him and the situation. I'd discovered a valuable tool to dealing with life.

When the coins came out a day or so later, I reached into the stool and mushed the turds with my fingers, extracting them one by one. I took the bar of my father's Lava he used every day after work and held it under the tap until the dried swirls of his oil and grime were rinsed off and then scrubbed the coins with it. For an hour I scoured them until they gleamed and shone a dull, lucent copper and zinc and aluminum. He never asked what happened to them and I have them to this day.

So it begins.

My childhood memories are sketchy. One of my former wives, Sheila, can remember her third grade teacher, for instance—me, I can't remember for sure what *state* we were living in when I was in the third grade, much less some teacher's name. Especially since I had several teachers, most likely, and lived in several states hat year. Our family was like the wind, blowing first here, then there. Home base was my mother's hometown of Freeport, Texas, although every couple of years we'd pack up a U-Haul or cram our latest used station wagon with our few possessions and head north to South Bend, Indiana, where my father was from. We were usually cruising on bald tires and almost always went through a series of flats and car troubles.

Everything we owned would be in the car and my parents spent a lot of time on those trips figuring out mileage and checking their stock of cash and worrying out loud if the car would give out before our money did.

We zigzagged back and forth like that, living the majority of the time in Texas until I was in the eighth grade and from then on my family lived in Indiana. Before that, We were never in one place for more than two or three years at the most, and even when we lived in one town, we were constantly moving from house to house. I tried to add it up once, and came up with thirteen schools I'd attended before high school, and I'm pretty sure I missed a few. My brother and sisters hated the moves, but I loved all of them, except when we moved from Texas. Texas was never boring, but Indiana always was. I found out quickly I could reinvent myself each time and avoid the social mistakes of the former school.

In Texas, we lived in the house with my grandparents. Grandpa Herman Vincent worked as a supervisor for the Freeport Sulfur Company. In my memory I see him in his yellow hard-hat and work khakis. What I remember most is that he was extremely quiet and stoic, especially compared to my Grandma Louise who was a ball of furious energy. The only other clear image I have of Herman is of the months before he finally died of cancer, of him sitting in the bathroom in the tub and my mom sitting on the stool weeping as she administered his shot of morphine for pain. I don't know why they chose that setting for their nightly ritual but they did. My memory is very clear of walking by the open door and seeing them so engaged and my mother spotting me, shaking her head vigorously at me to indicate I shouldn't be there, throwing a washcloth over his privates, and shoving the door closed. I assumed he sat in the tub because the warm water helped sooth him. I remember thinking it odd that he was nude in the bathtub with my mother there, but as a little kid you accept things like that. Now, I'm not sure what to make of that. He wasn't her birth father, but her stepfather.

I never recall him complaining or making a sound. From time to time, a look would come over his face and sweat would bead his forehead and he'd have to sit down, but he never made a sound. He was just strong and silent, the way real men were supposed to be in those days.

Grandma Vincent was a presence in all of our lives. According to Mom, she'd been abandoned by her husband when my mom and Uncle Buddy were just little kids. By dint of an iron will and the strongest work ethic I'd ever seen—besides my own father's—had succeeded in opening and running two very successful businesses: a restaurant/bar and a taxicab company. This was during an era when such things were almost unheard of for a woman. Somewhere along the way, she'd met and married Herman, who my mother always considered her "real" father.

Long before I was born, Grandma had begun her business as an ice cream shop and then a restaurant, but by the time I came on the scene in 1943, it had evolved into a drinking establishment where you could also get a great meal. They served everything from Texas-sized T-bone steaks to flounder, shrimp and red snapper to homemade gumbo. Even though beer was the restaurant's main moneymaker, it still went by the original name, "The Sweet Shop."

Freeport, as well as being a large base for the shrimping and sport-fishing industries, was also a port for off-loading Texas gas, oil, sulfur and other chemicals for the rest of the world. There was a constant stream of Norwegian and Russian oil tankers, and other international ships, arriving daily to load products from the Dow Chemical and Freeport Sulfur plants as well as from the oil refineries from up the road in Port Arthur.

Trying to raise two kids, Grandma saw the money to be made in catering to both foreign sailors and the local shrimpers, many of whom seemed to live for the joys of booze, so she turned the place into a tavern. Texas' drinking laws went by counties, and Brazoria County was a "dry" county, meaning they could only sell beer and wine. When sailors got as drunk as they could on suds, they were after harder stuff and the closest place you could get whiskey or vodka was either in Galveston or Houston, both about fifty-odd miles from Freeport.

Seeing a golden opportunity, Grandma introduced a cab service to take advantage of her customers' thirst. The Star Taxicabs would go out to the docks, pick up a load of sailors and take them to the Sweet Shop. After gorging themselves on fresh shrimp, flounder and gumbo and bottles of Jax and Lone Star Beer, along about midnight or so sailors were ready for Galveston Island or sometimes Houston, where they could not only purchase a bottle of hard stuff, but they could continue partying. Especially in Galveston. It was the honky-tonk capital of East Texas at the time.

A woman creating a business single-handedly in the 1920s was virtually unheard of. She worked in both the restaurant and the cab businesses, twelve to fourteen hours a day, seven days a week. A short, squat woman, built like a fireplug, she wore her hair in a net, a pair of wire-rimmed glasses and a cigarette holder on a chain around her neck. Except for one time, when my grandfather died, I never saw her dressed in anything but her white uniform. She smoked Pall Malls and Old Gold Long filtertips, and with the addition of her holder, you had to be careful to stay out of range if you didn't want to end up with a live ember in your eye or burn scars on your face. She had a habit of swinging around abruptly with a foot-and-a-half-long lit cigarette and people would duck. Every once in a while, she'd catch someone and sparks and cuss words would fly. As well as laughter from the others not wounded.

She kept a sawed-off Stan Musial-model Louisville Slugger behind the bar. I watched more than once when, after attempting to reason with a belligerent drunk to no avail, she'd reach over, grab the miscreant by the hair, yank her to him, and crank him over the noggin. Someone would haul his unconscious body out to the back where she had a weed-grown lot with a trailer one of the help lived in, and let him sleep it off. Occasionally, the guy would wake up and stagger back in and resume drinking. As long as he didn't cause further trouble, Grandma let him be.

As tough as she was, there was another side to Grandma. She fit right in with proper society. I remember when I was little, once a year she'd take me, Mom and my sister Jo with her to New Orleans to the department store, Maison Blanche. The store would be closed to the public that day, open only to Grandma. We'd sit in a room where we were served tea and cookies and models would parade in showing various styles. Grandma would pick out a bunch of dresses for her, Mom and Jo and spend several thousand dollars. I had to sit there and watch the show with them, but I hated it. It wasn't until I was older that I found out they didn't close the doors for just anybody. Only high-rollers. When she died, they found over twenty fur coats in her closet and I don't ever remember seeing her wear one. Eventually, my dad made Mom quit going because he couldn't pro-vide anything like that. They had a big fight about it and that was the end of it. I don't think Grandma ever went again after that.

Grandma wouldn't serve Yankees. She'd kick a northerner right out of the restaurant. Not many people came in from the north anyway, except a few fishermen after tarpon, as Freeport wasn't exactly a tourist town. Yankees had to find somewhere else to eat, because at the first hint of a nasal quality to their speech, out they'd go—asked politely at first to leave, but if that request evoked an argument or resistance, then she'd get tough. They always ended up leaving. I remember one time she'd told a Yankee to leave and he yelled that she couldn't do that. He said he was going to the police station and file a complaint. Sue her. Grandma just looked at him and said, "I'll save you a trip. The sheriff's right back there." She pointed to a back booth, where, sure enough the sheriff was sitting, easily visible in his khaki uniform. "Come on. I'll introduce you."

He left.

Grandma always hated the fact that my mom had married a Yankee. Some people in Freeport wouldn't even tolerate Texans from other parts of the state. East Texas is southern, while North Texas is...almost as bad as Yankeeland. And, to someone from South Texas, Dallas might as well be in Canada.

Yankees were pretty much hated by just about everyone I knew in Freeport. Every once in a while, they'd show a movie with a Civil War theme at the only theater in town—conveniently, for me, it was located next door to the restaurant—and whenever the Rebels scored any kind of victory over the Union, every man, woman and child in the audience would stand up and cheer at the top of their lungs. Except maybe the colored folks up in the balcony...We'd hear a murmur from that part of the theater but never any boos. That would have led to trouble for them.

I loved that movie house. Because of my grandmother's influence, I was able to land a job lugging the new movie reels up a flight of steep stairs to the projection room. Each week, a couple of new movies would arrive, along with that week's serial episode, cartoons, and a news reel. And those reels were big! There's an old picture somewhere, showing me lugging a reel up the stairs and all you can see of me are my fingers and the top of my head. My favorite serial was *Sheena, Queen of the Jungle*. It was the first time I remember being sexually aroused. I was eight, almost nine.

I asked the movie owner to pay me with free movie passes. My mother made me tithe ten percent of whatever I made to her church, and this way I got to keep it all.

My sister Jo and I were raised mostly by a series of black nannies. From my child's point-of-view, they all seemed enormous. One thing for sure, they were the Law. That was the Southern way. I don't remember Mom spanking me very much, if at all when we lived in Freeport. She was usually too busy talking to God. Discipline fell to my nanny. One, I remember in particular, Inez. I'd guess her weight at about three hundred pounds and I'd say she was at least seven feet tall, but that's probably an exaggeration. A strong woman in personality, as all the women from my childhood seemed, she was not to be messed with. If she said "sit," you sat. Right where you were.

Grandma would have our nannies switch jobs, back and forth, depending on what she needed. First, one might be a cook or dishwasher at the Sweet Shop. One job they couldn't have was waitressing. That had to be a white woman. Blacks could cook the food then but they couldn't serve it. Then, she would be a maid at the house. Eventually, she became our nanny, at least, some did.

I think part of the reason we were raised by nannies is that our mother didn't really know how to take care of kids, raise a family. Her own mother—Grandma Louise—had always packed my mother and her brother, Uncle Buddy, off to boarding schools. Neither of them had ever spent more than a week or two out of the year with their mother and stepfather. Grandma was too busy with work to fret over kids. And, when she and Uncle Buddy did live at home, Grandma had nannies to take care of them just like Mom did for us.

One day when I was about ten, Inez came to my dad at the restaurant. This day, he was driving a cab since a ship was in port—one of their busier times.

"Mister Edgy," she said, calling my dad by his nickname. "I want you to take me to the beach at Galveston. I think my husband's there with some gal. He's triflin' on me."

At that time, the beaches, along with everything else, were segregated. The blacks had their beach, white folks had theirs.

I didn't go along on the ride to Galveston, but I heard about what happened later. It seems Dad parked up off the beach (whites weren't allowed to go down on the colored beaches and vice versa) and Inez went down onto the sand looking for her husband. Dad didn't know Inez was packing a nine-shot .22 automatic. When she found her husband—sharing a beach blanket with his girlfriend—she stood there and methodically put all nine shots into his "triflin' body." Turned him into Swiss cheese. Didn't even look at the girl, who, if she was smart, was probably booking it down the beach as fast as she could truck. What was amazing was that the guy didn't die, even with nine pieces of hot lead in his body. Even more astounding, they stayed married. I don't think he messed around on her after that.

And she stayed my nanny.

There was a hearing of sorts. Dad, Mom, Grandma, Grandpa Herman and a lot of other folks testified as to her good character, and she was acquitted. The attitude was that black folks were always shooting and cutting each other and that was okay. If they messed with white folks, that was different.

Actually, that was the way most folks, black *and* white, solved their differences in those days. People didn't call the police that much but took care of things themselves.

The only black people I ever saw were my nannies and the kitchen help. Blacks just never made an appearance in our part of town, nor did Mexicans. Freeport was a sundown town, meaning people of color weren't allowed to be in the white part after sunset unless they had a legitimate job to do. Blacks and Mexicans lived in their own part of town, which was always referred to by us as "Niggertown." I don't know what the blacks called it—probably not that—and I didn't even know where it was. I'd never been there and didn't have a clue where it was. I can't recall ever seeing a black man or black child. Only my nannies or Grandma's cooks, dishwashers and maids. It never occurred to me to question any of this—it was just the way it was. The more I think about that, the more it feels really odd. It's like there were colored folks in the balcony of the movie theater but I don't remember ever seeing them arrive or depart at the theater and for some reason I don't even recall looking up to see them sitting there. They were just…invisible.

Adrenaline Junkie

* * *

One day after school—must have been eleven—I was sitting at a table in the Sweet Shop with Grandma, Inez, and the sheriff, Billy Watson (not his real name). Grandma was chewing Inez out for her showing me how to take the cap off my pop bottle with my teeth—chipped a front tooth doing that later.

The pay phone in the back rang and Inez got up to answer it. It was a call for Billy. I remember nearly every word of the conversation. "Oh, they are?" he said in his high, skinny voice. The way he said it, we knew it was something important. "I better get right out there, stop that." He hung up and came back to the table and said, "I believe I'll have another piece of that sweet 'tater pie." Inez got up to fetch it for him. "And, a glass of milk," he yelled to her. "Put an ice cube in it."

I remember thinking it was funny how he ate that pie—with little, tiny bites and little tiny sips of his milk. Finally, he finished, pushed back from the table, and announced, "I got to get out to Bryan Beach quick. They're beatin' some nigger out there, some white boys." He walked really slow to the door, went out, and climbed in his squad car and drove off as slow as could be.

After a few minutes, Grandma got up and said to Inez, "Well, you better clean this up." I saw Inez give my grandma a look and Grandma seemed to get mad. She said, "Well, Inez, Bryan is a white beach—you know that, child." Inez just kept looking at her, not picking up the dishes like she'd been told, and Grandma didn't say any more, just fetched her pack of Pall Malls in front of her, stuck one in the holder she kept around her neck and lit it.

Later that night, there was a news story about a black man from Houston they found dead out at Bryan Beach, killed by "unknown assailants" and then they interviewed Billy Watson who said there were no leads, but that "they'd get them. It don't matter what color a man is in this county, we don't tolerate murder."

I wrote a short story about this which appeared in my first story collection, *Monday's Meal*. I didn't understand everything that had happened at the time, but later on figured it all out.

When I was about twelve, Grandma let me be the night dispatcher for the cab company during my summer vacation. Most of the cabbies were drifters, alcoholics and small-time grifters who bootlegged whiskey and sold reefer on the side. My first night on the job, it being slow and all, they were having themselves some fun. A driver named Teddy started waving a dead rattlesnake at another cabbie named Lester who was terrified of snakes and told Teddy so. Again and again. Lester thought it was a live snake. After several minutes of tormenting his fellow driver, Teddy tossed the rattler at him. It wrapped around Lester's neck, whereupon Lester pulled out a pistol and shot Teddy in the throat. Killed him about as quick and as dead as it gets. There wasn't any question of that. At that point, it looked like my job as the dispatcher was to get on the phone and call the police, which I did. I remember thinking the whole thing was kind of cool.

Lester was acquitted, just like Inez. It was difficult to draw jail time in Texas at that time, it seems. Unless you were caught with marijuana. For a heinous crime like that, you could draw serious time. As for the shooting, the judge ruled it justifiable homicide and Lester left town shortly after. Probably didn't want to tempt his luck, as the man he'd shot had lots of friends and relatives in town.

By the time I was twelve, I had worked virtually every job the restaurant offered, from waiting on tables and serving beer to dishwashing. And if you worked for Grandma and were related, you were expected to work twice as hard, to provide an example for the others, meaning the blacks.

Even though my parents were very strict, in those days, nobody thought about such things as child molesters and kidnappers so no place was off limits for me. My best friend was Richard Barnes and we went everywhere on our bikes. We'd go fishing and swimming in the Brazos River, down by the shrimp docks and we'd ride out in the country and catch live rattlesnakes to sell to the local high school. They had an ongoing science project where they would buy live snakes and extract their venom and sell to labs that produced anti-venom serum. The going rate was fifty cents a snake, a lot more than you got for pop bottle empties at two cents each. You could get a sack full of rattlers easily in an afternoon.

One time, Richard told me he'd heard if you grabbed a snake by its tail and snapped it like a bullwhip, the head would pop off. The first one we caught, he had me hold its head down with the forked stick we used and he grabbed the tail. "Let 'er go," he said, and I did. He snapped it...and the snake disappeared. Just flat-out vanished. Richard stood there holding just its rattles. We were both having private little heart attacks. Carefully, we looked around, trying not to move a muscle. Finally, he spotted it about ten feet away. Coming toward us. Mad. At least I imagined it was mad. We didn't stick around to see if it was emotional or just confused.

We had an argument later where he maintained it was true about the head popping off—he just hadn't held it in the right place. He wanted to try it on another rattlesnake, but I talked him out of it. I don't really think he needed much of persuasion.

Richard and I and later on Tony Dorman, who'd moved to town and became one of our little gang, figured out a scam with pop bottles. We'd go out to the Piggly-Wiggly on Highway 288 where they stacked their empties along the side of the store in their wooden crates. One of us would be the look out. When the coast was clear, the other two would run up and grab a couple of crates each. We'd throw them in our bike baskets and make our escape.

Later, we'd put the bottles in large paper bags and take them back to the same store and sell them. Then, one day, we went to the store and they'd moved the bottles to the back room inside. That's when we began going after rattlesnakes in earnest.

Life was so much different then. There weren't as many laws, rules and regulations back then. There was a little medical clinic a block from where we lived and in the back, by the alley, they kept a pet alligator in an open pen. They'd feed it amputated body parts and we'd race home after school every day to see what they'd fed him that day. There were always bloody bandages in the gator's pen. Not exactly something that would be allowed in today's sanitized world. It was a thousand times better than TV.

Richard and I were out by the Dow Chemical plant and were playing on railroad cars on a sidetrack. I climbed up on a flatbed full of oyster shells on its way to be crushed and used for driveways and roads. It was a hot day and I fell asleep and Richard wandered off somewhere. While I slept, the train took off and I didn't wake up until it was a long way gone. I ended up in Dallas, a couple of hundred miles from Freeport, where someone from the railroad found me and turned me into the police.

When my dad drove up, several hours later, I was sure I was going to get a whipping.

I was right. No big deal. He applied the belt to me at about every opportunity he had and I was used to it.

Richard thought the whole thing was hilarious. "I saw the train take off," he told me later.

"Why didn't you yell at me?" I said.

"It was too funny," he said. "You were snoring to beat the band. I figured you'd end up in California and think you'd landed on another planet."

From time to time, I'd shine shoes to make money. Next door to the Sweet Shop was a honky-tonk named Red's after the one-armed red-headed owner who'd lost his limb to an alligator. Red catered to hard-core drunks and winos, and they were my best customers. Since kids were allowed in bars, I'd grab my shoe shine box and head for Red's and shine as many drunk's shoes as I cared to. They always tipped well—at least a dime and sometimes even a quarter. When you consider that fresh jumbo shrimp sold for a twenty cents a pound and you could get a Texas-sized T-bone and all the fixings for $2.95 in the early fifties, that was good money.

I also caddied at Freeport's municipal golf course. The bags were usually bigger than I was, but I loved it. In those days, there was no such thing as an allowance. If you wanted money, you figured out a way to earn it. I always tried to make extra since my mother made me tithe ten percent to the church of anything I made. I never considered lying to her about the amount I earned. Lying was the single worst sin you could commit in our house. I didn't even want to consider what might happen if I got caught lying about what I earned!

Richard and I would hunt and fish every minute we could. I had a pump air rifle and we would ride our bikes out to some property Dow Chemical had and hunt wood ducks in the marshes and bayous. We'd just shoot them on the water as they swam. The property was posted and there was a chain-link fence around what was probably at least a thousand acres or more, but we just dug a hole under it and used that. One time, his bike wasn't working, so we rode double on mine out to the marshes. For some reason, we got in an argument and he rode off on my bike, laughing. I told him to bring it back and he just laughed, so I pumped up my pellet rifle and shot him in the leg. The pellet buried itself in his calf and he bled like a stuck pig, but Richard was a tough kid. He just laughed and we made up and dug the pellet out with the tip of my hunting knife and went on our way.

Richard and I joined the Boy Scouts.

My Uncle Buddy gave me his Boy Scout Manual from when he'd been a scout, back in the thirties, and I read it over and over, cover to cover, dozens of times. I taught myself all the knots and spent hours trying to start fires by rubbing two sticks together—I never could.

After a few months, Richard dropped out, just before our troop went on a three-day camping trip to Garner State Park in south-central Texas. It was the coolest place I'd ever been. We went hiking and explored caves made of crystal. All of us went home with huge chunks we chipped out of the walls. I kept mine for years, but somewhere along the way, lost it.

They had a dance pavilion and we got to go there and it was there I heard my very first rock 'n roll song, "Maybelline" by Chuck Berry. Before that, all I'd ever heard was country music on Grandma's Wurlitzer and classical music on the home stereo that my mother played.

One of the things we did each afternoon was go swimming in the Frio River. There was a stretch they had roped off for use of our troop to swim in. It was shallow for about twenty feet out and then there was a steep drop-off, which was clearly marked. "If you can't swim, don't go near the drop-off," our scoutmaster warned.

I couldn't swim, but wouldn't admit that to anyone. I was terrified of the water, but I didn't let that stop me from getting as close to the edge of the drop-off as I could. This fat kid I'll call Waldo—I couldn't stand him; the guy was a born bully—came up to me and wanted to know why I wasn't out there swimming in the drop-off like the other kids who could swim. "I just don't feel like it," I said.

"You can't swim a lick, can you!" he taunted. He grabbed me and pulled me with him over the edge. We both went into the deep water and down, down, down. I scratched and fought like a wildcat. Somehow, I got my feet on top of his shoulders, holding him down, and I could see the light at the top and it looked at least twenty feet away.

    I remember thinking, just before I went out, that this was it. I was going to die. I recall clearly thinking that at this point my life was supposed to flash in front of my eyes, and it wasn't happening. I tried to force myself to make my life flash in front of my eyes. All I could remember was the time my sister Jo had fallen on a half-buried coffee can in a vacant lot we played in and cut her knee.

    Somebody pulled both of us out. They gave me and Waldo artificial respiration and brought us both back to life. All I remember is that everything was very peaceful, but the other Scouts said I was fighting like I was on Iwo Jima. I don't remember that part at all. They all knew what Waldo had done and were laughing about it, saying I'd got the best of his fat ass (no one else liked him either). They told me I'd been standing on his shoulders, shoving him down, and both of us were down deep.

    Waldo never fucked with me again.

    From then on, I would swim everywhere I could. It seemed to just come naturally to me.

    I quit Scouts shortly after that.

    One night, as I often did, I set up my pup tent in our backyard. I loved to sleep outdoors whenever I could. Around midnight, Richard showed up. I'd told him I was going to set it up earlier in the day and invited him over if he could. He crawled in and I could see he was trying his best to keep from crying. I asked him what the matter was and he told me his stepfather—a part-time shrimper and full-time alcoholic—had been wailing on his mother as he often did and Richard attacked him to try and protect his mom. The guy proceeded to beat Richard bloody. What really hurt was that his mother took her husband's side. I reached over to put my arm around him and give him a hug and at that exact moment, Dad thrust open the tent flap. He'd just come home from his shift of driving his cab for Grandma and I imagine he heard us talking.

    He went berserk, screaming at us that we were "little faggots" and began kicking me in the ribs. Richard scuttled away, lifting the tent bottom and he was gone. I got another beating—not a rare thing at all. I later wrote about the incident in my first novel, *The Death of Tarpons*.

Early on, it was discovered I was bright, had an I.Q. ranging from 158 to 163, depending on the day I took the test. They had me take it several times. The thing was, I read all the time. From the moment I learned, I was hardly ever without a book in my hands. Whatever turns my life took—and it took a few—the one constant was that I maintained a hunger to read.

By the time I was ten, eleven, I'd read hundreds and hundreds of books. Before junior high, I'd read all of Dostoevsky, Balzac, Dickens, Kafka—dudes like that. I gobbled up books, so many that I ran out of new material at the Freeport public library quickly. Grandma Vincent also had a terrific library. She owned such tomes as *The Rise and Fall of the Roman Empire*, which I went through at about the age of eight or nine. Most kids of my acquaintance—boys, especially—weren't into reading at all. They might glom onto a Hardy Boys mystery once in a while, but that was about it, for at least the kids I knew.

Reading caused me a lot of grief with my father. He constantly made remarks about "sissies who read." I don't remember him ever reading a book and in his spare time he'd rather be outside, working on a car. I tried to help him several times, but hated working on cars, more so when it was cold. Much rather be curled up inside with a book.

Of course I also had to read the Bible. Mom had us read at least three chapters a day on our own, and then every night we'd have family Bible reading hour, where she read and explained what the passages meant. As soon as we'd read through the Bible, starting at Genesis and ending with Revelations, we'd begin all over again. We read the Bible several hundred times during my childhood. We also had to memorize verses each week. I must have memorized hundreds of verses, but I can't remember any of them now.

Being above-average in intelligence and having read so much created other problems. Freeport Elementary skipped me from the fourth to the fifth grade. In the middle of the school year, we moved to Indiana, and South Bend's Oliver Grade School didn't believe in skipping, so back I went. Then, we'd move to another South Bend neighborhood and I'd go to Measle School and I'd get skipped again. Then, another move to Monroe School and...you get the picture. After a while, I just tuned out of school. No matter what grade they put me in, I'd already read all the books years before and none of the teachers seemed to really understand them anyway.

It was easier if I didn't get skipped in school anyway. Every time I did, my dad would openly sneer at the "little bookworm." He'd talk constantly about "book smart" and "street smart" and "common sense," and he made it perfectly clear he didn't have any use at all for "book smarts."

We constantly moved. Dad would have a job for a while and then quit or get fired. Usually because, as he claimed, he was "too honest." I remember a trucking job he said he quit because the boss wanted him to lie on his logbook about the hours he'd driven and he wouldn't lie for any reason, so the guy let him go. Stuff like that happened all the time.

Most of the time, because of all our moves, my only friend was my sister Jo, who was a year and a half younger than me. We fought like mortal enemies about as much as we played together peacefully. We just didn't have anything in common. She hated books and found them difficult to read. She hated school and I loved it. It was if we were from different universes.

One our houses in Freeport was across the alley from a Catholic grade school that had a playground. One summer afternoon, Jo and I were taking turns going down the slide. Jo got slick at one point and raced around me, stealing my turn. She was almost at the top of the slide when I grabbed her by her shirt and yanked her down. When she hit the ground, she broke her arm. We both knew it was broken—the bone was sticking out.

Jo started yammering and squalling about how she was going to tell Mom and Dad on me. I screamed, "If you tell on me, I'll break your other arm." She told anyway. I got one hell of a whipping for that one. It didn't help that I threw pomegranates from our bush at her as she ran screaming. I smacked her on the back of the head with one that raised a lump. Of course, she had to tell on me about that, too.

I hated Indiana. When we lived there, I was anonymous since South Bend was a much larger town than Freeport and we were poor; I was just another kid there. It wasn't like Freeport, where Grandma gave me everything I wanted and we ate all our meals at the restaurant—I alternated each night at supper between a T-bone steak and flounder. I'd come by after school with a group of friends and she'd give them free ice cream cones. Lots of times Jo and I would ride to school in one of the taxis.

Being Grandma's favorite was a constant source of conflict in our house when she wasn't around. "She's spoiling this kid!" Dad would yell at my mom. "She's the reason he's such a little sissy. He'll never learn to work for what he wants. She gives him anything he asks for. She's just trying to make me look bad because I can't afford what she can."

He'd go on at length. "She doesn't spoil Jo at all," he'd say. "Treats her like dirt, but...little *Butchy*, little *Sugarman*?" His voice would take on this falsetto, I can still hear today. "He gets anything his little heart desires." I knew he hated Grandma. Hundreds of times I heard he and Mom arguing that he wanted to leave Texas and get away from Grandma. His version was that she hated him because he was a Yankee and she'd wanted Mom to marry this rich guy she'd been "pinned to" at Baylor before she met Dad and married him instead. So, periodically, he'd get fed up and we'd move back to Indiana. Where he couldn't hold a job and we'd be dirt poor all over again.

In Freeport, lots of people in town knew who I was, mostly because Grandma was one of the most prominent business people there. Due to the nature of her business, we were treated with a double standard. One time, she donated a $50,000 check to the First Baptist Church for a new building. But the pastor and elders denied her membership because she served beer in her restaurant and catered to low-life sailors and shrimpers.

They cashed her check though...She could attend the church but couldn't become a member.

I wasn't allowed in "nice people's" houses...but I often saw the fathers of my classmates down at the Sweet Shop, trying to pick up women on the q.t. Sinners. And their judges.

Another lesson on adults and their lies.

I don't remember Grandma ever taking a vacation or even a day off. Seven days a week she was at the restaurant or driving one of her cabs. And those weren't eight-hour days. Even when her husband Herman died, Mom had to talk her into taking her white uniform she always wore off and changing into a black dress for the funeral. But as soon as we arrived back home, she whipped off the dress and got back into her uniform, climbed in her cab and went down to the shop to see if there were any fares.

And then, when I was grown and in the Navy, she met someone. Ray. *Mr. Personality.* Ray was one of those good-ol'-boys, who'd done everything, been everywhere and knew everyone. He'd just come up from South America where he'd worked as a welder for some international company. At least, that was the story he told.

Turned out Ray was nothing more than a fortune-hunter, preying on women with money. He romanced Grandma right into marriage. There was some uneasiness on everyone's part, but in the end, all the adults agreed Grandma deserved a little fun. When she was diagnosed with cancer, most of the family was glad she had someone to be happy with in her remaining days. It was after she died in 1962 that the shit hit the fan.

She left a sizable fortune. A hundred thousand in cash to each of us five kids, for starters. Even more to Mom and Uncle Buddy. As her favorite, her "Sugar Man," she'd always wanted me to go to medical school and become a doctor and my inheritance was earmarked for that. There were many other assets. Oil and gas stocks, two businesses, houses, property. As much as a million and a half. I was in the Navy, stationed in Bermuda when she died. I went back to Freeport to be one of her pallbearers.

As hard and tough a businesswoman as Louise Vincent appeared to most folks, she had a soft side to her. After her death, two cigar boxes were discovered. One held unpaid chits from sailors and others who were down on their luck, and the other contained loans to black people and meal credits. The I.O.U.'s totaled over a hundred thousand dollars in each and were uncollectible. It seemed certain she had never meant to collect them in the first place.

In her will, she had left her new husband Ray a settlement of $50,000, a fair enough sum for his "services" for roughly a couple of years. Ray had a different idea. By Texas law, the surviving spouse is entitled to half the estate, no matter what the will. He contested it and for the next five years battled the family in court. It ended when the lawyers for both sides had exhausted all the assets and at that point the suit was magically over. Seems like a common lawyerly thing. All that was left were a few small oil and gas stocks and some fur coats Grandma left to Mom and some other small assets to Uncle Buddy. The stocks provided an income of less than a hundred a month and Mom's religion forbade her wearing anything as prideful as a fur coat, so the furs just sat in closets. She finally gave them away to the Goodwill.

That wasn't the end of Ray though. A year or so after the money was gone, Ray romanced another wealthy widow in

Freeport, also terminally ill with cancer and whom he ended up marrying just months before she died. Again, Ray contested the will that left him what he must have felt was an unfair bequest. This time, that woman's son shot and killed Ray. It was common knowledge around Freeport what Ray had done to Grandma and this man didn't want to go through the same thing our family had, so he took the logical and sensible approach to the situation.

He was acquitted. The verdict was justifiable homicide. Different times. Times when some lawyers and politicians hadn't completely eliminated honor and common sense.

Strange is not a powerful enough word to describe my childhood. Dysfunctional is perhaps a bit more accurate, but still not quite the word. *Fucked-up* is the closest I can get and yet there are still nuances that description can't convey.

I guess the principal element that was always present was my mother's religion.

My earliest memories are of my mother lying on my parents' bed, a mound of yellow tissues piled up—from crying at her religious "guilt"—and her nose stuck in her Bible. Her eyes would be puffy and red and she always looked as if she was getting over a cold since she was forever blowing her nose.

We weren't allowed to "disturb" her when she was communing with God. Which was just about every waking minute. Mom was with God and we were alone. Her body was present but her mind was elsewhere.

I cannot remember a time when my mother was anything but the lowest form of excrement on the face of the earth. This was a given, in her eyes, and communicated to us kids a hundred different ways each and every day. By extension, we were dogshit, in the eyes of the Almighty and were told so, continually. Totally lost, depraved sinners.

She would drag herself away from her religious readings—

which not only included the Bible itself, but an ongoing blizzard of tracts and other religious writings—long enough to throw together a meal, many times silently reading the Word of God at the table and ignoring the rest of us. Since my father was absent himself because of the demands of whatever job he held at the time, mealtimes were grim experiences. As a very young child, I remember my mother's cooking as absolutely the greatest in the world, but as she became more and more submerged in religion, less and less effort went into meal preparation—or housework or anything else to do with family—until supper became reduced to whatever was easiest and quickest. She needed every minute she could steal to be with her "Lord and God." As noisy, bothersome kids, we intruded on the time God demanded of her. This life was just a way station on the way to the really important stuff—whatever awaited after death.

I raised myself and my sister Jo raised the younger kids. Mom was always secreted in her room, reading her Bible and weeping. It was mostly up to Jo to fix the meals and dress everyone. We all helped clean the house and do the laundry. It was funny—this was during the week, but as soon as the weekend came, Mom was up and about. Dad was driving a long distance truck, so he was usually out on the road until the weekend. As soon as he arrived home, Mom would be up and about.

The days before TV dinners, Mom invented them. Her religion forbade any kind of work on Sunday, so on Fridays or Saturdays, she'd cook up two meals and wrap them in tinfoil and put them in the refrigerator for us to eat on Sunday. A lot of times she had Jo make the meals. This way she wouldn't break the "Lord's law" by working on Sunday. For breakfast, we'd just have milk and a breakfast roll. And then, for lunch and dinner, we'd have those "TV dinners." It was always something she wouldn't have to heat up, like cold fried chicken or hamburger steaks. Cold meatloaf. I still can't stand to eat cold meatloaf!

In Freeport, it got worse and worse. Every few weeks, Mom

would announce that the church we'd been attending was the "wrong" church—"Satan-inspired" according to Mom—and off we'd traipse to a new one. And when we attended church, we *attended*. With a vengeance. Both Sunday school and church in the morning, along with the service at night. Wednesday night prayer meetings. Friday night Bible study classes. She joined every committee and class. The doors of a Baptist church hardly ever close. She'd be involved with Young Christians, Young Christian Parents, the choir, the Bible-study group...you name it. If they had it she belonged to it. And so did we. Also in most of the churches we attended, Mom was the organist for services, so we had to get there earlier than anyone else for her to set up her music.

When we weren't at church we were tiptoeing past her bedroom, on orders not to disturb her when she was reading her Bible. We also had to read many of the books. John Calvin, Martin Luther, John Bunyan. *Pilgrim's Progress* for "light reading" along with *Paradise Lost* and *Paradise Regained*. We were reading those books when other kids were reading *My Friend Flicka* and similar children's books. I doubt if any preacher's kids got a tenth as much religion as we did. And every single night, she'd read us chapter after chapter from the Bible, on top of what we were required to read on our own. I half-figured other kids didn't know the English language properly when they'd say "you should" instead of "thou shalt."

One of the particularly joyous requirements we had as kids was to get baptized on a regular basis. Whenever we'd pick up our King James's and march to a new church, we'd be coerced into getting baptized again. The "old baptism" wasn't any good any more, since she'd discovered they were a Satanic-based fellowship. And Baptists weren't like wussy Catholics with their little candy-ass sprinkling; no, hard-shell Baptists dunked your body all the way in. Some bald-headed, fat guy in a white robe would recite mumbo-jumbo over you, praying to the Lord for your soul, his hand an iron claw on the top of your head and then *whoosh!* under the water you'd go for a three- or maybe a ten-count if he was feeling particularly inspired and under the Holy Spirit that day. Everybody in the joint crying because we were all such depraved and useless sinners and were now going to Heaven.

We'd make every revival within fifty miles. The preacher would get all the folks worked up and then they'd have to go on down to the front and be "saved" all over again. Everyone would be bawling their eyes out, the minister up front screaming and ranting that we were all going to burn forever in hell, and away you went, swept up by the group emotion, taking your place in a long line. Behind Mom. As this was your mom, the person who formed your little personality and who had pretty much convinced you that she and she alone had the answer to life and all that—it was fairly natural that you would buy into the whole scene and hike on down with her, bawling your butt off, and getting "saved" along with a couple of hundred other lost souls. It's a wonder my skin wasn't permanently puckered from all the dunkings I went through.

It wasn't a nice God we were introduced to. No, sir, this was a fierce, warlike God, who threw miscreants into a living lake of fire. One afternoon, I was cooking something on the stove in the farmhouse we rented on Highway 6 in Indiana and Mom came up behind me, grabbed my hand, and stuck my fingers in the flame in the burner. She started crying and said she did it for my own good—so I'd have an idea of what eternal hellfire was going to feel like if I didn't get "saved." She ran cold water on it afterwards and then I had to go sit with her on her bed while she prayed out loud to God to give her the strength to "save" her son and do what was necessary to do so. Like turning my hand into shish-kebob.

Then there was my father, who was basically an atheist. Didn't have much use for God. God hadn't been around to help out when he was a young boy and had to quit school in the eighth grade and go to work during the Depression. Dad pretty much pooh-poohed the whole religious thing, made it obvious he thought Mom had a screw loose.

Even though Dad thought all this religious junk was in Mom's head, he would say he respected her right to her beliefs. Therefore, we lucky kids had to respect them too. It gets a little crazy inside a kid's head when you've got your two major influences at odds with each other, both saying we should respect the other one...even though they didn't respect or share each other's beliefs. Work that out, sometime. I've been trying to work it out all my life and I'm not much further along than when I started.

Mom got so bad when I was seven or eight that the powers-that-be, meaning my dad and Grandma and Grandpa Herman, huddled together and decided my mom the saint was maybe mental. They shipped her to a psychiatric hospital in Houston where doctors proceeded to give her electric shock treatments. The doctors urged Dad and Grandma to give them permission to perform a prefrontal lobotomy on her and they both signed the document, but at the last minute, Mom begged Dad not to and he withdrew his permission.

As it was, the experience completely transformed her but seems even the electric shocks couldn't shake her particular brand of faith in God. So they gave up and shipped her back home. From then on, it seemed like all the joy went out of her life and a strange light burned behind her eyes. I can vaguely remember her laughing before Houston, but never again. To this day, it's hard to remember a single time when my mother smiled. My image of her can only be described as solemn and *deadly grim.* The enemy had revealed itself to her and it was everybody she could see at a given time. She'd beaten the boys in the white coats and nobody was ever going to come between her and her Savior, not her husband, or her kids. And they never did.

Shortly before she was sent to the hospital, she'd happened upon a radio minister by the name of Leroy "L.R." Shelton, who broadcast his ministry from Algiers, Louisiana. As a child, she'd attended this guy's church when she, Grandma and my Uncle Buddy lived there before they moved to Freeport and Grandma opened her restaurant. Somehow, she found this guy again, radio station surfing, and began listening to his show on Sunday evenings.

This was The Guy. She embraced his message with every ounce of her being. He was the reason she went over the edge. That was when they sent her to get strapped down and jolted. Now, I understand this guy was running a cult, but then he was just another preacher-man in my mind.

When she came back, she was a different mom altogether. She'd passed the test of fire and her faith hadn't wavered. They hadn't been able to beat her. What little time she may have spent with her family before completely vanished. From that time on, it was "Brother Shelton," completely, absolutely and forever. To the end of time.

She received tape recordings in the mail of Shelton's sermons and we had to listen to those every Sunday night.

This was an especially grim time for my sister Jo and me. As my dad didn't believe in the same God my mom did, but believed in her right to do so (and drag her kids along with her), he'd drive us all to church and sit outside in the car and wait for us.

Eventually, my parents' relationship evolved. This is where it gets a bit tricky. First, my mother believed she had latched onto the only true God. Second, my father thought she was full of shit, mostly because she was a woman and had…well, you know, *that* kind of mind. A *feminine* mind. Third, my father also felt that even though she was bananas as far as what she believed in, she had the inalienable right to believe it. Like he could have stopped her! Fourth, my mother figured out that although my father was wrong about God, God also told her she had to obey him as he was the titular head of the household.

As a result, one week us kids would have to go to church with Mom, while Dad waited in the car. We're talking *hours* here. Since Dad was the head of the household, on alternative weeks we could skip church and sit with Dad in the car. It doesn't make sense to me then and doesn't now.

I was usually the only one who opted for car time. Jo usually went along with Mom, even though she hated church just about as much as I did. She just didn't want to get on her bad side. Sitting in the car for three hours with Dad wasn't a whole lot better than inside on a hard wooden pew. There was very little dialogue. This was in the days when my father still drank and usually he'd be more interested in the bottle he brought along than the pesky little kid that was bothering him. "Children should be seen and not heard," was a mantra to him. And I was scared to death of my father. Always was, always have been, and am now even though he's dead. When he said jump my only question was, how far. Or it'd get physical. Real quick. Around the age of ten, though he'd still beat me with a belt or a stick, he introduced a new "discipline." He'd sneer at me and tell me a "man" fought like a man and he wanted me to fight him. When I'd refuse, he'd smirk in satisfaction, and say, "I knew you didn't have the guts. Just remember—if you ever get big enough to where you think you can take me...you can't. If I can't whip you with my fists, I'll get a two-by-four. Don't ever think you can take me because you'll never be able to."

I have another set of memories from that time. I still have a hard time talking about those and don't think I ever will. Sometimes when he was drinking heavily, he'd come into my bedroom and make me do things. That's really all I can bring myself to say, even now. It was horrible, but I've learned that it wasn't my fault. I try not to think about it. I do remember him doing that when we lived on Miami Street in South Bend. I had my own bedroom and when Mom went to bed, he'd come in my bed, stinking of booze. What I remember most is that I could leave my body and hover above the bed, watching. It made it more bearable. I know that sounds nuts, but I remember doing exactly that.

It was while we lived on Miami that I had one of my few

good memories of Dad. There were three brothers who lived down the street from us—Dan, Steve and Roger Staley. They caused me daily misery. Dan was a year younger than me, Steve was my age and in my class, and Roger was a year older. Like every place I'd ever lived, I put in a vegetable garden. I took a lot of pride in my gardens.

Well, the Staley's discovered it and they began sneaking into our back yard and trampling down the plants. I went crying to my mom about it and she told my dad and he had a talk with me. You can't let these kids bogard you he said. You've got to kick their asses. But, Dad, I said—there's *three* of them! I heard you, he said, but that doesn't matter. You've just got to even up the odds. Get a stick or a two-by-four. If you don't they'll always own you.

I was scared but I was more scared of him and what he'd think if I didn't take care of this. The next time they came down to mess up in garden, I was lying in wait. With my hoe. It wasn't like a standard hoe. At the end was a traditional hoe end and opposite it was a three-pronged digging tool. I went after them and they ran from me when I clopped Steve up alongside his head, hitting him with the prongs and opening up a good-sized gash. I chased all three of them back to their house and got in several licks, drawing blood each time.

I went back home and Dad pulled in just as Mrs. Staley arrived with fire in her eyes to start yelling that I'd attached her kids with a weapon and nearly maimed one of them. She said she was going to call the cops on me.

My dad told her she was lucky I hadn't killed her little angels and if they ever came back to mess with me it just might happen. She left, ranting and raving. Dad sat me down in the living room. Damn, Butch, he said. I told you to get a stick or something—not a goddamned weapon! I thought he was mad, but then he grinned and told me he was really proud of me. That was the best moment I ever had with Dad.

When Dad died, I wasn't exactly in a state of grace with my parents. I'd left Sheila and my two daughters to go shack up with my girlfriend Patty and her two kids. They thought Patty was a whore. As any woman who "stole" a man from his family would have been.

On the day of Dad's funeral in South Bend, I was nervous, but Patty took her time getting ready. Afraid we would be late for the services, I rushed her, but she stood perversely in front of the mirror fussing with her makeup and hair. When we arrived at the church, we were half an hour late and the services had begun. There was no way I was going to parade in with a woman on my arm my entire family considered a Jezebel. Instead, we sat in the car, in icy silence, waiting for the service to end.

When the doors opened and people piled out, I waited for the last car and fell in behind. At the cemetery, I parked up on a little rise overlooking the burial tent and sat and smoked cigarettes. I recognized lots of relatives and friends and hoped they didn't recognize me. My ex-wife Sheila and our girls were there. I didn't want to think about what everybody was saying about me.

The last car to leave was the funeral home limo with my mother and my brother and sisters. After they left, I got out of the car and walked up to stand beside the mound of dirt that would soon fill the cavity his coffin lay in. I stood there, looking down on his casket, smoking. Waiting for some emotion to emerge. Nothing. No memories flooding over me, no tears welling up. Nothing. I felt stupid, standing there, so I walked back to the car, got in and drove back home. I stopped in Lakeville and got a cold six-pack of Miller's and a bag of ice. I put the ice bag on the floor, sliced it open across the middle, and stuck the cans in it to keep them cold—a redneck ice cooler. I drank five of the beers and Patty sucked on the remaining one on the way back home. I didn't feel sorrow or hatred or...*anything*. There just wasn't anything there. I was just irritated at Patty for being late. Deep inside, I was angry at myself. I had reached a new bottom. In life, I had been a constant source of disappointment to my father and now, at the final act of our relationship, I fucked that up as well. I couldn't remember a single time in life when I'd done something to make him proud of me and I guess I was just following form. From that day forward, my slide into my own personal hell accelerated. I just didn't give a fuck.

What I recall the most from when my dad died was the same thing that Barry Gifford reported in his own memoir, *The Phantom Father*. In it, he said when his father died "was the precise moment time began to pass more quickly."

Exactly.

When I was nine years old, I pulled my first "job." One Sunday morning, while everyone in Freeport was at church except those sleeping in with a hangover, my best friend Richard Barnes and I climbed up on the roof of a shed behind the Lack's Sporting Goods across the square from the Sweet Shop and broke a window.

We climbed in and went crazy. We were both fishing and hunting nuts and finding ourselves amidst dozens of guns and fishing tackle made us dizzy with excitement. I never stopped to think that my grandmother would buy me just about anything I asked for. But this was better than asking for something and getting it. We were robbers, outlaws. This was the most exciting thing we'd ever done. Looking back, I see this was one of my first stabs at establishing some kind of control over my life. Not to mention that the adrenaline rush was something like I'd never experienced before.

At first, we just ran around, ransacking the shelves. I grabbed a South Bend baitcasting reel and boxes of fishhooks—I was always running out of hooks. We both grabbed as much stuff as we could cram in our pockets. Then I saw the glass counter that held the handguns. It wasn't even locked. All I had to do was slide the door in the back over and I had in my hand the most beautiful .38 caliber revolver I'd ever seen. On the shelf behind it was a box of shells and all of a sudden we began sobering up. I had a serious killing weapon in my hands and the realization of what that meant hit home to both of us at the same time. Once I had that gun in my hand, everything changed.

"Let's get the hell out of here," Richard whispered.

We unlocked the back door and flew out. We decided to go to the old deserted, half-sunken barge where we used to play. On the way, I loaded the gun from the box of shells I'd taken—target shooting at seagulls was our plan.

Halfway across the barge when five teenaged Mexican boys emerged from below the decks.

"Hey, white boy!" one of them yelled. "We're gonna beat your ass."

"Yeah," said the guy next to him while grinning and pulling out his knife. "I'm gonna carve me some white meat."

As smooth and slick as Gene Autry, I lifted up the gun and pointed it at the head of the biggest Mexican kid about thirty feet from where we were. That stopped them cold.

"That's a toy gun," I heard one of them say.

"Don't matter, he won't use it," said another, and they started toward us again.

I pulled the trigger and my arm kicked back and I brought it back into line for another shot. The entire group of boys dove off the side into the river.

Richard and I just stood there, watching, and then we both started howling.

"You scared the shit out of them," Richard said, admiringly. "That Mex thought you were really trying to hit him."

"I was," I said, and his smile faded.

I loved living in Freeport. We had a lot of good times there. As much as we had to go to church, it wasn't all the time. It just seemed like it.

One time, my dad's Uncle Whitey came down from Illinois

to visit. Grandpa Herman decided to take him frogging with us, since he claimed to be this big hunter and fisherman. Herman, Dad, Uncle Whitey and me all gathered out at the shed behind the house and got our gear together to load on the pirogue. We loaded up the lanterns, the .22 rifles, the gigs and then Herman handed Uncle Whitey two lengths of stovepipe. They'd been cut in two length-wise and then reattached with hinges so you could open them and then snap them shut.

"What in the heck are these for?" Uncle Whitey said.

Herman explained. "You put them on your shins."

"Okay," Uncle Whitey said and then laughed. "What're they for?"

"Snakes," said Herman.

He explained that we'd be wading the bayou, pulling the pirogue along with us, shining our lanterns. If we "shone" a frog or an alligator's eyes, freezing them, then we'd either gig the frog or shoot the alligator. The stovepipe was for when snakes tried to strike us. Water moccasins, mostly, although once in a while a rattler might be on the bank or even swimming, and they'd strike, too. "Most people think snakes can strike pretty high, but actually, they can't," he went on, explaining to Uncle Whitey. "Only six inches or maybe a foot is about the highest they go. You'll feel 'em thumping against the stovepipe once in a while. It's pretty rare they'll get any higher."

Uncle Whitey decided he'd rather stay home.

As soon as he'd gone into the house, Herman just shook his head and smirked. "Yankees!" he said. "Pussies."

Another time they let me go dove hunting with the men. I was ten or eleven, already had my first shotgun, a single-shot .20 gauge.

Dove hunting in Texas is a big deal. There are huge fields where there were thousands and thousands of doves, and on opening day of the season there would be hundreds of dove hunters ready to strike out into the fields and shoot as many as they could.

Me, Dad and Herman arrived at the field where Herman hunted every year and got out of his pickup and began assembling our guns, loading them up. As far as the eye could see, there were hunters on either side of us alongside the road that ran in front of a thousand-acre field. We were asshole-to-belly button, as Herman used to say.

When Herman got out of the truck, he grabbed his twelve-gauge and something else. A bottle of Jack Daniels, three-quarters full. I'm sure I had a puzzled look, as I'd never seen Herman drink before. He started slugging down that Jack like he'd been in the desert a week without water, and trying to load his shotgun. He kept dropping the shells in the dirt and cussing and staggering when he bent over to try to pick them up.

All around us, men gave each other looks and began getting back in their own trucks, starting them up, and moving away. In maybe ten minutes, we found ourselves all alone. Our nearest hunting neighbors were a good hundred yards away on either side.

Five minutes before the game warden signaled with his whistle it was officially opening season, Herman looked around, smacked his lips in satisfaction and announced, "Perfect. Now we've got a little elbow room."

I found out later it was tea in the bottle and Herman did the same thing every year.

We each shot at least twenty doves, close to seventy altogether. Since there were no limits many hunters would shoot four or five hundred. We shot only what we could eat. I got twenty-three. They were great eating.

I also had to dress and clean them all. It was almost two in the morning before I finished.

I miss Grandpa Herman.

Once Dad took me and Richard gigging for flounder.

It was a rare treat. I couldn't remember the last time my dad had done anything with me. He was too busy with work. I got up at the crack of dawn most days and he was already gone, and he always worked until long after dark, much longer if there were tankers in dock and sailors to ferry to the Sweet Shop or to Galveston or Houston. It wasn't unusual for Dad and Grandma both to work round-the-clock and get only a couple of hours sleep a night, if that.

So, this was a big deal. Also, he let me invite Richard. I couldn't remember a time when I'd been allowed to have a friend along when we did anything.

The way to go floundering is to wait until the sun goes down because that's when the flounder swim up close to shore, looking for food. You wade along the shallows with a lantern and when you spot one, you spear it with a gaff. There are several kinds of gaffs. Some are tridents with three prongs. We used the old-fashioned kind which was basically just a cast-iron spear with no barbs. You had to spear the fish just right and then twist it and throw it up on the beach. It took some talent.

We had gathered all our gear and had just arrived at Bryan Beach. While Dad got the Coleman lanterns ready, lighting them and adjusting their wicks, Richard and I chased sand fiddlers on the beach, stabbing them with our gigs. I went after a sand fiddler and thrust down with all my might. And missed. But, I did spear something. My big toe. I put the gig clear through the middle of the nail.

Oddly, it didn't hurt. I didn't even feel it. The spear point was a bit bigger than the circumference of a large pencil and when it went through my toe, it took up about half the nail. I yanked at it to get loose and all I succeeded in doing was to lift my toe up off the sand. It wouldn't budge. I yelled at Richard to come help me and he came running over.

His eyes got as wide as those proverbial saucers! "Ohmygod!" he said. "What the hell did you do?"

"I stabbed my toe, dummy. Help me get it out."

We both grabbed my spear—which was as tall as I was—

Adrenaline Junkie

and pulled. Nothing. It just wouldn't come out.

I limped over to where my dad was. He hadn't seen what I'd done.

"Dad," I said. I was afraid to tell him because I knew I'd get in trouble for being so clumsy, but I knew there was no way around it.

"Good God," he said, a disgusted look on his face. "What the hell have you done?" He was about as original as Richard had been.

"I was going after a crab," I said. "We can't pull it out."

He stood up, walked over and put his foot on top of my toe. That hurt some, but not much. Then, he yanked and it came out.

Then it hurt! As soon as it was free, my toe was on fire. It was also spurting blood like nobody's business. Dad laughed.

"Well," he said. "Nobody ever died from stabbing their toe, but we better get you to the hospital. You're going to need a tetanus shot."

I hated getting shots.

"I don't need a shot," I said. "It'll be okay." Whenever we got a bad cut, my folks just took us down to the beach and had us soak it in the salt water. However bad the cut was, it always healed up right away.

"Naw," he said. "You got this one pretty good."

We packed up our gear and climbed back into the truck. Our outing was over. There was no talking on the drive back into Freeport.

When we got to town, Richard said goodbye and headed home. Dad took me over to the little hospital near our house, which was little more than a clinic. The nurse clucked her tongue when she saw what I'd done and then laughed when Dad told her how I'd done it.

"We need to clean that and get you a tetanus shot," she said.

She scrubbed it forever with something that felt like steel wool. The cleaning hurt worse than the stabbing had. Then, she pulled out a needle and that's when the fun began.

I ran.

She and Dad had to chase me down. They finally cornered me behind the examination table and Dad held me down while she poked me.

Afterward, we went over to the Sweet Shop where Grandma made a fuss over me and fetched me a Dr Pepper. But I was so shook up, I drank it without realizing it was a Dr Pepper. I wouldn't drink them because when I was little Mom told me they were made out of prune juice.

A bunch of regulars stopped by and Dad told them the whole story. He said, "The little sonofabitch didn't cry a bit when he speared his goddamned toe, but he bawled like a baby when the nurse brought out the needle!"

They all laughed. Except me. I hadn't cried when she came at me with the needle. I'd just yelled at her.

I can't remember the beginning of a single semester where I hadn't gone through all the books required by the end of the first or second week. The rest of the time I spent daydreaming. I'd sneak in books and hide them behind whatever text we were on. If the teacher called on me, I'd answer the question, even though most of my mind was on whatever I was reading. I'd discovered a trick. I could compartmentalize my brain, concentrate on two things at once. She'd be talking about the Civil War and I'd be reading Stendahl and I always knew where I was on both fronts.

I went to at least thirteen different schools, some more than once, before I entered high school. I say "at least" because I'm not sure of the count. Whenever I was trying to figure it out, say for a job application or something, another one I'd forgotten would pop up. Thirteen seems a good round number and probably close. Several of them I attended more than once, but I'm only counting those as one. There were six elementary schools in South Bend, one in Freeport, and then at least six junior high schools.

Junior high school was boring. English class, especially. The class would be on some book I'd already read and usually the teacher didn't seem to me to understand what the author was doing at all. I got into lots of trouble disagreeing with the teacher.

Then, I got to high school. It was worse. One, Tyner H.S., was literally run by the kids, especially the athletes. Especially the athletes on the basketball team and the baseball team, which were nine-tenths of all the jocks in school.

The teachers had zero authority. The principal had a zoo on his hands, but looking back, I suspect that all he cared about was keeping a low profile and finishing out his last year or so until retirement.

There was intense pressure from those kids who ran things against any guy who got good grades, except in gym class. You were ridiculed if you got anything above a C. Girls could get what they wanted, but any boy better not get a decent grade or he was ostracized. Do you know how hard it is for someone who had read all of Dostoevsky and Tolstoy before age twelve to get a C in English?

I was on the B-team basketball squad, but that didn't mean I was a great athlete. If you could get out of your wheelchair or iron lung, you were on the team. In fact, I played center for the tip-offs and then moved to a forward spot once the ball was in play. I was six feet and a half inch tall and playing center. There was another kid on the team who was six-two but could only jump about two inches with a running start. He took over the center position once I had jumped the tip-off.

I made Tyner's teams in basketball and baseball, and ran cross country. I was pretty good at baseball, hit for a good average but not for power. Cross country wasn't my idea of a sport. I hated running, especially long distances. But, since Tyner didn't field a football team, the basketball coach made his players run cross country to stay in shape. Myself and Jim Anglin, who was of the same opinion as I about running, would go out early in the mornings of our home meets and hide a pack of cigarettes and matches at the halfway point of our races. We always ran on the Robin Hood golf course up by South Bend for our home meets. When the race began, we'd sprint out way ahead of everyone—a terrible strategy, if one had a burning desire to win, which we didn't—get to the spot where the fags were and hide and smoke, while the rest of the field ran by. Jim and I usually ended up in last place. Probably close to where we would have placed if we'd run the more accepted way.

Hal Muncie coached all three sports and taught gym as well. Mr. Muncie was a god in our eyes. He reached that status in my own mind because of an incident in eighth grade.

I was sitting in his study hall one afternoon when I noticed Johnny Miller doing something weird. Johnny was a big, fat, nasty kid whom nobody had much to do with, except his faithful sidekick, another slimeball named Billy Thacker. Kind of an early version of Lennie and Squiggie, with a Lennie suffering with a thyroid problem. Johnny caught my eye when I was supposed to be studying for an algebra test. Our study hall was in the library. He was sitting clear up in front, away from everyone else. The teacher's desk was in the back and I was sitting near it.

Johnny had his head down on his desk like he was napping, but I could see he wasn't asleep.

I got up and strolled up his way. As I got nearer, I could see that was exactly what ol' Johnny was about—pounding his pud. He had it out and was spanking the monkey for all he was worth. I would have just laughed, but I happened to catch a peek at what was inspiring his ardor. It was a yearbook photo of the girl I was sweet on, Jane Mason.

I went ballistic. I grabbed him by his greasy hair and whipped his head back and started thumping his nose. I had him down and was pounding him pretty good when all of a sudden I was being lifted in the air by my belt. Coach Muncie.

He ordered both of us down to the office, but he called me back and motioned Johnny to go ahead on down.

"What was that all about, Les?"

We stood out in the hall and I told him my version. He laughed and said, "Between you and me, I'm glad you nailed that fat slob. I hope you got in a lick for me."

At that moment, I would have walked through fire for him.

I had to go down to the principal, but sure enough, just like the coach said, I didn't get in trouble. Johnny was expelled for three days.

When he came back to school, Miller started telling everybody he was going to get me.

As soon as I heard this shit, I went up to him. "Noon, Porky," I said. "Upstairs."

At noon, everybody went to the cafeteria or gym or downtown to a gas station to smoke cigarettes and the classrooms upstairs would be deserted.

Sure enough, Miller showed up with his faithful sidekick, Billy. Miller had a surprise for me. A pocket knife. He whipped it out and both boys backed me into the chemistry room and Billy closed the door. Not for a minute was I worried or even shaken up. Johnny was such a slowhead and so fat I knew I could whip him even if he was armed with a bazooka. And Billy was as gutless as they came unless he had a partner and they outnumbered the opposition.

I ran around, looking for a weapon, and came up with was a steel yardstick. I grabbed it and ran right at the fat fuck and whacked him in the neck with it. One whack and he dropped the knife and ran for the door. I ran after him, smacking him on the back of his head. All the way down the stairs he ran and I was right on his butt, putting dents in his skull. Billy probably fainted.

We ran all the way down to the cafeteria and burst through

the doors into where everybody was eating. He ran over to Coach Muncie and I was right behind him, taking divots out of his fat ass the whole way.

In the office, I told the adults what had happened, figuring I wasn't going to slide this time. Johnny was a bloody mess. Happily, I was wrong. When they found out he'd pulled a knife on me, he was expelled for the rest of the school year and I was let off with a lecture, although you could tell the principal's heart wasn't in it. It was just something he had to do. Coach Muncie even came up later and patted me on the back and whispered, "Way to go, Edgerton."

Like I said, I would have walked through fire for Coach Muncie.

These days, something like that happened, I'd be in juvie court, jail and taking "sensitivity" classes. We'll all be wearing dresses, by and by.

As an aside, that day may already be here. A year or so ago, a crime writer came up with this brilliant idea to ask a group of crime writers to contribute a short story to an anthology he was editing with one caveat: no guns could be used in the story. Instantly, I was reminded of an incident a couple of years previously in which I'd been invited to be a presenter at the annual Idaho Extravaganza. The headliner was a writer I admired immensely, C.J. Box. After C.J.'s talk, he held a Q&A and was asked a weird question.

A short time before, I'd been talking to my host, Aaron Patterson, about moving to Idaho. It just seemed like a really cool place. Don't, Aaron said, we're getting ruined here fast. He said the nature of the state was changing overnight. Hundreds of wealthy Californians were buying property and moving there and bringing a lot of fruitcake ideas with them.

The guy who stepped up to pose Box a question seemed to fit that description. A little baldheaded guy with designer glasses and a wool sweater draped around his shoulders, stepped up and said, "Mr. Box, does your character have a gun and if so, does he ever use it?" The crowd laughed, thinking this guy was joking, but he wasn't. It was also clear he'd never read any of Box's novels. This was one of Aaron's California transplants. He'd probably just wandered into the book festival thinking it was going to be featuring writers like Robert Waller or Nicholas Sparks. The way Box handled him was priceless.

"Well, sir," he began, "my character is a game warden and in my novels he always gets involved in murders and usually there's a confrontation between them. With guns. That get fired. You don't suppose they'd engage in pillow fights, do you?" The whole place exploded with laughter and Mr. Sweaters crept away.

So maybe that day when we'll all be wearing dresses has already arrived.

I noticed that C.J. Box wasn't listed as a contributor in that guy's anthology. Maybe there's still hope...

Dad didn't think kids should play sports. Instead they should get a job. So he and Mom never went to any of my games. That hurt. In fact, he was so against the idea of sports, he wouldn't give me a ride home from practice or let my mom pick me up either. Since we lived about twelve miles out in the country, that posed quite a problem. I was too embarrassed to tell anyone my folks wouldn't pick me up so I just ended up hitchhiking. I'd tell the guys my folks were on the way and wait until they all left and then get out on the road and stick out my thumb. I suspect my teammates knew, but they never let on.

Tyner was off the main highway, maybe seven or eight miles from U.S. Highway 6. That meant there wasn't much traffic, especially at night around six o'clock when practice let out. A few farmers, that was it. Sometimes it took more than an hour to get a ride just up to Highway 6. Once I got to the highway, I was all right. Highway 6 was a major trucking highway and I usually got a ride for the last leg pretty quickly from some trucker or salesman. When I got home, I had homework and chores to do. It was worth all the trouble though, just to be able to play on the teams.

I'd always loved sports. In Texas, I played Little League as a kid and my hero was Dizzy Dean. I played shortstop and was a better-than-average fielder. As I would be later, I was strictly a singles-doubles hitter.

I went out for football in the sixth grade at Freeport Elementary and the first practice the coach got us all around him and taught us how to grab a handful of sand burrs and try and stick them in the opposing running back's face in the pileups. They were serious about football in Texas! Football and baseball and, to a certain extent, track and field. Most Texans considered basketball a sissy sport at that time. They didn't even field a team at any level until high school and it was hard to get a complete roster together. Nobody went to the games. "A real sport isn't played in short pants," our coach used to crack.

Football was king. The high-school stadium at Freeport held 4,000 fans and was a classier structure than many college stadiums I've seen since. Better attended, too. My mom's brother, my uncle Buddy Vincent, had been a football hero when he was in high school and he was recruited by several colleges including the University of Texas to play ball before World War II came along and he joined the Navy.

My dad's family was loaded with outstanding athletes. He himself had been a star hockey player until the Depression came along and he and my Aunt Ruth had to quit school—Dad was in the eighth grade and Aunt Ruth was in high school—and go to work with my grandpa selling fruit. They'd moved from Canada to Joliet, Illinois, and then over to South Bend. Dad's mom died about that time and Grandpa remarried a few years after Dad and his sister Ruth were grown, and he had four more boys, all of whom were fantastic athletes. But Dad always resented sports after that, I suspect since he wasn't able to continue.

South Bend has a storied history in athletics and the Edgertons have always been among the biggest names. The reputation of my uncles helped get me on teams both at Tyner and later at Lakeville High School when we moved there my senior year. I was a decent athlete, just not in their league. But, man, I loved sports. Later on, the Edgerton name helped me land a part-time job as a sportswriter on *The South Bend Tribune* while I was attending the regional campus of Indiana University right after I got out of prison.

The happiest time of my childhood was spent with Bill and Rich and my grandpa and grandma. In the middle of seventh grade, we moved up from Texas and spent most of the year living with Grandpa Albert Edgerton and his family. Rich and Bill were the only two still at home and we all slept together in one big bed upstairs. They lived in an old farmhouse they rented out on Highway 20, between Mishawaka and Elkhart. Grandpa Al was still a fruit peddler and would go up to Michigan, buy fruit and bring it back to South Bend where he had a large market in downtown South Bend on Michigan Street and a roadside stand in front of the farmhouse.

Their house wasn't heated except for a wood stove in the kitchen and the only running water was a pump by the kitchen sink. No inside plumbing, not even a toilet. There was an outhouse out back. To take a bath, you had to heat water in tea kettles and pots on the stove and pour the water into a tub that sat right in the kitchen. We'd all use the same water, the older boys getting it first, working down by age to the youngest. My sister Jo got to take a bath with fresh water each time. Feminism hadn't reared its equality head then.

The year spent with my uncles at the farm was a wonderful time. I played sports daily with two of the best athletes in the state and my own game improved immensely. We'd moved in right after Christmas and I didn't go to school the rest of that year. Dad had finally had it with Grandma's unkept promises of a partnership in her restaurant and cab business and had brought us back up north. We had hardly any money and he had a hard time finding work. So we just stayed out of school. The next fall, when he got a job hauling Studebakers for Morgan Driveaway, we had enough money to rent a farmhouse by Walkerton, Indiana, on Highway 6 and that's when I started school at Tyner. By this time, I had two more little sisters, Ann and Kathy. My little brother John was on the way. At Tyner, even though I hadn't been to school the last semester, they let me go into the eighth grade anyway. My sister Jo started the sixth.

Shortly after I began classes in my new school, I became bedridden and had to stay at home. I developed ingrown toenails on both of my big toes. Don't laugh—these weren't like "normal" ingrown toenails. They started out as what would probably be called average ingrown nails. Something happened though and almost overnight they really swelled up. I was in a lot of pain.

My mother decided to take me to the doctor who had delivered my sister Ann a decade earlier, Dr. Arisman. Problem was, the good doctor was in his late seventies and prematurely senile. For some reason, he still kept his office even though he only had one patient. But Mom looked at him as a saint. It seems he'd saved her life during Ann's birth and so she thought he could do no wrong.

I still remember that first visit to him. I have a vivid picture of me sitting on his examination table and I could see Mom a few feet from me sitting in a chair in his waiting room. He had me lie down and removed my shoes and socks. With my toes exposed, he snipped down both sides of both my big toes and then took needle-nose pliers and pulled out the nail roots on both sides. Without deadening the toes. I can still see my mother sitting there, leaning forward, her head in her hands, tears running between her fingers and onto the carpet.

I didn't scream at all. It was the worst pain I'd ever felt before. I clenched my teeth and kept pretending I was a spy and was being tortured by my enemy. This sounds made-up, but not a bit of it was. Like I said, Dr. Arisman was senile and for all I knew this was the way they did these kinds of procedures back in his day. He bandaged me up and sent us home.

My toenails grew back and were infected. Back we went to the good doctor. Same scene. Except this time it was worse. My toes were more infected than the first time and this time I knew what was coming. I can't begin to describe the pain.

They grew back again with even worse infection.

This time my father stepped in. No more Dr. Arisman, he said. He looked up podiatrists in the phone book and found one in River Park a neighborhood in Mishawaka, Indiana. When we walked in, workmen were still installing his equipment and carrying in his office furniture. I wish I could recall his name but I can't.

The doctor looked at my toes, expressed his disbelief than a "real" doctor had done what he had and began what was to become a weekly procedure. He froze each toe in turn with liquid nitrogen, squeezed the pus from each toe, applied a salve that he described as a kind of acid that would eat the diseased material from each toe and bandaged them up. We were told to return each Saturday where the same routine took place each week.

In less than a month, my toes not only hadn't gotten any better, they kept swelling up until they were both bigger than golf balls. I couldn't walk without the aid of crutches and was in constant pain. The podiatrist gave my mom a note to give the school to gain permission to keep me home as I was in no shape to make it to classes. I spent my time either in bed or on the couch, mostly reading and writing stories. I was thirteen and a half and the year was 1956.

Two of the stories I wrote while lying on the couch included one I titled "A Mother's Love" and later changed to "Hard Times," and another was one I titled "Broken Seashells," both of which were later published in literary journals and ended up in my first story collection, *Monday's Meal*. I wrote at least a couple of dozen more stories during my stay on the couch, most lost or misplaced.

After most of the summer, my toes got worse and worse. I was still going to the podiatrist each Saturday and he'd go through the same routine each week. The pain, which had always been considerable, just got worse and worse.

Then, one day my father returned from one of his long-distance trucking hauls and came into the front room to see me. I had a sheet over me and he pulled it off to look at my feet and immediately became furious.

"Dottie!" he yelled. "Come here and look!" My mother came running in and he lifted one of my legs. "This boy's got gangrene." Both Mom and I saw right away what he was talking about. There were faint white lines running from my toes up into the calves of my legs.

"I'll call the doctor," she said.

"Fuck that," Dad said. "We're going there right now." He picked me up in his arms and half ran, half walked out to the car. My mother came running behind and jumped in the front seat while Dad placed me on the back seat.

He sped the whole way up to River Park. Along the way he laid out to Mom what he'd just figured out. That the podiatrist had just been using us to pay off his equipment with our weekly visits. As it turned out, he was spot on.

When we reached his office, Dad picked me up again and raced into his office, which was full of patients. Spotting the doctor back in his office, Dad yelled at him to come out. When the doctor came out, Dad was livid.

"This boy has gangrene!" he yelled. "You're bleeding us to pay your debts. I want you to fix him right this minute. If it takes an operation you better get busy."

The doctor tried to calm him down. "Sir," he said. "I can do an operation but not today. It takes time to set one up. And, you can't sue me," he added, probably after realizing the room was full of waiting patients. He didn't know my dad.

"You motherfucker!" my dad roared. "We don't sue. If this boy loses his legs I'll break your goddamn neck. I don't care what you have to do but you get this kid cured or you're a dead man." The doctor must have believed him—which was a smart move on his part as Dad would have done exactly what he said. I was never more proud of my dad in my life than that moment. He had Dad carry me back to one of his office rooms and put me on the examining table. He told the nurse to cancel all his appointments. He examined me and then started to make phone calls, obtaining an operating room and time and contacting another doctor to assist him. The soonest he could set it up was for the next day but he got me checked into a private room at Memorial Hospital.

Early the next morning they wheeled me into the operating room. The doctor told us what he was going to do and he planned to put me under. I begged him to just give me a local and let me watch the operation. The doctor was shocked. I imagine no one else had ever made such a request. He didn't want to grant my request, but Dad talked to him and he reluctantly agreed to.

He'd called in another surgeon to assist him and there was another man there with a camera. Turned out it was a photographer hired to take pictures for the podiatrist monthly magazine. It seems mine were the worst case of ingrown toenails the good doctor had ever seen and the operation he was about to perform was very unusual at the time. I imagine he got paid for the article and photos.

Way it ended up, they didn't put me under, just gave me a local in both feet, but I didn't get to watch. He placed a wire frame with cloth stretched over it and placed it over both ankles so I couldn't see over it. But it was still cool. I could hear everything going on. They cut the swollen flesh on both sides of each nail away and then removed the nails on each side—pretty much what Dr. Arisman had done sans deadening the nerves. Although I couldn't see or feel him cutting the flesh, I could feel him holding each toe and cutting the meat. It sounded like someone cutting leather and felt like that's what he was doing as well. They had a porcelain bowl on the floor and each time he cut, I could hear the blood running into the bowl and then go drip, drip, drip. It was just really, really cool.

They sewed me up, bandaged me and sent me home. I was to return to the guy's office the following Saturday for a post-op exam, which I did. He took the stitches out and pronounced me cured. He also took more photos, for the magazine article, I assume. I don't know if there's any way to get a copy of the issue my operation was in, but I'd love to see it. I wonder if the article says anything about the circumstances of how I came to get the operation but I'd bet a bright shiny new five-dollar bill it didn't.

The doctor didn't charge us for the operation.

A week later, it was as if none of it had ever happened. Except for the weird way my big toes looked. My daughter Sienna came down with ingrown toenails on both of her big toes just as I had and I didn't wait a single minute but took her immediately to a podiatrist (different one in case you wondered) and got her the same operation I'd had. Lot less pain and drama for her, though.

We were living on a farm on Highway 6 out in the country. To get money I had to be able to walk or ride my bike to wherever I could find a job until I turned sixteen. I worked dozens of jobs over the next couple of years and eventually earned enough saved to pay for a used car. I also had to pay for the insurance and plates before Dad would let me get one. He picked it out. It was my money, but he said I'd just pick something bright and shiny and he wanted to be sure I got a good, sound automobile. I ended up with a gray 1950 Plymouth four-door for a hundred bucks. Four-door cars were the kiss of death if you wanted to pick up girls. I argued like crazy, but it didn't do a bit of good.

Dad was the boss.

In a way, I was happy just to get wheels. Wheels meant freedom. I spent hours waxing that Plymouth but it still had four-doors and was gray. I wanted to take the outside door handles off the back doors to make it look more like a two-door but Dad wouldn't let me.

With a car, I was able to get a regular job. In a week, I had a job at Kroger's in Plymouth, Indiana, about ten miles from where we lived. I stocked shelves, bagged groceries, and once a week, on Wednesdays, the owner would lock me in the store after it closed and I would strip the floors and wax and buff them. I loved that part of the job. I had it arranged each week with a buddy that after I'd been working on the floors for about an hour he'd pull up to the back door and we'd load record albums, cartons of cigarettes and cases of beer in his car. Next day, we'd take it to school and sell the stuff to the other kids. I always made sure to keep our pilferage to a certain level so the owner wouldn't catch on.

I was knocking down about forty a week in the summer, after taxes and union dues and other deductions, and my dad made me pay twenty of that for room and board. I argued with him, telling him no other kid paid room and board but it didn't do much good. He said I should try and to rent an apartment and feed myself for that much. He said it was a pretty good deal I had for only twenty bucks. He was teaching me to be self-sufficient and understand the value of a dollar, he told my mom. Mom got into the act too, telling me I had to tithe ten percent of my earnings. Not ten percent of the twenty I kept, and not even ten percent of the net, but ten percent of the gross, which was about fifty-two bucks. I had to send it to Brother Shelton, at his church in Algiers, Louisiana to help pay for their radio broadcasts. As an added insult, I had to sit and listen to it every week.

With the money I had left, I had to buy insurance, gas and oil for the car and purchase my clothes as well. In short, I had to buy anything I wanted or needed. If I went on a date, I paid for it. Never in my life did my father ever say, "Here, Butch, here's five bucks. Go have a good time." If you didn't earn it you didn't get it.

I wouldn't have had much left to spend on myself if I didn't have my theft game going on. God and my family got most of my legitimate pay and I got what I stole. Crime does pay—sometimes.

I had to pay for my own haircuts every two weeks whether I wanted one or not. Worse, my mother went with me and told the barber how she wanted him to cut it and sat there while it was cut so I wouldn't talk him into something else. When I'd say it was *my* money, Dad would say that as long as I put my legs under his table he was in control. It wasn't until I was twenty-two and out of the Navy that I had the first haircut in my life the way I wanted it. It's excruciatingly embarrassing when you're a high school senior sitting in a barber shop with a bunch of other guys, men and boys, and you're the only one that has his mother sitting there with you and you're the only kid getting a flattop. I wanted a "Detroit flattop" in the worst way. It's cut flat on top but the sides are long and you greased them back into a duck's ass, or D.A. as we all called them. It was what passed for cool in those days, but my parents thought that only hoods wore their hair that way so it wasn't allowed. What they didn't know, was that I was one of the biggest hoods in school. I just didn't have the haircut.

I felt like I was in prison for most of my childhood. Nobody else I knew had as many rules as we had. Years later, I came up with a theory on what had made me a criminal. Everybody I've ever met who'd run afoul of the law had one thing in common: we just wanted control over some part of our lives and most of us felt we were always at the mercy of others. To rob something, shoot somebody, pull a knife on somebody, represented the one moment when we could take an action and be in charge, even if it was only momentary. Even knowing the consequences wasn't enough to overcome that feeling of being God, however brief the moment might be. Living by the rules didn't give you that feeling. Not in this society. I really believe that's why most people turn to criminal activity. It's something about the helplessness and frustration. The more I think about it, the more I think that's the root cause of much bad behavior, much more so than heredity or environment. The person who feels he's in control of his life doesn't commit antisocial acts.

That was the theme I used in a novel I wrote—*Just Like That*—and Cathy Johns, the assistant warden of The Farm at Angola, Louisiana, read it and said that I'd delivered the most accurate account of the criminal psyche she'd ever read.

My senior year in high school was a hoot.

In the summer between my junior and senior years, we moved from Tyner to Lakeville, a little town just south of South Bend along U.S. Highway 31. This was a rough little town of about six hundred residents, the kind that would have fit in nicely in Texas. It was 1960.

At Lakeville High School, I had another opportunity to reinvent myself. I loved moving to new places. Whatever problems I had at the old address, I could lose at the new one. First impressions, I realized, were what most people judged you by. Perhaps for the rest of your life.

Inch by inch, I was reformatting myself into a hood.

I entered my senior year determined to make a big first impression. What I wanted to be was both cool *and* tough. The first day, I picked a fight with one of the baddest kids in school. David Rierdon. In the gym, during lunch, I walked by him and stumbled into him like it was an accident. He turned and snarled and I came unglued. There was a push broom standing nearby and I picked it up and swung it at him. Unfortunately, a teacher was standing in the bleachers and I caught him up alongside his head with the broom handle. Down we went to the principal's office.

While waiting in the outer office, Rierdon told me what he was going to do to me after school, how he was going to whip my ass. I just looked at him with this blank look, no expression. "I'm gonna kill you, fuckface," I said very quietly, as if I was telling him what time of day it was. "I'm gonna kill you. First, though," and I paused a second and leaned over very close to him, put my face right up in his, "I'm gonna put your eye out. I'm gonna pop your eyeball like it was a grape." I never blinked or changed expression and there wasn't a hint of anger showing on my face. I was the picture of calm. Inside, it was a different story, but he couldn't know that. He gave this little snort and looked away but I could tell I'd psyched him out. Then, the principal came out and ordered us to come into his office.

The principal listened to whatever lie we told him—how it was just an unfortunate accident from horsing around—we went back to our classes. By the time school let out, the whole student body knew we were going to rumble. When the last bell went off, I ran out to the parking lot and grabbed a rock about the size of a baseball. I stood on the outside basketball court waiting for him. Dozens of kids came by and they all knew what I was waiting for. Rierdon waited until almost the whole school had emptied and I saw him come out with three of his buddies.

I figured I'd catch him off-guard, smack him alongside his head with the rock, try to scramble his brains before he knew what hit him. Usually, when guys got it on, there's a lot of trash-talking about how bad they're going to whip the other guy's ass. I figured Rierdon was like that. The first time he opened his mouth I was going to cold-cock him. He wouldn't be expecting that.

A funny thing happened. Instead of coming over to where I was waiting in plain sight, he and his friends went right to his car and jumped in. They drove by me, all of them giving me the finger. I gave it back and yelled something at them when they went by—"cocksucker" or something original-diginal like that—but they kept on going.

I'd bluffed him out.

The next day, Rierdon came up to me in the hall just before first bell, acting like nothing had happened. He asked if I wanted to eat lunch with him and his friends. "You're all right, Edgerton," he said, and laughed, but it wasn't the kind of laugh that was merry. More like nervous.

"Sure," I said, a cocky look in my face to let him know I owned his ass.

I ate lunch with Rierdon that day, but never had anything more to do with him the rest of the year. If I'd see him, I'd say hi and he'd do the same, but we never hung together. Once in a while, he'd act as if he wanted to fuck with me, but I'd just look at him with that blank look. I think he thought I was nuts, more nuts than he was, and that was enough to keep him from messing with me.

That was all there was to it, no fight or anything, but from that moment on everybody knew I wasn't to be messed with, and I never had to fight anyone the entire year. In school, anyway. I had plenty of fights after school. We'd drive up to South Bend or some of the little towns near Lakeville and get into fights constantly. Each time I picked a fight, my father was there, perched on my shoulder. Or, so I imagined...and wished.

Every week, there were dances at a couple of places we'd go to. Bremen, Indiana, had a dance on Wednesday nights at a place downtown. If I didn't get kicked out for fighting, I got kicked out for dancing the "dirty boogie." There were also dances at Tippy Gardens in Syracuse, another weekly one at the ski lodge at Mount Wawasee, and one in South Bend at the Presbyterian Church. We made them all.

At Tippy Gardens, there was a freak from Fort Wayne who called himself Jesus. He had long hair and a beard just like the picture of Christ you always see. He also wore a long white robe. I found out one night when I pushed him that he carried a machete. I had been trying to instigate a fight and he whipped out this huge blade. He chased me all over the grounds but never caught me.

There were always knife fights at the Presbyterian dances. A group of Mexicans always came, and before that night, me and my buddies would get into it with them. I got a bad cut on my left arm one night when a guy stuck a knife in it. Luckily, it wasn't much more than a penknife or it might've done more damage.

On a spring day in our senior year, three of us decided to skip school. Me, Dale Fansler and Andy Burkhart. We tried to get Ronnie Hampton to go with us but he begged off. I had a fifth of flavored vodka so we just hopped in my car and took off, cruising the country roads around Lakeville, heading north drinking booze.

About a half hour after we'd left the school, we were starting to get a little buzz on and we were driving down Miami Road, just outside South Bend. Andy, who was just one tough Polack, started razzing me about my car—how it didn't have any pop in it, couldn't outrun a Schwinn, shit like that.

I got pissed, said I bet it was fast enough I could knock him off the hood. Naturally, he took the bet. None of us could turn down a bet or dare like that. He crawled up on the hood and I took off, Dale in the front seat with me. I got it going just over sixty and hit the brakes and Andy just rolled off like this huge tumbleweed in a windstorm. He went flying end over end up into this yard and smacked right into a big-ass tree.

I pulled the car over and Dale and I ran up to him where he was lying. There wasn't any blood, but there was a huge lump on his forehead where he'd hit the tree and he didn't seem to be breathing. I tried to feel for a pulse and then Dale did too. He put his hand over Andy's mouth and said he couldn't feel anything, no breath at all. I did the same, but couldn't feel anything either. I looked up and down the road to see if anyone had seen anything but there wasn't anybody out.

"Let's go!" I said to Dale. "He's dead, man. They'll put our ass in jail. This is murder."

Dale didn't want to go. He wanted to knock on somebody's door, have them call for an ambulance, but I just started walking back to my car and he finally followed. We turned around and headed south on Miami, passing the bottle back and forth. Dale kept arguing that we should go back and help our buddy, see if he really was dead. I kept saying that wouldn't do Andy any good, since we knew he was dead for sure, and that all that would happen would be we'd get sent to prison for life. He wouldn't let up so about halfway to Bremen, I said fuck it, turned the car around and headed back to where we'd left Andy. The whole time I was driving back, I could see my dad's face when he found out I was in jail.

Just as we pulled up to the yard, Andy sat up and began to rub his head. We jumped out and ran over to him. He'd just been knocked out is all and was coming to. We'd been gone at least twenty minutes, arguing and shit, so he had taken one serious thump to the noggin. Five minutes later Andy was good as new and we were cruising back down the highway, figuring out where we could buy more booze.

Fucker wouldn't pay me the dollar we bet, though. I can't believe he welched on me like that. Twenty-five years later, I saw him at a class reunion and he still wouldn't pay me.

He was one tough Polack. Tough head, anyway.

We constantly played chicken in our cars. Twice, at least, it almost got me killed, or someone else. I must have done it at least twenty times, but always, the other car would veer off before I got close. Not once was I the one to turn. Still two times it turned out bad.

Both near-misses happened in almost exactly the same spot

on Lake Trail in Lakeville, although months apart. Dale Fansler was riding with me both times and in fact, was the one who dared me to play each time. I never turned down a dare like that. Not once. If the thought of doing so ever crossed my mind, immediately the specter of my father calling me a sissy, exed out the thought.

The first time, I had just picked up Dale at his house out on Lake Trail Road, a winding, curving road just outside of town that came up on Highway 31 on the south end of town by Lakeville Lake. It had more esses in it than Mississippi. I had just backed out of Dale's driveway and put the pedal to the metal when Dale said, "I dare you to play chicken with the next car that comes along." Less than a minute later, we rounded a curve and there was this humongous green Buick Roadmaster in the other lane maybe a couple of hundred yards away. I moved into the opposite lane and hit the gas. Whoever it was in the Buick wasn't moving. They stayed in their lane. Maybe thirty yards from a sure collision, I just closed my eyes and stayed in the wrong lane. I was sure we were going to die, but there was no way I was backing off. At that age, I would rather be dead than called a chicken. As soon as I closed my eyes, Dale started screaming. Whatever he was screaming was incomprehensible, but I got the message. He must have kept his eyes open and later he told me he was sure we had bought it.

At the last possible second, the other car veered sharply in front of us, and shot down a steep incline on the other side and sheared off a telephone pole, hitting it dead on. I didn't see any of this as I still had my eyes closed, the gas pedal floored. Dale filled me in on all the details later.

We didn't know whether the driver was dead or not, but there was no way in hell we were going back to check. I just drove on to school and we went in to our classes.

Over the next few weeks, we told a bunch of people about it, and I was eating it up. If you played chicken and didn't back down, you were big shit. After a while, we just kind of forgot about it unless somebody mentioned it. But I was getting tired of telling the story.

A couple of months later, Dale and I and some other guys were hanging around the Dairy Bar when somebody brought up the story. An older guy, Tim Donovan, was sitting with us, and he stood up and got this crazy look on his face.

"That was my grandpa, you assholes," he said. My heart started beating like nobody's business, especially when he went on. "That was my grandpa and he broke his collarbone and had to go to the hospital. When he was in the hospital, he got pneumonia and died."

Fuck.

I felt terrible. Also scared. Tim was a couple of years older than I was and truly a badass. I figured my life was over at that point. If Tim didn't kill me, I'd end up in jail for murder or manslaughter. Same thing.

All of a sudden, Tim started laughing like a crazy man. I thought he'd flipped out or had gone insane and was going to tear me apart from limb to limb. He got his laughter under control and then said, "Fuck it. I hate my grandpa. I'm glad the fucking drunk's dead. Fucker used to beat my ass all the time when I was a little kid. He's the meanest cocksucker I ever knew." Later, he went out and got a pint of cherry vodka and shared it with Dale and me.

The second time, on the way to school we were flying down Lake Trail and played chicken with a farm tractor who had gotten off the road as soon as he saw what I was doing. I had just passed the tractor and we were laughing and I had the gas floored when we went around a curve—almost on two wheels we were going so fast—and just as we hit the straightaway there was a woman with two kids walking on the side of the road. They appeared so quickly, I didn't have time to swerve. But the woman was quick—maybe she'd heard us coming and anticipated danger—because she grabbed her kids and hit the ground alongside the road, all three of them tumbling down the ditch. We just barely missed hitting them.

That kind of shook us up, but by the time we got to school we were laughing about it. Nobody had gotten hurt and I think our laughter was just relief.

Third period, a kid came into my history class and told the teacher I was wanted in the office. When I got there, a woman was sitting there along with the principal, Mr. Street, and a county sheriff. It was the woman I'd almost hit.

She was the wife of a county deputy sheriff and she'd had the presence of mind to get my license number, or at least enough of it that they were able to trace me, combined with the description of my gray, four-door, 1950 Plymouth sedan. She was mad. I can't say that I blamed her since I had nearly killed her and her children. I was scared to death. I could clearly see long years in prison in my future.

I started running this story that my foot had slipped, that I thought I was hitting the brake and I'd hit the gas pedal instead. I went on and on about how sorry I was this had happened; that I had a brother and sisters myself and that I felt terrible about how close I had come to hurting her and her family. I tried my best to work up some tears, but couldn't.

They bought it, although she was still upset, but after talking awhile, she decided not to press charges and left. After that episode, I still drove fast down Lake Trail, but only on the straightaways. On the curves, I slowed down.

This was 1960, before Indiana instituted the point system for traffic violations, and you could get an unlimited number of tickets for speeding and not get your license revoked. In my senior year at Lakeville, I had a contest with Harold "Hairs" Miller to see who could get the most tickets. Hairs was the James Dean of our town, the guy we all wanted to be like. There was a justice of the peace who was also one of the two town barbers, and he would let you pay your tickets off in installments. There wasn't a single week I wasn't walking down to his shop to make a payment.

Hairs and I decided to put all of our tickets up on our bedroom walls and whoever got the most owed the other five bucks. I got a wall and a half of my bedroom covered. A lot of tickets. Actually, I was a piker. Hairs covered his entire bedroom, all four walls. A lot more tickets. He won our bet easily.

We were just wild with cars. We didn't go anywhere without drag-racing, even when you had a pooch like mine. You still had to try, even though you knew you'd lose. This was when the speed limit was sixty-five miles per hour, and nobody went under seventy to eighty, and usually a lot faster.

I don't think I ever stopped at a stop sign at night in the country. You'd just turn your lights off and if you didn't see lights coming you just blasted through. Once in a while, the thought would arise that maybe someone coming along the cross road was doing the same, but I didn't think much about that possibility. Most of us just thought we were invincible.

We'd have drag races almost nightly on one of the many country roads around town. Someone would stand about twenty yards in front of the cars and give the signal to go. Those of us driving would see how close we could come to the starter—the boys and girls who would stay in the middle of the road. Their guts would be determined by how close the cars came to them, as well. I did both. Raced and stood in the road and gave the signal. I couldn't count how many times cars actually brushed my clothing. Each and every time I wished Dad could have been there and seen me.

Several of my friends were killed doing stunts like that. There were some fast cars around town. I never had a fast car, but lots of my friends did and they used to let me drive their cars in races. I was nuts, never showed fear in a car, and would do things nobody else would.

One time, I was driving a guy's car against the hottest car in town, a '55 Chevy owned by Runt Miller, an older guy who had won lots of stock car races. I was driving Rodney Scott's '57 Ford, which had a Police Interceptor engine in it, a pretty hot car. Rodney let me drive and he sat in the passenger seat, even though we were giving weight away for the race. He didn't want to let his car out without him, and besides he wanted to be there if his car beat Miller's. We were out on 31 South, and the speedometer just topped out at a hundred and twenty when Runt pulled around us like we were standing still. Runt had always claimed he could get one-fifty out of that Chevy and I guess he was right. When he went around us, he hit the middle berm in the highway and went airborne and crashed into a tree on the other side of the highway about two feet above the ground. Killed instantly. Rodney and I got the hell out of there and the police never found out who he was racing. It's doubtful they were even aware he had been racing as there had been no traffic on the road during the run and Rodney and I sure never told anyone we were involved. It was too bad Runt got killed because everyone knew he was going to hit the big time in racing eventually. He might even have ended up at Indy. He was that good. The best I've ever seen with an engine and if I thought I had driving guts, I was a piker compared to him. I'd drive one-twenty, but my heart would start to beat fast when I got over one-ten if I was sober. I don't think Runt ever had a sweaty palm, no matter what the speed, drunk or sober.

    I had a South Bend friend named Ole Galloway who became a drinking buddy. Ole was a helluva football player who set the all-time rushing record for Riley High School and received a full scholarship to the University of Kentucky, but got kicked out for drinking all the time. Ole's dad owned a body shop and when I was a senior in high school we met and became friends. He bought a used Studebaker and worked on it with his dad. They hooked up a bar so you could steer the car with your knees. Then, they fixed the steering wheel so you could take it off. We'd get a guy who didn't know about any of this in the car and drive out west on Lincolnway drinking beer. I'd sit in the back seat, Paul would drive and the new guy would sit in the front passenger seat. Out by the airport, Paul would start weaving the car when we were doing at least eighty-ninety and then say, "Oh, man, I'm getting' woozy…I'm goin' out…" and lift the steering wheel up and hand it to the guy and say, "Here, you steer," and slump over like he'd passed out. I've never laughed as hard in my life as I did those times…

During my year at Lakeville, I fell in love for the first time in my life. Oh, I'd had crushes before, but those weren't love.

At Lakeville, I fell head over heels in love. With Cheryl Marker. It was her eyes that did it for me. Blue, blue eyes with the longest eyelashes I'd ever seen. She had another feature I couldn't resist. She was tiny. I'd always been drawn to small girls, way back to Freeport when I was enamored with a miniature lass named Dixie Bell. I think it was Dixie's name as much as anything that caused me to be swept under her spell.

I dated a couple of other girls and then got up the nerve to ask Cheryl out. She accepted!

Our first date was to a bowling alley in Walkerton. We doubled with another couple, friends of hers. Bill something and I can't remember his date's name. Most of what I remember was that Bill and his date both got sick from a bottle of cherry vodka we were drinking from and threw up all over my back seat.

We'd gone to the bowling alley at my suggestion. I was working there part-time after school and on weekends as a pinsetter and figured I could impress Cheryl since everyone there knew me.

Pinsetting was a hazardous job. You sat, crouched in a fetal position, on a ledge just behind and elevated above the pins. As soon as the ball cleared, you jumped down and set the pins and sent the ball back. If you were conscious, that is. Pins would jump all over the place when struck. You'd get hit on the shins all the time and once in a while, if you weren't quick with your reflexes, one would bounce up and catch you in the chops.

There was one regular bowler who used to take great delight in knocking out the pinboy. We weren't paid by the bowling alley, so we depended on tips for our wages. It was just like caddying for golfers, which I'd done as a young boy in Freeport. All of us pinboys tried to cultivate regulars who would ask for us. If you were smart about it, you'd set the pins so they'd have an advantage in picking up splits. Once the bowlers learned who could give them a good placement, they'd always ask for that setter.

There was one guy we all dreaded. This asshole couldn't care less about what he scored. His only aim in life was to erase pinboys. He'd haul off and throw the ball as hard as he could. I've still got scars from where he nailed me. None of us gave him good placements, but that didn't matter to this guy. He took particular delight in creaming my skinny butt and usually asked for me. He was a lousy tipper, too.

Anyway, I think the fact that Cheryl and I were the only ones who didn't puke during our date bonded us. We became a couple.

Cheryl was as interested in writing and reading books as I was. That really made me fall in love with her. I fantasized about us getting married and sitting around in the same room, writing novels. We talked about it endlessly. We also "made out" endlessly.

And that was all. We never actually made love, although we came close several times. Each time we were at the brink of actually "doing it," it was me who put the brakes on. I wanted us to save it for marriage. My romanticized idea of the course true love should run. We would both be virgins on our wedding night. I think I was reading *Ivanhoe* at the time and it had rubbed off. Not to mention my mother's influence. One minute I was convinced I'd burn in hell for sex outside of marriage and the next I was trying to shut that thought out.

We'd lie on her couch together, for hours on end, making out and talking. It was probably the most exciting time in my life with a girl. That magical time before you become jaded and cynical. Everything about Cheryl was beautiful to me. Her mind, her smile, her eyes, the way she smelled, the way she laughed.

We had fights, sure. Our family had moved from across the street on Highway 31 to a house adjoining the high school parking lot. Each morning, I'd pull out of our driveway, turn right, and drive twenty feet to the school parking lot entrance and park near the edge of our lawn. The only reason I drove to school was so that I could take Cheryl home from school. And have a place to smoke during lunch. In those days, you could smoke in your car in the school parking lot without getting into trouble. (Before that, at Tyner High School, you were allowed to smoke in the bathrooms during lunch hour. Different times...) Cheryl's stepfather, Kenny, wouldn't allow me to pick her up in the morning and he forbade her to ride home with me most of the time, but she'd do it in defiance anyway. In the mornings, he was still home, so she had no choice but to get on the bus, but when school let out, Kenny was at work, so she'd let me drive her home.

Once, when he came home from work early and caught me dropping her off, he lowered the boom. The next day, she told me what happened and that I couldn't take her home that night. She was afraid he'd be waiting for her and she'd get in worse trouble.

I wouldn't take no and all day I pressured her to ride home with me. She didn't. She got on the bus and that's when I really messed up. I followed behind the bus in my car and every time the bus stopped, I stopped just behind it. By the time we reached her house, she was boiling mad. All the other kids on the bus had hooted and razzed her every time the bus let off somebody.

She got off the bus at her house and I jumped out of my car. I was just going to talk to her, calm her down. She ran up to me and swung her purse at me, trying to hit me, but the purse strap broke and everything in it went flying.

I couldn't help it. I started laughing. Everyone on the bus

had witnessed the act and everybody, including the driver, began laughing, too. Cheryl was utterly humiliated.

We broke up that time for almost a month.

When we finally got back together, it was different. About a month before the prom, I went to school one day and everybody and their brother made a point of coming up to me and telling me what Cheryl had done. She'd gone out with another senior, a guy I had always liked, and they'd had sex. The bus incident and the fact that I kept turning her down when she wanted sex had finally done it. At least, that was what I imagined.

I was heartbroken. I had been the noble one—in my mind—and kept us chaste and pure and Cheryl had betrayed our love. That's the way I looked at it for a long time. Ever since that, I've never been able to put another girl on that kind of pedestal. It was more than twenty years before I finally realized that Cheryl had just been a normal, healthy human being, with the same wants and desires as anyone else and that my expectations of a relationship were totally unrealistic, but, boy, did that experience fuck me up! From it, I not only developed a truly unhealthy view of the opposite sex, but acted on it as often as I could. For years and years, I treated women about as cavalierly as I could.

Thirty years later, I saw Cheryl again for the first time since high-school graduation. She'd just moved to Fort Wayne because of her job and someone in her new office had recommended our hairstyling salon. I was booked too far ahead to do her hair, so my wife Mary put her on her book.

Prior to her coming in, I was a nervous wreck. After all, this had been the first great love of my life! Even though Mary is extremely level-headed and mature, she knew Cheryl had been my first love and I'm sure she was a bit nervous, too.

When Cheryl came in, it wasn't the Cheryl I remembered at all. She was very nice, even still beautiful, but there was absolutely no emotion on my part. Time had healed all wounds. We had a nice reunion, brief, but that was all right. She'd done well in her life and I was happy for her.

She did tell me something that made me murderous for a while. Shortly after I'd gotten out of the Navy, I got in a fight with a guy where I'd swung at him and missed, falling off a porch and breaking my ankle in two places. I spent the next two months in bed. Cheryl told me she'd heard I was home and came by to see me but said my mother wouldn't let her in to see me and told her I didn't want to see her. This was the first I knew about this.

The next time I saw my mother I asked her about it. Surprisingly, she admitted to it. He reason? Cheryl wasn't the girl for me.

I guess it was good several decades had gone by since then. I was mad but not as mad as I would have been at the time. I was married to Mary and deliriously happy. Later, as I kept thinking about how my mother was still running my life at the age of twenty-two and a four-year veteran, I got madder and madder.

Cheryl came in several times for a few months after that, but then disappeared. I don't know whether she got transferred again or just decided to go to another salon.

At one time, I would have died for her but now she's just another citizen. It's funny, about love.

II
THE NAVY

Ever since I could remember, I'd wanted to join the Marines. Mostly to impress my dad, show him I could be as tough as he was. Secretly, I wanted to go to college and study literature, but I could never admit that to my father. My son, the sissy poet, is what he would have said about that.

I still occasionally had thoughts I might go to college until Cheryl and I broke up. From that moment on, I got it in my head I was going to join the service and get as far away from her as I could. What was going on in my head was a mixed-up, crazy notion that joining the Marines would be kind of like joining the Foreign Legion. Once she heard the news, she'd be sorry!

I was young and read a lot of romantic bullshit in those days.

One day, during my senior year, I drove to the recruiting offices in downtown South Bend. It was around noon and everybody was out at lunch. The Marine and Navy offices were together, just two little rooms that sat side by side, connected by the same main door. I went in and sat down. I'd neglected to see what service was marked on the door. A few minutes later, a Navy chief in his khaki uniform walked in and sat down behind the desk. I honest-to-God thought this was the Marine guy. I thought all swabbies wore white or blue bellbottoms and sailor hats. Didn't have a clue what a chief's uniform looked like. Didn't have a clue what a chief was! He was ten minutes into his spiel before I realized I'd made a mistake and I was talking to a representative from the wrong branch. I thought about getting up and leaving and coming back later when the Marine was there but didn't want to admit my mistake and get laughed at. Besides, the chief had really given me a beauty of a sales pitch. He made the Navy sound like nirvana.

I was "guaranteed" a Class A photography school. I thought I wanted to take pictures—a recent interest. Become a photojournalist for *Life Magazine* when I got out with all that free training. A buddy I worked with at Kroger's in Plymouth was enlisting at the same time—upon graduation—and I mentioned Jerry Botorff's name and the chief threw in another "guarantee." I'd be going in on the buddy plan with my pal. I signed up.

In the first week of boot camp, Jerry came down with pneumonia and had to go to sick bay. The company commander called me in and told me my choices.

"You can get set back a week and continue with your buddy," he said, "or continue with your present company and graduate on time." After seven days of boot camp I knew enough then to know I didn't want five more minutes of boot camp than I was required to take.

That was the end of the buddy plan guarantee. I haven't seen Jerry since.

Photography school? Hah! One of the things you do in boot camp is take a test called the G.C.T. It's basically an I.Q. test. I'd scored a 72, just three from a perfect score of 75. That cost me photography school.

Again, the company commander called me in.

"Seaman Edgerton," he said. "We've guaranteed you photography school but there's a problem. There aren't any openings in photography school right this second." He explained that there were openings in Class A Radioman's School. Electronics was just beginning to surface in the Navy at that time and anything (like radio school) that had to do with electronics was considered what they called a "critical rate." Meaning there weren't enough bodies with the sufficient mental ability to fill the slots. Meaning I had the requisite brain power, as evidenced by my score on the G.C.T. Meaning, as this kindly man explained it, that, "I could go out into the fleet and scrub decks for maybe two years until an opening occurred in photography school, or..." he beamed at this, "I could go right into the brand-new jazzy radio school." He praised my intelligence, telling me only a select few were chosen for the electronics schools, and that's all it took. Sharp cookie—knew the key to my heart was through my ego.

That was the end of my photography school guarantee.

Upon graduation from radio school in Bainbridge, Maryland, I was then selected to attend an advanced school in Newport, Rhode Island. Cryptography school.

This was well and good, but the main subject you studied in radio school was math. I scored high on I.Q. and G.C.T. tests *in spite* of my horrible math skills. I mean, my verbal scores were so off the wall I could have flunked the math portion and still been in the upper two percent. I wasn't an idiot in math. I just wasn't much better than average. I could give them the answers they wanted—well, most of them—but I never understood any of the concepts. And I *hated* math. Absolutely abhorred it.

No problem. The Navy needs you there, you go there. I got through it but never really understood the mathematics part.

Some funny shit happened in boot camp.

The first day at the Great Lakes base, we were given a lecture and demonstration by the cat in charge of the drill team. I wasn't much interested until he mentioned that if you were on the drill team, you got to skip morning calisthenics and all the other moron stuff you did before noon. Like assembling and disassembling your .45 ninety-eleven times, getting pecker checks, and all the other inane crap the Navy thought was important.

My new best friend, Bill Worthington, and I had the same brainstorm and signed up for the team. The first day of practice, we discovered they didn't have a roll call. Bingo. Light bulbs went off. That was the last time we attended drill team practice. For the entire nine weeks of boot, we never set foot on the parade ground again. We finagled sick bay chits to hang on our lockers and bunks and that meant we didn't have to stand daily inspection. As soon as chow was over, Bill and I would head back to the barracks and just hang out there all morning, listening to the radio and smoking cigarettes. Busting a gut laughing at all the other chumps in our company who were up on the grinder doing pushups and other silly stuff like that.

Looking back, I'm not sure if it was really worth it. Sure, we skipped just about all of boot camp—the tough stuff—but we were in a perpetual sweat, worrying daily when we were going to get caught. Which would have meant a Captain's Mast or even a Court Martial and certain brig time. Not to mention, we'd receive dishonorable discharges. Whenever any noncom or officer came into the barracks, if we couldn't hide in time, we just brazened it out. Told all kinds of lies about why we were there instead of out on the parade ground. We were blessed. Not once did anyone check up on our stories.

Then something happened we hadn't figured on. Graduation day came. And we discovered we were expected to march with the drill team.

Fuck! In nine weeks, these guys had gotten *good*. They were doing all kinds of nifty shit, like snappy Queen Anne Salutes with *real* bayonets. Drills where if you weren't in tune with the rest of your compadres, you ran an excellent chance of severing the neck of the guy in front of you. We'd watched these guys from the barracks windows many times in the preceding weeks and they were good! If we were to have a serious dumb-ass attack and actually join the team for the graduation day soiree, somebody was going to get mutilated for sure. Not to mention our scam would be exposed and we'd end up with dishonorable discharges...or worse. Brig time?

All night the night before, Bill and I didn't get a wink of

sleep worrying about what we were going to do. Going to breakfast felt much like I suspect it does on Death Row when you get your last meal.

When we returned to the barracks, everyone was getting into their dress whites, all happy and joyous at the big day. All but two of us. You could pick us out easily. We were the two boots with the white-as-a-sheet pusses.

Bill and I finally decided our only recourse would be to pretend to leave with the rest and then sneak back to the barracks one more time.

We were the luckiest idiots ever. We spent the entire ceremony, which took hours, in the barracks, peeking out at the goings-on. Then, when everybody threw their hats in the air and rushed to meet their families and sweethearts who had been watching proudly from the grandstand, we ran out and joined the melee.

I found my parents and they were overcome with pride. It seems they'd picked me out in the drill team right away and had focused on my expert machinations with rifle and bayonet the entire time. They'd even taken a couple rolls of pictures. That was just too wild.

I did the only sensible thing. I went along with the program, told my mom and dad, sisters Jo, Ann, Kathy, and brother John, just how hard it had been to train to be this good. As far as I know, Bill and I were the only ones to miss fully half of boot camp and graduate with our scheme undetected. An early lesson in how easy it was to fool authority figures.

From boot camp, I was sent to Bainbridge, Maryland, for Class "A" Radioman's School. Six months of Ohm's Law and other scintillating electronics and communication lore. Anybody need a guy who can send and receive Morse Code at thirty-two words per minute on a speed key?

From Radioman School, I was selected to go to Newport,

Rhode Island, for Class "C" Cryptography School. Three months of learning to decode and encode messages in various crypto systems. That was a lot better than electronics.

At Bainbridge, we'd come back from weekend liberty and there were always a couple of girls on the bus who were new recruits on their way to boot and they always seemed to be lookers. The next day, we'd see the same girls on their side of the chow hall and they'd undergone an amazing transformation. Their hair was cut and their makeup gone. We used to laugh that they'd been put through the "Ugly House."

My best buddy Don Walker was a good guy. He was from Buffalo and had been the state welterweight boxing champion before he joined the Navy. Every bar we went into in Boston and Newport, we'd start a fight with the Marines or the Coast Guard guys and never lost a single one. Of course, Don would take care of two or three while I was pretty well wrapped up with my one jarhead. We used to go to New York City some weekends, Washington, D.C. others, but there wasn't a single liberty we didn't end up in a fight. It's just what you did in the service. I loved it.

We were always playing tricks on each other. Once, we'd gone to New York and when it came time to return to base, Don was falling-down drunk. Instead of helping him onto our bus, I "helped" him board another bus...one going to Norfolk. He ended up getting a Captain's Mast for being AWOL at Bainbridge. I thought he'd want to knock me out when he got out of the brig after a couple of days. But he just laughed and told me not to go to sleep—he was going to get even in a big way. He never did but I tried to sleep with one eye open after that...

Don and I were split up after a weekend in New York. He left our room at the 42nd Street YMCA Sloan House to go try and roll some queers. In those days, the term "gay" meant a mood. We did that once in a while to get some extra money. I was too tired or drunk or something and passed. When it came time to leave, Don never showed up. A couple of days later, I found out he'd been shipped to the brig at Quantico. Seems he'd stabbed some guy he was trying to roll and the guy died. Personally, I think he was set up. I never saw a guy Don couldn't whip with his fists and I never saw him with a knife. He didn't need anything like that.

After crypto school, I was stationed on the island of San Salvador in the Caribbean for a year. I was nineteen. During that time that the Cuban Crisis went down. We were closer to Cuba than Miami and everyone was convinced we were going to nuclear war. We learned our base on San Salvador was first on Castro's "hit list." Without our sonar, the U.S. wouldn't know where Castro's navy or the Russian subs were so our base was going to be taken out first. Our base and the one at Gitmo. We were on twenty-four-hour alert, sleeping with loaded .45s on our bunk posts. All liberties were canceled and we were on patrols and watches everywhere. It was all pretty intense. Most people don't understand how close we came to war.

Our mission on San Sal was the sonarmen would track Russian subs and the radiomen and cryptographers would relay the information to Shit City (Norfolk) and other places. Most of the messages were sent encrypted, which meant not everyone could see their contents. I was one of a handful of noncoms who were designated "Crypto Officers" and had "Crypto" clearance, which was higher than "Top Secret" clearance and nearly as high as "Eyes Only"—top secret messages only the C.O. could read. I was the crypto officer on a watch one day when a top secret crypto message came in and this reserve officer, Lt. Clock, decided he was going to come into the crypto shack to read it. The comm shack was a large room with most of the communication gear—on- and off-line teletype machines, ratt gear, photofacsimile (fax) machines, and all the other communication equipment. Inside this large, central communications center was the crypto shack—a steel-enclosed room with a heavy steel door—in which all the crypto operations were performed. There was an armed guard inside the crypto shack, twenty-four hours a day. Only those with crypto clearance were allowed in the crypto shack. Of which Lt. Clock was not one.

"Get your ass out," I ordered him. "Sir." He got extremely angry and told me in no uncertain terms that not only was he coming in since he was the X.O., but that he was going to write me up on report and I was going to get either a captain's mast or court-martial for my tone of voice toward him, a superior officer. Superior, my butt.

"Get your ass out or I'm going to shoot you, Lieutenant Clock. You're not allowed in here," was my answer to that. I picked up my .45 and chambered a shell and pointed it directly at his chest. My crypto partner said, "I'd leave, Lieutenant. Edgerton'll shoot you. And if he misses, *I'll* get you." And my buddy picked up *his* .45 and cocked it. Lt. Clock left.

Within five minutes, the commander of the base himself was there, a red-faced Lt. Clock behind him, his mouth going a mile a minute. He was one pissed-off dude!

Commander Wells came into the crypto shack and closed the door behind him. "What's your account of this, boys?" he said. When we were done telling him, he nodded and opened the door and came out.

"You are one fucking asshole, Clock!" he thundered. "You're lucky these men didn't shoot your stupid ass!" I had never seen an officer dress down another officer in front of the enlisted men before. But this guy told Lt. Clock he was one hundred percent in the wrong, that we were fully in the right and that if he ever stepped foot in the comm shack he'd be court-martialed. Commander Wells was aces! I'd have died for that man, as I bet any of my compadres would have, too.

As I said, our mission was to track Russian subs and relay the intelligence to Norfolk. Weekly, the Air Force would send low-flying planes from Rosey Roads in Puerto Rico out to take photos of the subs we'd tracked. Once in a while, the Navy radiomen could trade places with the Air Force radioman and get to go on the plane that took photos. It was a real treat for us. Their box lunches were ten times better than what we got for regular chow. We'd fly what seemed like twenty feet above the water, with the bays open and fly over the subs when they surfaced and take photos. It was terrific! One day, after the Lt. Clock incident, I got to go up in such a plane and the pilot told me he'd heard about it. He told me that all the Air Force guys hated Lt. Clock maybe even more than we did. Said he was always parading around like he was some kind of real soldier and they had all decided if they got a chance they were going to throw his ass out the open bay into the Caribbean and claim it was an accident.

A USO show came to the island to entertain us and during the first show, Lt. Clock was all over one of the entertainers, a singer and dancer named Britt Ekland. At the time, she was just a B-actress but drop-dead gorgeous. Lt. Clock made a fool out of himself trying to impress her but she didn't want much to do with him.

During their break, they mingled with the sailors and I began chatting Brit up. She had a great sense of humor. One thing led to another and before I knew it, we found ourselves in a closet, the door closed. And, our clothes off. Getting busy...Lt. Clock just happened to open the door and found us and began yelling all kinds of crap. Someone ran and fetched the C.O. and he came and took us all aside to get our stories.

The way it turned out, he just shook his head and told Lt. Clock it looked to him like he just got outplayed and that was the end of it.

Brit ended up marrying the film star Peter Sellers a couple of years later and then had a big romance with rocker Rod Stewart.

There were about a hundred men at our station. About thirty each of sonarmen and radiomen and the rest were support personnel, cooks, Seabees, electricians and things like that.

We loved to gamble. Besides drinking, there wasn't much else to do. We'd have poker games that went on for weeks. When you got off your watch, you'd head to the game and those who had to go on duty left. It went like that for weeks and weeks. We'd bet on anything. You'd bet a hundred bucks you could throw a paper wad at a waste basket and make it.

I'd gotten deep into debt gambling. I had about a month before my tour ended and I was in debt over $5,000. I owed most of it to one guy so the others just transferred their share of my debt to him. Since we were both going to the same next duty base—Bermuda—they figured he had the best chance of collecting.

About this time, the movie *The Hustler* with Paul Newman and Piper Laurie came out. I happened to be the best pool shooter on the base and everyone started calling me "Fast Eddie" (from the movie). It was to remain my nickname the rest of my time in the Navy. The guy I owed the money to would give me a chance to win some of my money back any way I wanted... except in pool. He wouldn't go near a table with me.

One night, I got a brainstorm. I bought a case of beer and collected the guy I owed the money to and we went out on the cachement basin. The cachement basin was this huge concrete "bowl" that captured rain water for the base's water supply. We sat up there and drank the whole case and he got roaring drunk. When he was drunk enough, I started matching quarters with him for a hundred bucks a pop. In an hour, my entire debt was wiped out.

That's when he sobered up and realized what he'd done. I didn't know if we were going to fight or what, but he wasn't much of a fighter. Instead we went down to the rec room where a couple of guys were still shooting pool and I had him sign a paper with them as witnesses that I didn't owe him diddly. After he signed the paper, he practically begged me for a chance to get some of his money back. The only way I'd do that, I told him, was to shoot pool with him. Hundred a game. I had him by the short hairs. He was so sick over losing $5,000 he agreed. In an hour, he owed me $1,000! In front of witnesses.

The next morning he was one sick puppy. Not only from the

beer but from the realization of what he'd done. Technically, he owed me a grand, but I never mentioned it to him nor tried to collect, even when we both were in Bermuda. I figured I'd done enough to the poor guy.

A bunch of us caught crabs because of poker. One of the guys who liked to go down to U.E. and hook up with the prosties got transferred to another base and for a few days his bunk sat empty. We used it to sit on during the games and at the same time half a dozen of us came down with a case of crabs. From this guy's bunk, it turned out. They are one miserable bug.

The Navy had erected a small Quonset hut half a mile from the base on a beach and furnished it with a few chairs, coolers for beer and a jukebox. We'd head there on our days off, lie on the beach, and drink rum and beer. Sometimes, we'd go snorkeling or scuba-diving and hunting with spear guns. There were no laws then against spear hunting like I understand there are now, so we hunted everything that swam.

San Salvador was where I really learned to drink. I don't remember a sober moment, even when I was on watch, during that year. We had rum bottles stashed all over the comm center. Officers looked the other way, since they were all juiced, too.

There were no freshwater springs on the island—hence the need for the concrete cachement basins—and the Beewees got theirs from rain funneled off the roofs of their shacks into tanks that looked like fuel oil tanks. This meant water was too precious for the natives to waste on bathing. It had to be hoarded and used for drinking and cooking. And they wouldn't swim in the Caribbean that was all around them since they were terrified of the barracuda. It took a while to get used to their body odor.

The significance of all that to us was that the women didn't bathe. *Ever.* You had to be stationed there for about two months before you got horny enough not to care about the smell.

That wasn't the only unusual thing about the women. You could get laid for a bar of soap. They didn't use it to bathe but to *eat*. The natives had developed a taste for soap! You'd ride by their houses on your bike and every so often you'd see a woman sitting on her front porch, foaming at the mouth. I don't know whether the men ate soap as well. I never did see a man eat a bar of soap.

One time, a friend and I were taking turns laying the wood to a local girl when her husband came home. He chased us all the way back to the base on his bike, waving a machete. We just barely made it inside the gate, visions of being decapitated turning us into Olympic cyclists.

From San Salvador, I went to Bermuda for the last two years of my hitch. It was 1963. It was paradise!

Beginning just before Easter each year and lasting until early winter, hordes of East Coast college girls descended on the island for a series of drunken revelries called "College Week." There was one radio station on Bermuda and one disk jockey, a cat named Everett Charles DeCosta, or, as he called himself, "EDC," who opened up each morning's broadcast with the number of women to men on the island that day. He'd check the passenger lists of the airlines and the ships and the ratio of women to men stayed right around 35:1. We were surrounded by rich, beautiful young women from the mainland who were there only to get laid and we obliged them.

We'd have week-long "swizzle" parties and it was normal for most of us to get laid four, five and six times a day, every day. There were just that many women, all of them out to have a good time away from the eyes of parents and teachers. Swizzle parties were parties held at private cottages where the owner would scour out the bathtub, fill it with gin or vodka, and then throw in boxes of swizzle sticks. You just dipped your cup into the tub for your drinks. Weed was everywhere, as was heroin and other drugs. These parties were so enormous you had to literally crawl through a window to get in since every square inch of the cottage would be packed with gorgeous young female bodies in bikinis.

These were women from exclusive East Coast colleges like Vassar and Bennington and the like. A different breed of cat from the largely Midwestern girls who went to Florida. More sophisticated and with a lot more money to spend.

You never bought a drink in Bermuda if you were a guy. Girls were so anxious for a guy to party with you just walked in the hotel bars and went from table to table to see who would buy you drinks and who would screw you. It never took more than a couple of tables to connect with someone willing and usually they'd approach you the minute you walked in the door.

This was about the time the movie *Where the Boys Are* came out, and we laughed our asses off about how tame Fort Lauderdale was, compared to what was going on in Bermuda. Lauderdale was kiddy-time.

I became fast friends with a native guy, Butch, who was a local bandleader who played at the Bermudiana and Princess Hotels and was a big deal on the island. Butch had several albums out and the tourists loved him and his band. His signature song was "Yellow Bird" and whenever I hear it, I see him again in my mind. Our friendship led to tons of parties I might not have been able to attend on my own.

There was another guy, a black local, who was a big figure on the nightclub scene. I can't remember his name so I'll just call him Danny. He was a serious player and we hit it off as well. The top nightclubs in Bermuda were called "key" clubs and Danny helped me gain membership—my own key—to them. There were three key clubs we hit regularly. One was a jazz club, the E Carte, which was one of the coolest clubs I've ever been to. They seated about thirty patrons, had a small bar and tables, and the only served basic sandwiches. It was geared toward serious jazz fans. I was privileged to see Miles Davis, John Coltrane, McCoy Tyner and a bunch of other jazz giants. It wasn't like a club in the U.S. where people were talking and laughing and making noise when the groups played. These were serious jazz fans and the atmosphere was always quiet and respectful when they played. And, they only paid scale to these major figures in jazz, but it had such a great reputation, guys like Miles would gladly play there for peanuts.

The Jungle Room was another club down on Front Street and it was more of a traditional big-venue club. One night I won a twist contest with Little Eva as my partner and they gave me a bottle of cheap champagne. This was the club my black friend Danny mostly hung out at. On one side of the club was a tiny opening that led back to a patio and a small bar there. For a while, I tended bar and it was unlike any place I've ever bartended. If you met a tourist and wanted to take her to a room or whatever, you put a sign out that you were gone and patrons were on the honor system. There was a basket to put their money and tips in and anyone who came in could just serve themselves. As far as I know, no one ever cheated.

The other key club I spent a lot of time at was near the Jungle Room. I can't remember the name of it, but it was mostly just a cool drinking club. One afternoon, me and a couple of buddies were sitting there and in walked Steve McQueen. He was in a T-shirt, cutoffs and flip-flops. He told us he'd just sailed his boat over from New York. We spent the rest of the afternoon drinking with him and swapping stories and it was uber cool!

There was one other club we went to a lot—the 40 Thieves on Queen Street at the harbor. That was the largest venue club. All the big-name U.S. acts appeared there. A couple of years later, my then-girlfriend Joyce and her best friend, another nurse, stopped in for a drink in the afternoon and as it happened B.B. King was there, setting up and running through a practice session. They all met since they were the only customers in the club and he ended up inviting the girls and their dates to be his guests for the show that night. Joyce and me and her girlfriend and her date all sat at the table with B.B. and had a blast. He was a big, rotund man and for that gig was dressed all in green satin. I kept calling him "The Jolly Green Giant" and he loved it. Really a cool, cool guy and we partied down later at his hotel suite.

There was another club we used to take dates to, a second-story loft that was just a big room with wall-to-wall mattresses on the floor and the owner showed stag movies, one after another. There'd be dozens and dozens of naked bodies fucking, sucking, whatever, all over the place. Guys on girls, girls on girls, guys on guys, threesomes, foursomes, whateversomes. Cost five bucks an hour. Nothing like that was happening back home in Indiana, far as I know.

Bill, a buddy, and me went to the James Brown concert they had in a huge hall. We were the only white people in the entire audience. Whites weren't aware of who James Brown was at the time, but a couple of black friends of ours had introduced us to his music. Near the end of the show, he started going into what we learned later was his regular schtick, where his handlers would lead him off the stage and he'd "fight" them and return and keep on singing. He'd do this several times, whipping the crowd into a frenzy. Finally, he started taking off his cufflinks and scarves and throwing them into the audience and people—young girls mostly—went nuts. Girls were diving over chairs to get at these souvenirs, and Billy and I both got scratched up and bruised from the flying girls. "Time for the honkeys to book!" I yelled at Billy and he nodded and we fought our way out of there.

I got my clock cleaned good one time. A Navy friend of mine from New Jersey and I picked up a couple of tourist girls at the Bermudiana Hotel and took them down to Horseshoe Beach for a little beach blanket bingo. We were just beginning to romance these lovelies, when some asshole Marine with a bunch of his buddies started yelling at us. They were all up on a generator blockhouse behind us.

I wanted to go fight right off the bat, but Jerry was a bit more cautious. Well, actually, he was a chickenshit. Nice guy, but no guts. There were just the two of us versus seven or eight of them. But even if it had been even he would've backed out. I could have gone myself and faced them, but I didn't. Maybe a little bit of chickenshit in me as well.

Anyway, we took the girls back to their hotel and then Jerry decided to call it a night and head back to the base. I couldn't. I'd been embarrassed in front of the girls—there was no way I was ever going to face those two again—and I was getting madder and madder at how those jarheads had fronted us.

I went back. Sure enough, they were all still there. I walked up to the blockhouse and asked who the bigmouth seagoing bellhop was.

It didn't take long for my question to be answered. The biggest motherfucker I'd seen outside of the gorilla cage at the Chicago zoo came down and informed me he was the bigmouth. This guy was huge!

I reached behind me and grabbed a handful of sand and threw it in his face. He must have been royally drunk to let me do that. Then, I hit him with everything I had. Best punch I've ever thrown in my life. He was so big, I had to jump up to hit him in the face. He went down like he was poleaxed and I jumped on him. I was astride him and must have hit him twenty-thirty times. I hit him so much in the chops that I literally couldn't lift my arms any more they were so tired. There was absolutely no energy whatsoever left. He gave a little "oomph" and pushed up, flipping me off of him. I jumped up about the same time he was standing up, just in time for him to hit me with a roundhouse.

It knocked me out. It's the only time I've ever been knocked out by a punch. I don't know how long I was out, but when I came to, there were all these Marines standing around and their girlfriends. The moose who'd knocked me out, slapped me on the back and helped me up.

"You're a tough little fucker!" he roared. In his mind, we were now best buds. He gave me a can of beer which was hard to get down being as I was in the middle of throwing up. Somehow, I managed to choke about half of it down and we ended up sitting around on the sand, swapping war stories. He kept saying I had more guts than any ten guys he knew, to pick a fight with someone as big as he was. And to front the whole bunch of them by my lonesome. Where's that other little chickenshit, he kept wanting to know.

Eventually, he let me go and I got back to base about half-dead. Every once in a while I'd see this guy out somewhere, in a bar or somewhere, and he'd have to tell everybody the story all over again. He'd always buy me a drink, too.

I learned to be careful around island women. In Bermuda, the first year I was there I hooked up with a girl whose family had emigrated from Portugal and had become Bermudian citizens. She was a wild one. The night I met her, she took me home and we made love on a pallet on the floor where the whole family slept. Her parents were sacked out there, just a few feet from us, along with a bunch of little kids, her brothers and sisters, I suppose. I was kind of nervous but she acted like she did this all the time, so I went ahead and did the nasty with her.

That must have made her think we were engaged or something, because I couldn't lose her after that. I went out with her a couple of times, but then stopped calling her. About a week later, I saw her across Front Street and she saw me and smiled and crossed the street toward me. She had this big grin on as she came up to me and just as she reached me, she put her arms up like she was going to give me a big hug. Something flashed in the sun just as she extended her arms and I ducked. Lucky me! She had a single-edged razor blade between her fingers and if I hadn't ducked, she'd have cut the tendons in the back of my neck.

I was telling a Bermudian friend what happened the next day and he said, "Yeah, that's what the Portuguese babes do. They hamstring your neck." He said I was lucky I hadn't gone to bed with her after I broke it off. They hide a razor blade in their pussy, he said, and you can imagine what happens when you put your Johnson in. Both of you look like you're on your period.

While I was living there I was having sex just about every day and almost always with a different girl. Lots and lots of times I'd end up in bed with two or three different ones in the same day and there were times, when I was doing drugs I'd end up screwing four or five even. Women were everywhere and vastly outnumbered the men. There were a few women I saw on a regular basis, even though I continued to fuck around constantly. It was like the Garden of Eden for a male nymphomaniac!

One girl I happened to fall hard for was Marilyn, a black Bermudian. (The "proper" term is "Bermudan," but the natives always referred to themselves as Bermudian.) We hit it off so well, she ended up becoming my first wife. Marilyn was just about the most beautiful woman I had ever seen in my life up to that point. She was the color of semisweet chocolate but that was the only Negro feature she possessed. Her nose was thinner than most white people's and her lips, while full, were not the kind of fullness you usually see in black folks. She had totally white physical features except for her color. Even her hair wasn't kinky, but fell in soft waves.

I went nuts over Marilyn.

I was sleeping off a drunk in my bedroom in the cottage I shared with two other guys. While I was sleeping they brought some girls over to have fun with and Marilyn was with them. They talked her into undressing and crawling into bed with me and screwing me while I was asleep. I awoke to this gorgeous female on top of me, going to town, doing the nasty.

I stayed drunk most of the time in those days and in fact was in the third day of heavy drinking, which must have been why I didn't wake up when she first got in bed with me. When I did wake up, I was lying beneath this gorgeous girl who was fucking my socks off. She told me later we'd been screwing for maybe two-three minutes before I even came to.

Afterward, I just started shaking. I shook so hard my teeth chattered. A shot of rum calmed me down. Marilyn and I lay in bed together and just talked about a million things. I was stone in love, almost immediately. About an hour later, a friend of hers, another black girl named Betty, came in and asked if she could join us. All three of us got it on and while we were screwing, my two buddies walked in—the ones who had brought the girls over—and sat there and watched. The other girl who'd come with them had just left. We—the girls and I—just kept doing what we were doing and they sat on chairs, watching, cracking jokes, and drinking rum.

It was my first threesome. I was a few months shy of being twenty-one years old.

Marilyn and I got married, secretly. For a couple of reasons. I'm ashamed of this, but at the time I didn't want my family to know I had married a black woman. And two, I was still in the Navy and if the military had known what I'd done there would have been a lot of trouble. To get married, you're supposed to go to the commanding officer and get written permission and the Navy was extremely reluctant to give permission for sailors to marry local women, especially if they were of a different race. This was 1964. Also, I would have caught living hell from my shipmates. It would have gotten out quickly that I'd married a prostitute, a black prostitute at that, which is what most of them would have considered Marilyn. If she'd been white, she would have been thought of as just another girl who liked to have sex, but being black automatically made her appear different in their eyes. She wasn't a hooker at all. She just liked to have a good time, same as most of us guys did, but that wasn't the way they'd see it.

Marilyn agreed that we ought to keep it secret. She was never aware that I was ashamed of her race, which, in a way I was and in another way I wasn't. I just knew it would tear my family up. Her reason for keeping our relationship a secret was that she felt that if she married a Navy guy openly, the Navy would consider her its property as well, and if I got stationed somewhere else she would be forced to go. And she never wanted to leave Bermuda. Smart girl. That's what broke us up, eventually. About seven months after we got married, I wanted to go back to the States on leave and take her. She said there was no way she'd ever go there. She'd been to the States and couldn't handle the racism, so we decided to split up. It was a friendly parting. We saw each other from time to time, but never resumed our previous relationship.

When I returned from leave and was divorced from Marilyn, I started seeing Joyce, a nurse from Nova Scotia. We were quickly engaged. Joyce and a nursing friend of hers from British Columbia had just come to Bermuda as part of a British Commonwealth program. Any nurse or bobby (policeman) could go to any other country England had ties with and that country guaranteed a job. They just had to agree to spend two years in that country and got the job. There were four of us who hung around together. Joyce and I and her friend Nancy and Nancy's boyfriend, William, who was a bobby from London and in the same program. Joyce and Nancy had already been to South Africa for two years before they came to Bermuda and this was William's first post in the program. It was a terrific idea, sort of a forerunner to our own Peace Corps.

During this period, I worked as a bartender and at whatever odd jobs I could find. I worked at Danny's Hideaway for one night. Actually, for *one hour.* Danny's was on the second floor and I was hired as the bouncer. That was some optimism on the owner's part. I was twenty-two and must have weighed all of a hundred and fifty pounds. I guess nobody else was answering his ad. I had this cockiness, though. Thought I could whip anybody. Except huge Marines although I was game enough to give it a shot.

The first night on the job, maybe an hour after I started, the bartender told me to throw out this sailor who was being loud. This isn't cool, I told myself when I saw the guy. He looked like he could break me in half. I tried diplomacy and that didn't seem to work, listening to the things this guy was saying. What saved me from getting my face busted was the guy was seriously drunk. Falling-down drunk. I got him to the door at the top of the stairs by talking to him and he had one foot on the first step going down when he decided I wasn't the guy to keep him from coming back. Purely by instinct, I popped him and I must have hit him just right because down the steps he went, end over end. Looked and sounded like he hit every single step on the way down.

We rushed down to him, lying at the bottom and couldn't find a pulse. He didn't appear to be breathing, either. The bartender kept saying, "He's dead, man. He's dead. Why'd you kill him?"

Excuse me? I thought that was my job. Not to kill him but to kick him out. The bartender kept saying I was going to prison for manslaughter. I didn't know Bermuda even had a prison, but I guess they must have. Somebody called an ambulance but right before it arrived, the guy started moaning and then sat up. He'd just been knocked out. Not by my punch, surely. The fall down the stairs, I'd guess.

We both left about the same time. I don't know whether he ever went back but I sure didn't. One more place that owes me wages.

At least I got paid for the stag movies I made in Bermuda. They weren't called porn movies then and there wasn't much to them, artistically speaking. This was when I first arrived in Bermuda in 1963.

A shipmate and I were walking along the beach by the Princess Hotel and a guy came up to us and asked if we wanted to be in this sex film. He'd pay us fifty bucks apiece, he said. Of course we did. Are you kidding me? I was twenty years old at the time and the biggest thing about me was my ego.

When we got to the "set" which was just a room in a cottage the guy had rented, there were five girls there. Our co-stars. We all got undressed and I caught a woody and the guy in charge got all freaked out at my size.

"Man!" he said. He wanted to measure me but there was no way a guy was going to touch my dick, so he had one of the girls come over and check it out. That was fine. It's eleven and a quarter inches long, she said. Six inches in circumference. Years later, I read this article that talked about the old black myth, and the article said the myth was technically true, but barely. The average white guy's penis was five and a half inches long, erect, and the average black guy's was just under six inches. It's stupid, of course, but I always took a lot of pride in my size, especially after learning my circumference was more than the average black guy's length.

And, I have to laugh at the one stereotype black guys are quick to embrace—that half inch seems to be a giant source of pride. Go figure...It's a funny thing about stereotypes. Ones that seem to make a race look bad are dismissed, while the ones they think paint them in a positive light, they embrace...Pretty much an indictment of human nature.

The guy was so impressed by my equipment he had me make two more films. Mostly just fucking. No dialogue. Put on a white lab coat. Walk here, stand there, knock on this door. Walk in, shuck your clothes and fuck the girl who's whipped off her nurse outfit. That kind of thing. I couldn't see much difference in any of the three. I made a hundred and fifty bucks and my buddy made fifty and our egos made about a million. The girls were good-looking, too, although one couldn't have been much more than fifteen. Probably closer to fourteen, but she was well developed and acted like she'd been doing this for years. If you passed them on the street you'd think they were heading on up to the high school football jamboree.

This little episode caused me some embarrassment a few years later, after I had gotten out of Pendleton and was trying to become respectable. I was at a bachelor party and the best man had these stag movies he was showing. I wasn't paying much attention, concentrating on getting drunk and playing poker in the game that was going on, when somebody said, "That's

Les!" Sure enough, it was.

"Bullshit," I said. "That guy doesn't even look like me." Somehow, I convinced them it wasn't me, or at least I think I did. The copy he had was pretty scratchy and the lighting wasn't very good either, but mostly they didn't believe it was me because they couldn't imagine it. Story of my life...Secretly, I was sort of proud of the movies, and thought about admitting it was me, but the guy getting married was a friend of the girl I was engaged to at the time, Sheila, who became the mother of my two daughters, and I didn't want her to know I'd done this kind of thing. Later on, I would tell her myself.

Joyce and I had been engaged about six months, when I came back to the States. I'd bought her a huge diamond ring, over a full carat and flawless, and the plan was I was going to go to my folks' place in Lakeville, find a job and start saving money. Joyce would finish up her nursing job obligation in Bermuda and go home around June and we'd get married August 15th at her mother's home in Nova Scotia. She was an only child and her mother was a widow. A very wealthy widow. She owned her own private island just off the coast of Nova Scotia, which is one of the reasons I got engaged to Joyce. I fancied myself at the time as some kind of hustler who had conned his way into serious money.

What happened was I went home and didn't even try very hard to get a job. Amend that to "not at all." Mostly, I just partied and tried to get into Indiana farm girls' pants. They were much tougher nuts to crack than the girls I'd been used to in Bermuda! Not quite as sophisticated. They were all holding out for marriage. There was this "three date rule" they all followed. Meaning, they wouldn't screw anybody until the third date, less the guy think they were "easy." Stupidest thing I ever heard of. Like that made them moral or something. Bunch of bullshit. This drove me crazy, especially after leaving an island

Adrenaline Junkie

paradise where all you had to do was walk into any hotel bar and girls were climbing all over your ass.

Anyway, all this time I'm screwing around like crazy, and Joyce still thinks we're getting married. She'd write maybe nine or ten letters to my one, but I never told her what I was doing, only that it was hard finding a job because we were in a recession. The truth is, I liked her a lot, even if I didn't love her, but I couldn't tell her we probably weren't going to get married. I guess I was hoping she'd lose interest so I wouldn't have to make a decision and confront her. Only it didn't go down that way.

The weeks went by and the letters got farther and farther apart, but they didn't stop and she was still planning on our marriage. In June, I got a phone call from her that she was back in Nova Scotia, on her island, and she had sent out wedding invitations.

I just ignored it, put it in the back of my mind, and went on my merry, partying way. Then, I got a phone call from her the first week of August and her tone was somber.

"Are we still getting married?" she asked.

We were, I assured her. I'd be there in a week. I'd already bought my plane ticket.

Big fat lie.

I kept burying my head in the sand, hoping this would all just go away.

It didn't.

The night before our wedding date, she called again. From Nova Scotia. This time, her voice was definitely somber.

"You're not coming, are you?" she said, dully. I lied again. "Honey, I'll be there in the morning," I said. I felt like the biggest chickenshit of all time and the worst heel in history, but I just couldn't bring myself to tell her personally it was over. She had people from all over Canada who were already there to attend the wedding. She had her dress and her mom had hired a caterer. It was turning into this horrible nightmare. She was in something way beyond a nightmare, but I tried not to think about that. I was too busy being a Class A jerk.

About eight o'clock the next morning, the phone rang and I ran to answer it before my folks did. They didn't have a clue what was going on. Didn't even know there was a Joyce.

It was her.

"You're not coming, are you, Les." She didn't ask it; she stated it as a fact.

"No," I said. "I'm sorry, Joyce. I really am." I couldn't think of anything else to say. There was a silence for a few seconds and then she hung up.

I can't think of anything I'm more ashamed of in my life than what I did to that girl. She was absolutely the sweetest person I've ever known, not a bad bone in her body.

We'd never had sex the whole time we were together. She said she was a virgin and I believed her. That's the only good thing. At least I didn't take that away from her on top of all the other horrible shit I did to her.

That wasn't the end of it.

About two weeks later, I had gone out in the afternoon to Lake of the Woods near Bremen, Indiana, to go swimming with a girl I'd been seeing. When I came back home, I went into my bedroom to take off my clothes and take a shower, get the lake gradue off of me. Nobody was home, but there was a blue suitcase sitting by my bed. I wondered what it was doing there, but didn't give it much thought. I think I thought it was my mom's and she was just cleaning out closets or something and had forgotten to put it away. It didn't dawn on me that I'd never seen that suitcase before. I went to the bathroom and took a shower, brushed my teeth and shaved. I had another date that night with the girl I'd gone swimming with.

When I came out of the bathroom, I heard voices in the kitchen and figured it was just my parents. I went to my bedroom and got dressed and came out and went into the kitchen. It was my parents all right.

And Joyce.

They were all sitting at the kitchen table.

If I'd been an old man then, I would have had a heart attack. There's nothing worse for a coward than to be confronted by the person he has crapped on. It's worse when his parents are there, to witness his bastardness and total worthlessness.

My folks knew the whole story by now. Since I'd talked to Joyce, she and her friend Nancy, who was to have been maid of honor, had driven to New York City for a few days of partying—in a car Joyce had bought with the money she got for selling her engagement ring. Then, she had decided she wanted to face me.

My father was in a killing frame of mind. His whole life had been built on honor. Dad was a hard man but he was straight down the middle. No gray areas for him.

He was livid. He said, "I ought to kick your ass all the way down the street, doing what you did to this girl. You're not a man, you're nothing but a punk. I wish you had never been born." For a while I thought he was going to do just that—kick my ass all the way down the street.

I had to sit there and explain to Joyce and Mom and Dad why I had done what I had. I didn't have a good reason. I didn't even have a bad reason. The whole scene was pretty horrible.

Finally, she left. At least Joyce got some bit of vindication. I wish she could have gotten more. She didn't deserve what I did to her. My father was exactly right. The next day I moved out and got my own apartment. It was a long time before I went back home to see my parents, and clear up to his death, I was never able to look my father in the eye.

I was out of control, a totally heedless, hedonistic, selfish piece of garbage. After the event with Joyce, I just went downhill, faster and faster.

A couple of weeks later, I met a girl in South Bend at a bar and we ended up getting an apartment. Sarah was quite the party animal—as was I—and we spent most of our time high or drunk. Or both.

We'd joked about getting married and then woke up one Sunday morning, both of us hung over, and decided to do just that. We drove up into Michigan where they had the justice of the peace system, drove around until we saw a sign for one outside of Niles, went in, and the guy married us.

When we got home, we had a little "honeymoon" after which I took a shower and put on a sport coat and dress pants.

"Where are you going?" Sarah asked.

"To the concert," I said and she kissed me and told me to have a good time.

The concert was the last of the season event for the South Bend Symphony and I never missed one. Sarah liked some forms of music but not classical so she had no interest in going with me.

When I returned home a few hours later, she was gone along with all her stuff and she'd left me an angry note saying I was a selfish ass, leaving her on our wedding day and she never wanted to see me again.

I figured out pretty quickly she'd probably just gotten cold feet and had probably run home to her mother's and I suspected that if I just went over there and copped a few deuces, she'd come back with me, but I'd gotten cold feet as well. Instead of going after her, I called an old friend of mine in Bermuda, Weldon Burgess, and within two minutes he invited me to stay with him and he'd also give me a job in the photography store he owned in downtown Hamilton, and two days later I was winging it across the Atlantic on a Pan Am flight.

Wendell was a truly good friend. He had a bit of an ulterior motive for his invitation. Wendell was a young black guy and he was thoroughly gay. We'd been friends for the whole time I lived in Bermuda and it was clear he wanted my booty, but I wasn't worried at all—I knew I could handle him and he wasn't the violent type. I stayed with him about a month and, while from time to time, he put the moves on me, he was easy to brush off. The truth was I started to feel guilty about leading him on so decided to head back to the States.

I probably should have stayed in Bermuda...

The longer I stayed in Indiana after that, the more I realized the best I could expect for the rest of my life was to work at the Uniroyal plant and the most excitement anybody my age seemed to be into was getting a six-pack of beer and taking one of the few girls that hadn't already gotten married to a drive-in theater and groping her in the back seat. Not enough for a true adrenaline junkie. Not after Bermuda.

A few weeks returning home, I met Dave "Rat" Braniff out drinking on what turned out to be a fateful night. We hit it off and he wanted to know if I wanted to break into this place with him. Sure, I said. We did and I was hooked. The adrenaline was back. I was "controlling" my life.

I don't know if I actually thought that at the time. I know I *felt* like I was in control. Looking back, this was precisely when I began the opposite, began sliding down into the pit.

III
CRIME YEARS

Between the time I was discharged from the Navy in 1965 and the day I entered the outer iron-barred gate at Pendleton Reformatory in 1967, I had committed over 400 burglaries, along with some other crimes. If I had been sentenced on just the ones they actually knew about, just under a hundred burglaries, drug dealings, armed- and strong-armed robberies, I would have ended up doing over 500 years hard time. Luckily, they don't do it that way. They reduce them all to just a few and that's what you go to jail for. It's called "plea-bargaining" and in my case at least, it wasn't quite the same procedure as you might see on television. I was twenty-two years old when I began my little "crime spree" and I had never gotten caught for much more than speeding tickets in all the years before.

The way to be successful at crime is to be fearless. That saying "guts of a burglar" has a lot of truth in it.
 One summer night at around two in the morning, for example, I was driving home after robbing a couple of places, and I went through Bremen, a little town south of South Bend. In the middle of town was a small strip center and near one end was a twenty-four-hour laundromat. It was about three in the morning and not much traffic on U.S. Highway 6, which went through the center of town. When I drove by, I suddenly remembered laundromats had coin changers. I wheeled in, my purpose to break

Adrenaline Junkie

them open and get the bills inside. There was one slight problem. There was a side street on the end by the laundromat and directly across that, a gas station, and sitting out by the pumps were two state police cars. Both troopers were outside their cars, just sitting on their hoods, smoking and talking to each other. They were maybe sixty yards away and in plain sight of the laundromat.

I thought about leaving and then said, fuck it, and went on into the laundromat. There was no one inside and I walked back to where the coin changers were. I tried to pry them open with a screwdriver I had in my back pocket but it wasn't big enough. I went back out to my car and opened the trunk and got out a tire iron.

It wouldn't work either. I was getting a bit discouraged but finally decided to just break the steel bands that held the machines to the wall. That action made a lot of noise and the front doors of the place were wide open, but I didn't care. It took a while, but I was able to break the bands loose and the first machine fell to the floor. I got the second one loose and then picked it up and carried it out to my trunk and put it in. The cops were looking at me. I gave them a little wave and went back in for the second machine and brought it out, put it in the trunk with the first one, slammed the trunk closed and went around and started the car.

I turned back out onto Highway 6, the way I'd come, and drove right by the cops, just for the hell of it. I gave them another big wave as I drove by and smiled. They both waved back. I drove to the end of the next block, which was Highway 31, turned left and headed home to Lakeville where I was living then. About halfway there, I pulled into a lane of a deserted old farmhouse and got the cash machines out and fucked around with a hammer and the crowbar for about a half hour until I was able to jimmy them open. It was all change, since these weren't dollar machines but quarter machines and I ended up with about fifty bucks in nickels, dimes and quarters.

It felt better than robberies where I'd gotten a lot more, just because I'd done it right under the noses of two troopers.

All during this period of time, which went on for many months, I just had this feeling of invincibility, that I could do anything and wouldn't get caught. It was an attitude and it felt great.

Right around this time, Dave Mikesell, another outlaw I'd met, Rat and I were driving around one night, breaking into gas stations and stuff, and about one in the morning, we ended up in Argos, Indiana, a little town maybe fifty miles south of South Bend on Highway 31.

We totaled the town. There were nine businesses and we broke into all of them. Gas stations, a drug store, a bar, a cleaners, and a couple of restaurants. Two or three places, like the drug store and the bar, we broke into twice. Not a single alarm in that entire town. Nirvana for thieves. All night long, we just roamed that town, breaking into places, going back and going in again. No one ever came around, no cops, no town marshals, nobody. Months later, when we got busted and my rappies rolled over on me, they told the cops about that night. After I was out on bail months later, I was driving through Argos on my way to Indianapolis and decided to stop and get a beer at the only tavern in town. I walked in and sat at the bar. The bartender walked over, looked closely at me, and then said very politely, "You have to leave," before I could even order a drink. He reached down under the bar and pulled out a baseball bat. I couldn't figure out what the hell he was talking about. I'd never seen this guy before. I asked him why and he pointed the bat at a newspaper clipping tacked up at the other end of the bar. I walked down and just about fell out. It was the story in the *South Bend Tribune* the day after I'd given everybody the bird and it was all about our arrest. My picture was there too, big as life. There was another article below it, one that had come out a week or so later, and it named all the places we'd broken into, the ones Rat had given the cops. The town of Argos was named and all the places we'd broken into there. This bar was one of them.

All in all, I'd say the bartender was fairly good about the whole thing. He never once got nasty with me, but it was clear that he wanted me to leave, so I did.

I was by myself one night, just cruising around. I'd burglarized a couple of bars already, and hadn't gotten much, change mostly, some bottles of booze, and I was ready to call it a night when I came over the St. Joe River bridge, by the Farmer's Market, and saw this little bar sitting right on the river bank.

It was maybe three a.m., dark as hell, overcast and snowing just a little and the place looked like it'd be easy to get into. It was bitter cold. There was nothing around the bar itself, just the river behind it, a Dog 'N Suds across the street and on the other two corners a deserted parking lot and a restaurant that had long been out of business.

I parked my car a block away on Mishawaka Avenue and took just a crowbar and screwdriver with me and walked to the bar, going around to the back door on the river side. Not a single car passed me on my walk. It looked like the easiest way was just to punch out a little side window, so I hit it with the crowbar. It broke easily, but then the stillness of the night was punctured with an ear-splitting alarm.

I didn't panic, just stuck my crowbar up under my jacket and began walking back to my car, across the street and down a block. Just as I got ready to cross the street, a police car came around the curve. The alarm from the bar was deafening. Calmly, I crossed the street just before the police car passed me and when they went by, I gave them a little wave. *I'm busted,* I figured, but the car kept on going, past me and then the bar. It was so cold they had their windows up and obviously didn't hear the alarm. I got in my car and beat it the hell out of there.

***

Another time I decided to hit a bar I'd been casing for quite a while. Instead of breaking in, I decided to try out something else. I went in about two hours before closing and sat there and drank until about fifteen minutes shy of closing time. Then, I went to the bathroom and perched up on one of the stools in one of the stalls.

I stayed there about an hour. I could hear perfectly what was going on out in the bar. Heard the bartender opening and closing the cash register, heard him walking around, and then finally heard him close and lock the front door. Luckily, he never had to use the john.

As soon as I heard him lock the door, I crept out and the place was deserted. I found the day's receipts in the usual place, buried halfway down in a plastic garbage can they used for dirty bar towels and aprons and stuff. You could almost always count on the bartender or owner hiding money in a place like that. Another favorite was the trash can. Rarely was there anything but change in the cash register, but once in a while someone got sloppy.

They'd had a good night. I got almost a thousand dollars. After I found the money, which was in minutes, I poured myself a draft and sat at the bar and drank it, watching the street. I should have got the hell out of there, but I liked to push it. I drank the beer, taking my time, and when I finished, I just went over to the back door, unlocked the dead bolt and let myself out and went to my car which I'd parked a block over.

I would have liked to have seen that bartender's face the next day when he tried to find his money. Since it didn't look like a break-in, he probably went nuts, figuring he'd hid the money in a different place than he remembered. I bet he tore that joint apart.

***

There was some strong-arm robberies I was charged with, too, that were later dropped when I copped a guilty plea.

One wasn't a robbery at all, but they put it down like that.

One snowy winter night I ran out of gas three blocks from where I was living with Sherry, my third wife, on Lincolnway West. Conveniently, I ran out on the street just in front of a gas station, one of those places that sold gas only, no repairs. A Clark station, I think.

The attendant was closing up, inside counting his day's receipts. I walked up and told him what had happened and asked if I could buy just a buck's worth of gas so I could get home.

The asshole got shitty with me, said he'd just locked the pumps and wasn't about to unlock them for a buck's worth of gas. Told me to come back in the morning when they opened.

I started walking home and got halfway there when I turned around and came back. Every step of the walk home I'd been getting madder and madder. I'd seen a pickup truck parked by the side of the station that I figured was the attendant's and when I got back, sure enough it was still there and he was sitting inside, all slumped down and taking tokes on a bottle.

That really pissed me off. It wasn't as if this guy had to rush home to the little woman or anything. He was just a lazy cocksucker, didn't want to help me because he was anxious to start drinking.

I went over to my car and got out the tire iron where I kept it under the front seat and walked back over to this guy's pickup. He had the window down and was lying scrunched up in the seat, his back to the window. He never saw me.

I thumped him over the head with the tire iron a good whack but it didn't knock him out. He came out of the truck with a good mad on, but he was dazed and couldn't see too well on account of the blood running down into his eyes. I gave him a shot in the ribs with the iron and when he doubled over, I hit him on the back of the neck and he went down, this time out for the count. I went through his pockets and got his billfold and it had maybe twenty bucks in it. But, on the passenger seat was a money bag and in it was almost five hundred bucks.

Then, I kind of sobered up and figured I was going to have to move my car since he knew it was mine. There was a payphone at the end of the lot so I went over and called Casey, one of the guys who lived in the duplex next to our place, and he came down and together we rolled my car all the way home.

The guy wasn't dead or anything, just dinged up, and never would have figured out who I was until we got busted and made the front page of the *Tribune* with my picture all over it. He called the cops and told them I was the guy who had busted his head. They called it strong-armed robbery, even though it wasn't as much of a robbery as it was a righteous grudge-fuck. In my opinion, anyway. Turned out all right, though, since they eventually dropped the charge during my plea bargain. That's one crime I've never felt much remorse for. I still feel the creep asked for it, not helping me out with a lousy dollar's worth of gas.

One night, cruising around back roads and stopping every so often to break into these country bars, which were everywhere around South Bend, Rat and I passed a grade school stuck way out in the boonies.

We'd never robbed a school before and didn't know whether they kept money in the office, but it looked like an easy hit so we pulled in and broke into the front door.

We were walking down the main hallway, big as shit, figuring we had all the time in the world since nobody's going to be in a schoolhouse at 2:00 a.m., when all of a sudden somebody at the other end of the corridor jumped out and fired a shot at us. It sounded like a cannon going off in that empty school! Rat and I each jumped into a room on either side of the hallway and yanked our pieces out and started firing at the other end where the gunfire had come from. We were whispering back and forth and came up with this master plan that we would trade fire with the cops—that's what we figured they were—and then we'd run for the car and try and outrun them. I had my T-Bird then and there wasn't much could catch it.

We'd each shot four or five shots and were just about to make our break when this voice yelled, "We give up!" I looked over at Rat and he at me and I said, "Cops don't give themselves up, do they?" He started laughing and said, "Fuck no."

"You cops?" we both yelled down the hall.

"No!" came a voice back. "Are you?"

It was two other guys with the same idea who had broken into the other end at about the same time we had. You can't make this shit up. Things like this only happen in real life.

We talked to each other a few minutes and then Rat and I said we were going to get the hell out of there. Even though the school was way out in the boonies we figured maybe some farmer had heard the shots and might be calling the cops. For a few minutes it had sounded like a war zone, after all. The other two guys said they were going to go ahead and check it out, see if there was any money. Rat and I got in my car and booked. I don't know whether those other guys ever got busted or not. I didn't buy newspapers in those days and we didn't have a TV. I hope they made it. They seemed like nice guys once they "gave up."

I was picking up girls left and right and hitting the clubs every night. One of my hangouts was an after-hours black club in Elkhart named the Fieldmouse but everyone just called it "Mousey's." An old high school friend, Giff Torbenson, introduced me to it. We were always the only white guys there whenever we went. It opened up around 2:00 a.m when the legitimate clubs began to close.

One night, about 3:00 in the a.m., we'd just pulled into the parking lot, when we saw about ten black guys pushing some poor sap's car off the bank a few feet from the club and into the St. Joe River. That night didn't look like a good night for white boys, so we booked and went somewhere else. The Green Onion, another black after-hour's club a couple of blocks away.

Mousey's was one of the best honky-tonks I'd ever hung out in. It was basically just a big room with a couple of bathrooms. No bar, girls just walked around with ice coolers with beer in them and you bought from them when they came to your table. Sometimes there'd be a pick-up band playing, always R&B, and an area they'd cleared off to dance in.

One night, we'd just got there, sat down and grabbed us a beer, and some guy started mouthing off to another black guy and it was heating up pretty good, the way guys go at it before the punches start being thrown. The two guys were standing about two feet away and fights always made us a little nervous, being the only white guys in the place. All of a sudden, the bouncer came out of nowhere and shoved the two guys apart. One of the guys went down on his knees and I saw him reach for something in his sock and he came up, quick-like and took a punch at the bouncer. At least it looked like a punch. The bouncer must have thought it was a punch too, 'cause he put his fingers on his cheek where they guy'd smacked him only his fingers disappeared inside his cheek. Turned out the guy'd hit him all right, only not with a fist, but with a straight edge. Laid his whole cheek open. The bouncer yanked his hand back and stared at it and it was solid red and now his face was, too. He let out a yell, pulled out a pistol and shot at the guy only he missed him and the whole crowd. The razor guy ran for the door and the bouncer was chasing him and as soon as they got outside, I turned to Giff and suggested we leave, which he agreed with and we got out there as quick as we could.

For years, I carried a straight razor myself, in the same place as this guy did, in my sock. I'd wrap a rubber band around it so it didn't come loose and end up slicing my ankle. Every once in a while I see a movie where razors come out and mostly it was clear the actors didn't have the foggiest how to use a razor. They'd hold it in their fingers the same way you'd hold a shank and slice at each other. A method pretty much guaranteed to amputate about four fingers. The way you use a straight edge is you fold it back around your knuckles and hold the tang with your thumb and do just what the guy that night did, smack someone in the face with it like a pair of brass knucks. Any other way, is a fool who doesn't think much of his fingers as it was about 100% guaranteed that if you tried to slice anyone, the blade would be sure to come back closed and there went your digits. I do love the fiction you see in a lot of books and movies...

I always had a couple of ice picks in my car in those days and still carry one in my car even today.

It was a lively place and we had a lot of fun there. Got in our share of fights but none with knifes or guns although we always had both with us, and win or lose, the black guys always treated us just fine. There were some fine-looking women there and we had our share, usually out back in the back seat of our car and sometimes just up along the outside wall of Mousey's.

It was the dead of winter, February, and we had just busted into a bar and got away with a portable black and white TV, a sack full of rolls of quarters and a case of beer, Budweiser bottles. A trophy. Some bowling thing Danny McGowan wanted for some stupid reason. We were in my '62 T-Bird. My pussy wagon. It was burgundy with a white leather interior. A car I'd bought with the money my grandmother had given me for my high school graduation.

I had just come around the curve on Ironwood, heading south when the red light came on behind me. It was me, Dave Mikesell and Danny.

"Fuck," I said.

"Shit, we're cooked," said Dave.

"Hold on," I said. I just punched the gas and shot across Lincolnway through the red light. Just past Lincolnway, Ironwood went almost straight up to this railroad crossing. I hit the crossing and happened to glance down at the speedometer and saw it was pegged right at one-twenty. That was as far as it went. It felt like we flew half a block before we came down, sparks showering, metal screeching, and I was able to hold it on the road even though it wanted to swerve. We screamed down Ironwood, through a residential area where it seemed every other street was a four-way stop, my foot all the way to the floor. The fact that it was icy didn't seem to matter as fast as I was driving. We just kind of flew over the slick patches.

Danny started yelling he wanted out. *Stop*, he kept yelling from the back seat. Sounded like he was crying. "You want out, there's the door," I said. I looked over at Dave and he was just grinning. The cop car was far in the distance in my rearview mirror. Guess he didn't like driving that fast on ice.

"Get down on the floor," I yelled at Dave and Danny. We could hear Danny in the back and he was sobbing. He opted to stay in the car. We were flying down this narrow-ass street, cars parked on both sides, stop signs at every corner, snow and ice lying in places on the street. At a hundred and twenty mph. At least that's what the speedometer said. We might have been going faster. The adrenaline was coming in buckets and I felt this incredible *power*. Nothing was going to catch my ass, not in this car.

Just when I could barely see the cop in the rearview mirror, I saw the reflection of red lights flashing in the sky ahead of us. It was about two in the morning.

"They radioed ahead!" I yelled.

Dave popped up and looked around. "Turn at the next street!" he said. "I live around here. I know this area. We'll lose them, you turn."

I hit the brakes and we slewed sideways but I kept it on the road and we made the turn.

Into a cul de sac.

Wrong fucking street.

"Oh, man," he moaned. I cussed. Danny wept. The whole

scene was fucked.

We could hear the sirens now, coming from both ways back on Ironwood.

"We gotta hit it on foot," I said. It was for sure we didn't have time to get back on Ironwood and find another street. They sounded close and red lights were filling the sky.

All of us hit the silk. I grabbed the sack of quarters and we all rolled out. I didn't even look to see which way the other two went. It was every man Jack for himself. Just behind the houses on the cul de sac, I could see what looked like trees and a big open field. That's what I headed for. It was dark as hell, cloudy, only a little bit of a moon out, but the snow on the ground helped visibility some.

I was maybe twenty yards into the field and running for the line of trees at the far end when I saw someone running next to me about ten feet away. It was Dave. We ran and yelled at each other.

"You're going right. Keep going this way—I live this way."

I'd been to Dave's house maybe twice and I realized he was right. It was also the direction to the Shirley Motel a block away from his house, where Danny and I had a room and where all our stuff was.

On the way, we ran, then walked, then ran some more. There was nothing behind us we could see, but we couldn't tell for sure. We were both soaked and freezing to death. There must have been a foot of snow on the ground and some of the drifts we kept running into were waist-high. It was impossible to see them until you were in the middle of one of them. We made a half-ass plan as we ran. We'd go to Dave's house, where he and his mother lived, go in, get fresh clothes and his mom's car and then go to the Shirley Motel. We hoped Danny'd had the same idea and was heading there, too.

We'd hook up with Danny and head to New York. We knew they'd get the registration on my car quick and know who we were—at least who I was. I don't know why I thought of New York, but I had this idea it was so big they'd never find us there. We'd wait until the statute of limitations ran out—we figured that for a burglary and running from the cops it'd be seven years—and then we'd come back to Indiana. Don't ask me where I got all that; I wasn't exactly a criminal Rhodes Scholar. You hear more twisted logic than that on any Saturday night in Cellblock J in Pendleton, believe me.

We ran and walked more than five miles before we got to Dave's house, half a block off Highway 31 in Gilmore Park. The Shirley Motel was just around the corner, up on 31, maybe a block and a half from his house. We changed and grabbed a loaf of bread and a jar of peanut butter and Danny went through his mother's purse and grabbed some bills and then we went out and got in Dave's mom's car. She never woke up the whole time we were there, just lay passed out on the couch in the living room. We made plenty of noise, too.

"She's drunk," he said. "She'll never wake up." She didn't, either.

We drove over to the all-night gas station next to the Shirley and filled up the car. Between us we had about a hundred bucks with what Danny got from his mom's purse and what we already had on us, plus the rolls of quarters, maybe eight or nine rolls. We're looking up and down the street, the whole time we're in the car and then when we were filling it up, but everything looked normal. Not a cop in sight. We were home free.

Dave drove the car over and parked in the motel parking lot. We walked into the motel and there was just a guy sitting tipped back in a chair behind the desk, asleep. There was a magazine lying on his lap about to slide off. Our room was on the second floor.

When we got to the room I went to try the lock, thinking maybe Danny was there already. The door wasn't even closed, just standing ajar an inch or two, but it was dark inside. Now, I was convinced Danny was inside, having beat us there somehow. In my mind, I was thinking he'd run past us while we were at Dave's and was packing his stuff. I figured he had the light off so as not to attract attention.

I pushed the door all the way open and then the whole place just fucking exploded. Lights went on everywhere and cops were all over the place. They were in the room and in the rooms around ours—they just came charging out. It was a stakeout. Pretty good one, from their point of view, I guess.

This one cop smacked me between the shoulders with his baton even though I had my hands up and I went down on the floor like a sack of flour. Motherfucker! He put his knee against the small of my back and told me to give him my hands. I did and he slapped the cuffs on me behind my back. There was a little couch out in the hallway and he grabbed me by my hair and pulled me over there. I put my face down in the couch (I was on my knees) and he shook me down.

Then, from somewhere, came this German shepherd and started gnawing on my back. The cop had his revolver out and laid the muzzle on my ear and laughed and just let the dog chew away. After a few minutes of this fun one of the other cops came over and said why don't you give this kid a break, and so he put his gun back in his holster and pulled the dog off and jerked me up. We're going down the stairs, me with my hands cuffed behind my back, the cop holding my bracelets and the mutt trying to chomp on my gonads.

The cop said, laughing, "They're trained to go for the nuts or the throat. I guess he can't reach your throat." I'm doing the Watusi all the way down the stairs and then we get to the squad car and he shoves me in the back and then PUTS THE DOG BACK THERE WITH ME. The cop who's been orchestrating all this revelry climbs in the front with his partner and says, "This is Joe (meaning the dog) and he just graduated from the Academy today. He was at the bottom of his class. Kind of hard to control. He ignores me a lot." He thought this was about the funniest thing he'd ever heard, even though he was the one who said it. The way the dog just sat there on the seat beside me, growling the whole time, it's a wonder I'm still a dog lover.

We get to the jail and there are TV crews everywhere. The big one, Channel 21, is there and the cops take the cuffs off me and recuff me in the front and start to take me in down the perp walk. I looked at the bright lights and cameras all lined up and lifted my handcuffed arms and gave all of Channel 21's viewers the finger. That's how my present girlfriend, Cathy Czakany, the news editor, found out I was an outlaw. Later, she told me she fainted when my face came up unexpectedly in the editing room in the strip of news footage she was working on.

I wondered if my dad and mom were watching TV when that came on...

In my cell I lay on my stomach for two days before they finally took me over to Memorial Hospital and let a doctor look at my back where the dog had chewed it up. He said it was too late for stitches. He had a nurse scrub it down which I swear hurt worse than when the dog bit me and then put some stuff on it and bandaged it up. In about a week, I was as good as new, could even sleep on my back. It was during that time that one of the cops told me that the cop who'd put the light on me was only pulling us over to tell me I had a taillight out. I don't know if he was just fucking with me for laughs or not. Cops do shit like that...

I couldn't believe the dog had chewed through all I had on. A flannel shirt, a sweatshirt, a T-shirt and a light jacket. It was like the wrapping on a candy bar he wanted, far as he was concerned.

For two days, detectives questioned me over and over, for hours on end, about what "jobs" I had pulled. They had a bushel basket full of unsolved burglaries they were trying to clear up. They'd bring out a sheet, ask me if I'd done that one and I'd tell them to go fuck themselves. On the second day of this, on a Sunday, the sheriff, Billy Locks, cuffed me and took me outside the jailhouse. There's a little side street, not much more than an alley, between the jail and the courthouse and it was there he took me. There was literally not a soul on the streets, maybe an occasional car that passed on the main street. Everybody was in church or home in bed, nursing their hangovers.

Billy took off my cuffs and pulled out his revolver. He told me to run for it, that he'd count to ten before he fired. He said that if I made it without him shooting me, they wouldn't come after me. I'd be free and clear. I guess he was a bit testy because I hadn't cooperated.

"Nah, Billy," I said. "I'm sticking like stink on shit to you."

I was convinced he was going to shoot me anyway. After a couple of tense moments, with just us three standing there—me, Billy and his gun—he gave out this little snort, and clopped me alongside the head with his gun and I went down, blood running into my eyes. Then, Billy put the cuffs back on, yanked me up and led me inside. He told the desk sergeant to book me for resisting arrest and told him to tell the other deputies not to bother questioning me anymore and they took me back to my cell. When they left, I just stood in the corner and shook. The sweat poured off my body and my scalp was still bleeding. After a while, the turnkey brought me a wet bath towel to clean up with.

They eventually dropped the resisting arrest charge. Big whup.

It turned out I didn't have to confess to anything. My two rap-partners took care of that for me. They copped pleas and spilled everything they could think of. As it turned out, I was charged with eighty-two burglaries and ended up being the only one of us who was sentenced to prison. The court gave both of them probation. Eighty-two burglaries were all my "friends" could remember. There had been at least double that number with those guys, and then, too, I'd pulled a lot of jobs by my lonesome or with other guys that they knew nothing about. All told, over four hundred.

My "trial" was a complete farce.

***

Don't even talk to me about the American justice system. All I can do is repeat what countless others have said about it. It doesn't involve an even playing field.

I had gotten out of jail on bond after my first arrest, and then was arrested again a few months later, coming out of a gas station with Rat out in the country. It was about three in the morning and the station was closed. Rat wanted to break in to steal some really nice rims he'd spotted there one day. Dave Coffel was our getaway driver and he did just that—got away. Minus his buds. While there had been a good chance of probation after the first bust, the odds of that this time were greatly diminished. However, Sam Mirkin, the public defender who had been assigned to my case, assured me that I still had a reasonable chance at avoiding prison since I hadn't any prior convictions. Just arrests for which I hadn't yet gone to trial for.

While I was in jail awaiting my bond hearing on the second bust, the turnkey pulled a gigantic practical joke on me. He pulled me aside one day and gave me some inside dope. Or so I thought at the time.

He said, "You ought to get rid of Mirkin. He's a terrible lawyer. All he'll do is go through the motions and you'll end up in the joint." He had this other guy he said was just terrific. I'll call him "Max."

"Yeah, Max is your guy, all right," my jailer said. "He wins all of his cases. South Bend's answer to Perry Mason."

I bet he and the other guards tore their prefrontal lobotomy stitches loose laughing at that one. Max was a stone alcoholic and probably hadn't won a case in decades. What did I know? It's not like lawyers come with cards like baseball players with their won-lost records and E.R.A.'s. That's not a bad idea though, is it?

Crime hadn't paid all that well recently, and my parents were coming up with my bail money, but I knew they wouldn't spring for a lawyer's fees. I called Max up, explained my predicament and he couldn't have been nicer. Drunks always have the warmest personalities. He said he'd take my case and I could just make payments to him.

Wonderful news.

I made bail and got a job at the Uniroyal plant in Mishawaka. First thing, I repaid my parents and then started giving Max payments on his fee. Big mistake. I learned later that you never pay a criminal lawyer in full until he wins your case. Not a lawyer like Max, anyway. This is good info for you neophyte outlaws out there. I wish someone had let me in on that little secret.

As the weeks wore on, I had various meetings with Max. At each meeting, he'd outline his brilliant strategies and I'd nod enthusiastically at his plans and hand him some more money. There were a number of court appearances during this period. Max's genius strategy at each of these was to waive various of my rights. We waived my right of a speedy trial, then waived my right to a jury trial in lieu of a bench trial, then waived my right to a change of venue, and then waived...Well, we waived a whole bunch of things and then I paid him the last bit I owed and the next time we went to trial he convinced me my best bet was to plead guilty and throw myself on the mercy of the judge.

Mondo mistake. But then, Max had all the money he was entitled to from me and from this point forward, my case would only be cutting into valuable Happy Hour time, so it was time to Make A Deal. Which he did. He was able to join his cronies in time for "twofers" and I was on my way to Pendleton.

Later, I found out Mr. Mirkin was one helluva lawyer and that my man Max was the poster boy for AA. Turned out, it was all a big ol' practical joke my turnkey pal had sprung on me. Along with everybody (except myself) in town, he knew how lousy Max was as a barrister. I know I laughed for hours when I found out how I'd been tricked. Really funny stuff.

I had already cut a pretty good deal on my own with the prosecutor's office just before my sentencing.

While I was out on bond from my second bust, I hadn't exactly eliminated my criminal activities. I wasn't pulling a couple of jobs a day like I had before, but I still kept my hand in. I had also obtained gainful employment at Uniroyal on the boot line. Rubber boots were my game.

I ended up meeting a rookie cop, Darryl, and we decided to get an apartment together. I met him at a bar one night when he was off-duty and out of uniform and we hit it off. He didn't know I was an outlaw or out on bond. All he knew was that we got along great and that I worked at Uniroyal.

Darryl was perhaps the most naïve guy I've ever known. Really a nice guy, but innocent as all shit. I had a way with the ladies though and he really liked that. He was a gangly, pimple-faced doofus that would never have gotten laid on his own. I think they'd hired him to play the role of Barney Fife for the force.

One night, while partying, I fell asleep on the couch in the living room. Darryl got up in the morning and went off to work, catching parking meter bandits or whatever he did. For some reason, he got off early and came home about four in the afternoon. And, found me passed out with the apartment on fire.

The night before I was smoking when I fell asleep. The cigarette had fallen into the couch cushions and basically smoldered all night and most of the next day before it burst into flames. I'd awakened just as that happened with the apartment full of smoke and it was just a small fire at that point. I'd jumped up and had been running back and forth from the kitchen with panfulls of water to put it out when the smoke got to me and I went out. That's where Darryl found me when he walked in. He carried me out and the ambulance came and they revived me. Usually, he didn't get home until around six so somebody was looking out for me.

The apartment couldn't be used until they took care of all the smoke damage, so Darryl and I parted company and I haven't seen him since. Hope he's had a good life—I sure owe him mine. He reads this I imagine he's going to be a bit surprised to learn he'd been sharing an apartment with an outlaw.

I found out that dying from smoke inhalation was about the same as drowning. Both experiences featured no pain at all—you just went out and never knew a thing.

I met a new girl just after that incident. Sherry Whitney. She was to become my third wife.

There was an incident that happened with my third wife, Sherry, in which I used her as a shield against a pissed-off guy. Well, the *possibility* of a pissed-off guy.

We weren't married at the time, just living together and I was doing a lot of heavy-duty gambling. Each week, I was averaging about eight thousand dollars in bets, mostly on football and basketball, in season. I wasn't winning or losing that much—that was just how much changed hands in a week's time, on average.

I also ran a poker game with one of the guys who lived in the next-door duplex. Every Friday night we held the game and this guy and I would "brother-in-law" during the game and split up afterward. "Brother-in-lawing," for those who may be unfamiliar with the term, is when two people in a poker game keep raising bets each hand until most or all the others drop out. One of you would then rake in the pot. Or, if someone stayed, you still had a good chance of beating him. I would also deal "seconds" from time to time. I couldn't stack an entire deck like I've known some people to be able to, but I could stack one card at least, and deal myself or my partner that one for a hole card when we played five-card stud. We made a lot of money on those games and nobody ever tumbled. Maybe because we chose our "guests" carefully. Mostly straights who worked straight citizen jobs and fancied themselves expert poker players. I remember one guy always had out this little card that gave all the betting odds on the various hands that he constantly referred to. And, continually lost...

Here's a piece of wisdom you may want to consider if you play poker. If you can't spot the sucker...it's you.

We'd also furnish the booze and sandwiches, which Sherry would serve. For that, she took a small cut on each pot.

Whenever I'd have an especially good week, we'd jump on a plane and fly to Las Vegas. One week, I hit nine out of eleven bets on pro football games and was up about $4,500, so I came home and told Sherry to get her shit together, we were going to Vegas. We were gone three days. Did about what I usually did in Vegas, ended up losing about a thousand. That was pretty good, considering the amount of action we had. Most times, we didn't hit the hotel room except to screw, spending most of our time at the tables. I loved the craps tables and Sherry would play the slots, although she could roll the bones, too.

When we got back to South Bend, Sherry said she had to stop by her folks' house to pick up something or other. We walked in the front door and her dad was sitting in the living room in his easy chair and when he saw Sherry, he went white as the proverbial sheet and started gasping for air like he was having a heart attack.

When Sherry's mom heard the commotion in the living room she came out from the kitchen and she did pass out when she saw her daughter. Crumpled right to the floor.

They were under the impression that Sherry was dead.

While we were in Vegas, a girl had been found shot and murdered and dumped in a field just outside of Niles, Michigan, a little town just over the state line from South Bend. There was no identification on the body, so the police had her photograph published in the area newspapers, including *The South Bend Tribune.* Sherry's dad and mom saw the paper and "recognized" it as their daughter. They went down to the morgue and positively identified the dead girl's body as being Sherry's. That's how much this girl looked like her.

You can imagine their shock when Sherry and I walked into

their house a day later! They even had a funeral date set up for three days from then. The police had to conduct an autopsy first.

We all went over to Niles to the police station to tell them a mistake had been made and it got really confusing. Finally, it got cleared up, sort of. An ex-boyfriend of Sherry's, who'd been on the scene with her before me, was the insanely jealous type. He'd swore that if she ever went to bed with anyone else, he'd kill her and him. He was kind of a violent dude, Sherry said. He used to beat her up regularly. She figured the cops thought it was reasonable as well, was that since this girl looked so much like Sherry—I mean, even her own *parents* had identified the body as her—that this clown had thought it was her as well and whacked her.

The upshot was they picked the guy up but ended up having to cut him loose. He was a biker and a bunch of his outlaw buddies testified he'd been with them, partying hearty at the time they figured the girl was murdered. This wasn't good news as far as either I or Sherry was concerned. Now, he knew she was alive and he knew who I was from the newspaper reports. This didn't make me feel too comfortable.

We were living in a duplex apartment where we had a combination bedroom/living room and kitchen and shared the connecting bath with the duplex apartment next door. Our bed was a couch that folded out. Before this incident, I always slept on the side nearest the side window. After all this went down, I made Sherry sleep on that side. I told her straight out, "It's your deal, not mine. If this guy comes by and shoots in the window, I don't think it's fair I be the one who gets killed. I'm an innocent bystander." She didn't like it, but what could she say?

The guys next door and I were making some drug deals during this time. Mostly marijuana, but we also dealt heroin. In the mid-sixties, in a Midwestern town, this was pretty risqué stuff for white boys. Everybody did grass, but heroin wasn't the drug of choice for most Hoosiers, at least not in our corner of the state. At that time, it was primarily a black drug and even more specifically a black musician's drug. Other than a couple of times while I was in Bermuda, this was the first time I'd run (shot up) drugs. We did other stuff, too. Mescaline, peyote, 'shrooms, acid, prescription drugs, and pills. Basically, anything that could get you high.

While I was with Sherry, I was introduced to drug "salad" parties. We'd have a bunch of other fun-time druggies and party animals over and everybody would bring an assortment of pills with them. We'd all drop our stash into a salad bowl and mix 'em all up and then, without looking, reach in and grab five-six pills and swallow them. There were some interesting chemical experiences that came out of those parties.

One night, somebody slipped Sherry a hit of acid. No big deal, except Sherry hadn't experienced acid up until then and whoever gave it to her neglected to tell her what it was. Acid was fairly new in our part of the world.

When it kicked in, she started hallucinating. She thought she was going insane. Movies started playing on her mind's Sony. Going insane was one of her constant fears. Looking back over our time together, I can see it was a legitimate concern. Seeing a rubber room in her future, she did the only logical thing she could think of. She tried to kill herself. By jumping out of the window. The problem was, in her mind-altered state, she forgot we were on the ground floor and she made another small miscalculation. She forgot to check to see if the window was open. It wasn't.

She got cut up pretty bad when she went through the glass.

That was an interesting period, living with Sherry. I met her downtown right after I'd made bond from my second bust.

I picked her up at the Bonnie Doone drive-in restaurant and dazzled her with my repartee and we went to a motel and she fucked my eyes out. We got the apartment the next day.

There were three people living in the other apartment, the one we shared the bathroom with. Two guys and a beautiful Irish blonde girl with the greenest eyes I've ever seen. She was drop-dead gorgeous. The guys were your basic street hustlers. The girl, Maureen, worked in some insurance office as a secretary. Casey and Charles made money hustling pool and playing cards in a regular game at this bar just down the street from our apartment. It was with them that I ended up running the "brother-in-law" poker game at our apartment.

I was more of a pool hustler, though, and the bar we all hung out in was great for that kind of business. In the Navy, I made a lot of money shooting pool and had always loved the game. I usually played the money game, nine-ball, although there was always somebody who wanted to play straight pool or eight-ball. Nowadays, it's all eight-ball, which, far as I'm concerned, is a chump's game. Nine-ball's the only true hustler's game, and forget straight pool. That's pool for the tournament guys. Too slow to make money on. I've even played billiards but that's a game that's a major snooze.

Anyway, Maureen came up pregnant and her two boyfriends went ballistic. Sherry came up pregnant about the same time, but I didn't care. But Casey and Charles didn't want a pregnant girlfriend, so they did everything they could to make her abort. One time, they asked her to paint the cupboards in their kitchen and Casey came over and said, "Come over and watch this." I went over, not knowing what he was up to, and when we came in the kitchen, I saw him wink at Charles. Maureen was up on a stepladder with her brush and bucket of paint and Charles just went over and kicked the ladder out from under her. She went down and hit her stomach on the counter and screamed. It didn't work; she was still preggo.

Another time, they made her drink paregoric. That didn't work, either. One time, I heard a thumping noise on their side of the bathroom door and went over. They had Maureen standing up against the door and Casey was tossing these professional throwing knives he'd bought, all around her, like you see in the circus. She'd let these guys do anything they wanted. Beautiful, but dumb as a box of rocks.

Casey was the reason I got sent up. Well, part of it.

We were all dealing drugs. Lots of shit. Acid, weed, hash, heroin, you name it. This was before the cocaine days. In fact, this was in the mid-sixties, way before the serious drug days at all.

We'd been raided several times before and the cops had never found our stash. We had a place in the toilet tank where we'd run and tape it to when they knocked on the door. Now, that'd be the first place the cops would look these days, but remember that this was in the early days when cops weren't as hip on hiding places as they've become. They never even went near the toilet.

The three next door had a big fight and Casey left. The day after he was kicked out by Charles and Maureen, the cops raided us and this time they went straight to the toilet and found our drugs. They didn't even go through the pretense of looking anywhere else. I'm sure Casey snitched us out.

We were all busted—me and Sherry and Charles and Maureen. We all made bond and my lawyer said not to worry about it, I would still get probation, but that isn't what happened.

About a week later, a detective dropped by the apartment while Sherry was at work and told me I would probably walk on my charges, get probation like my lawyer'd said. He said I'd beat them. Then, he dropped a bomb on me. He said that even though I had a good chance of walking, they were going to go after Sherry and would make sure she got sentenced and did time at the Indiana Women's Prison. He told me some things about her past that convinced me the judge probably would give her at least six months in the joint. The detective said the only way I could save her ass was to plead guilty and if I did that, they'd drop the charges completely on Sherry. He also spent a lot of time telling me what would happen to her down at the Women's Prison in Indianapolis. Things other inmates would do to her with broomsticks, stuff like that.

This stuff got to me. Sherry was pregnant with our child and this guy kept telling me our kid would be born in prison and end up in foster homes being abused. Stuff like that.

I decided to plead guilty. The deal was, I would cop to one count of second-degree burglary and they would drop all the other burglary counts, plus all the other charges, the armed and strong-arm robberies. I might still get probation, I was told, but even if I didn't, the most I'd get would be a two to five-year sentence or maybe a one-to-ten on the burglary thing.

That was a laugh. They weren't even considering probation. As soon as I pled guilty, I was let back out on my original bond for two weeks while they did the presentence investigation and when I went back, I ended up getting a two to five and sent over to the jail to await paperwork and transportation to Pendleton Reformatory.

During the two-week period of the presentence investigation, Sherry and I got married and I made arrangements for my sister Jo and her husband Jim to take Sherry in during her pregnancy in case I got sent up. They lived in Lakeville and had two kids of their own, but both of them had big hearts and didn't even hesitate when I asked them to take her in. Sherry hadn't wanted to get married, but I didn't want our kid being born a bastard.

Once I was in Pendleton, Sherry visited a couple of times and then I didn't see her any more. Her letters stopped as well. Normal shit for cons. Then, I got a letter from a lawyer asking my consent for a divorce. I wouldn't sign it, and then my sister wrote me a letter saying they had had to kick Sherry out. It seems she was eight months pregnant and one day my brother-in-law Jim was painting the living room and she walked up to him on the ladder and grabbed his johnson and told him she wanted to screw him. He was a righteous dude and told her to get fucked and also to pack her shit and leave their house, which she did. Jo apologized over and over for having to kick her out, but I thought she showed remarkable forbearance, as did Jim, for what she'd done. I signed the divorce papers, but a few months later, I was served with some more papers asking if

I'd allow Sherry to put the baby (it was a girl) up for adoption. I refused to sign them, and wrote my sister to see if they would consider keeping the baby until I got out and could care for her. They immediately agreed—great sister!—but Sherry told all of us to get fucked and put the baby up for adoption anyway. It turned out they didn't need my signature to do that, even though I was the legal father. You forfeit all such rights when you're in prison. So our little girl was adopted and I've never seen or heard of her since.

When I got released a couple of years later, I went to a minister and told him my story. I wanted to know if he thought I should try to locate my daughter and get her back. He advised me to leave things the way they were. "She's in a good home now," he said. "Parents who love her and who she thinks of as her mom and dad. You can't take care of her at this time, so leave her alone. She's better off." I saw he was right and did as he suggested. Many times since then I have wondered if I did the right thing. I also wonder if she'll ever try to look me up. I hope her life turned out all right. I hope if she ever does look me up she'll understand why I didn't try to find her.

I only saw Sherry one more time after that. About two years after I got out, I walked into a titty bar in South Bend one afternoon. It was bright sunshine outside and dark inside and when I walked in all I could see was the barmaid behind the bar and one girl sitting in the middle of the bar, but I couldn't make her features out that well. I sat on the end of the bar and ordered a drink and then I looked at the girl sitting there. She looked cute, so I asked her if I could buy her a drink and then if she minded if I sat by her. Cool, she said, so I picked up my drink and walked over and sat next to her and asked the barmaid to give her a drink. When she got it, I looked at her and said, "You're going to think this is the corniest line you've ever heard, but I swear to God, you look familiar." The girl looked at me and laughed and said, "I should. We used to be married."

It was Sherry. When that dawned on me, I grabbed the drink

I'd bought for her and said, "I'm not buying you any drinks, bitch," but then I cooled down and we talked some. It turned out she was working at this place at nights as a dancer and had just stopped in to pick up some money the owner owed her. We talked a little bit and then I left the bar. Haven't seen her to this day. Hope I never do.

A few years later, I told my story to a lawyer I was drinking with and he said I'd made the biggest mistake of my life by listening to that detective. He said, based on what I'd told him, Sherry never would have got sent up and that with a decent lawyer, neither would have I. Other than changing my plea to guilty, all they had on me were the two times they'd caught me at the scene of a crime and while they could easily prove those, two crimes wouldn't have been enough to get me sent up. I should have gotten probation, he said. I saw he was right but then it wasn't a big deal. I'd given up a couple of years of my life in a misguided effort to save Sherry from prison, but I just chalked it up to a valuable experience for my writing. Still seems like a fair tradeoff.

I was brazen for years, bolder than bold, thought I had balls of brass. One time, for instance, I went into a little club down by the St. Joe River where a band was playing, and started talking to a cute girl at the bar. She was drunk. Ten minutes after meeting her for the first time, we got up to dance and I just backed her into this little space behind the bandstand and laid her down and fucked her there on the floor. People were dancing by, looking down at us.

She kept saying, "Can anyone see us? Is anyone looking?"

"No way," I said. "We're completely hidden." I think the entire population of that club danced by before we were through, laughing and pointing at us. She never saw any of them. Until we got up and she pulled up her panties and we walked out and the whole place burst into applause. She ran out and I've never seen her since.

Another time, a girl drove by Michael's Hairstyling where I was working, saw the sign and walked in and asked if she could get a haircut. During the shampoo, I just came out and said, "You know what? I'd like to eat you till your nose bleeds." Her hair was dripping wet as we made our way out through the back room to my car and screwed in the back seat. People kept parking their cars and walking by and doing doubletakes. Twenty minutes later, we went back in and I cut her hair. I never did get her name and she never came back for another trim. I think she was embarrassed. Sounds crude, but those kinds of lines worked a lot of times. Usually best on the "Ice Queens," girls so beautiful that most guys were afraid to approach them, and when they did, treated them with this cockamamy respect. It wasn't the lines as much as the boldness and the cocky attitude I always had at that time. I just expected them to say yes to whatever I wanted and they usually did.

There have been many, many casual sex incidents. I had a shop in a small town in Indiana in the mid-seventies and about a month after I opened for business, the mayor's wife came in for her appointment. First time she'd been in the shop. I had just finished blow-drying her hair and we were talking about something mundane—the weather, perhaps—when out of the blue, she leaned over and grabbed my cock through my trousers. She was maybe fifteen years older than I was, but still very attractive. A minute later, we were on the floor fucking. After, she walked to the front door to leave, and as her hand was on the doorknob, I said, "Didn't you forget something?"

"What?" she asked, a puzzled look on her face.

"You didn't pay for your haircut," I said.

"You want me to *pay* after what we just did?" she said, incredulous.

"Well, yes," I replied, grinning. "You don't want me to think of you as a whore, do you? Somebody that does this for money?"

She paused in thought for a moment and then said, "I guess

you've got a point," reached into her handbag and placed some money on the counter.

She didn't tip though.

One night, we were out burglarizing a gas station—me, Rat and Tim Coffel. Tim drove the getaway car for two reasons: One, it was his car and it was one of the new Plymouth Hemi's and it was fast, and, two, he was too chickenshit to actually break into a place with us.

Rat and I had just rolled a pair of tires off the display rack and had gone out the back door into the field that lay between us and the side road where Tim was parked, motor running, when Rat stopped and said, "Listen."

I didn't hear anything at first and then I did. It sounded like a rifle to me. Rat thought it was a shotgun, but then he wasn't much of a hunter. Then this voice boomed out from the darkness, "Lay down, motherfuckers, or I'm going to blow you away."

We complied.

We couldn't see where the voice was coming from. It seemed to be from a house at the other end of the field. Probably where the owner lived and he probably had some kind of alarm hookup that rang in his house. We figured that all out pretty quickly.

We still couldn't see anybody and the voice sounded like it was some distance away but we just couldn't be sure. We kept looking at where Coffel sat in his car and could hear the motor running. He was completely unaware of what was going down. So near and yet so far.

"Let's go for it," I said.

"Fuck you," Rat whispered. "That asshole'll shoot us."

"He's too far away," I said. "Chances are he can't get both of us anyway."

"Fuck that shit," Rat said. "I'm four inches taller than you. Who you think he's gonna pick?" If he wasn't pretty much on the nose with that observation, it would have been funny. Actually, it still was.

We kept arguing like that back and forth and then we heard the siren and a second later, the cop car's red light bouncing off the night clouds. Coffel sat in his car, oblivious to it all. He had a bitchin' reverberator on his radio and we bet he was listening to some Young Rascals or something and couldn't hear the siren. Some getaway driver.

The police car was in full sight now, barreling down the highway and Coffel must have finally spotted it since he laid about fifty feet of rubber getting out of there. Left us high and dry. Didn't even hesitate. Nice guy. For a long time, I wanted to look him up and thank him for everything.

I never liked Coffel to begin with, hadn't wanted him to come on the job, but he was Rat's friend so I let Rat talk me into letting him come. Coffel was a big fat slob whose dad owned a big construction company in Elkhart and bought him new cars, whatever he wanted every year. Daddy's little fat fuck. He had a big mouth that matched his body. His cojones were where he got cheated on size.

The cops must have made a decision to go with the two birds in the hand rather than chase Coffel. Maybe they saw what he had and knew they wouldn't catch him in a month. In a second, they were rolling up to the gas station and running over to us, revolvers drawn.

Now Rat was the big motherfucker. Sat in the back seat, handcuffed, cracking jokes with the cops. I was quiet. I knew we were in big-ass trouble. This was my second bust.

Sure enough, I keep my mouth shut, Rat sang like a...well, a *rat*, even gave up his buddy Coffel. Since this was my second bust, I went to Pendleton, Rat got probation and Coffel got charges dismissed. Rat blew the whistle on Dave and Danny, too, what he knew about their part in various jobs. They got probation, too. Since I was the oldest of the bunch, they said I must be the ringleader.

IV
THE SOUTH BEND JAIL AND MY RAPE

I was raped in the South Bend jail. For many, many years, no one besides myself and my attacker knew what had happened. It isn't something a guy goes around talking about. It wasn't until one day in Vermont when I told my MFA advisor I was planning to write a memoir and then told her about what had happened to me that no one else in the world was privy to it. I knew then that I would have to write about it. As I said earlier, I *want* to write this. See if it's the kind of therapy folks claim it is.

My body, as I tap the words onto the screen belies that last statement, about wanting to write down my experience. My hands perspire; no, they flat-out *sweat*. My stomach aches in that spot where my ulcer always shows up. I've cleaned up the mess on my desk, dumped my wastebasket, fed my son's beagle, Buddy, watched a baseball game I wasn't remotely interested in. I'd clip my toenails again, but they're down to the quick from the three times I've already clipped them. I've done everything I can to avoid this. My feet are dripping and I keep moving them to a dry part of the carpet. It soon becomes wet, too. I may get electrocuted by my computer before I can write about it. One can hope...

Deep breath. Plunge into the water. Don't think about how cold it will be.

***

It's kind of funny, what goes on in a guy's mind when a razor blade is held to the tender skin of his throat and he is being fucked in the ass...against his express wishes. That an erect penis forcibly entering the anus is not unlike that of a proctologist's fingers. Or, in my more immediate experience, that of a prison guard conducting a gloved body cavity search. Those were some of the thoughts that swept through my mind while I was being raped, early one morning in the South Bend city jail.

A kind of detachment separated my mind from my physical body as my butthole was being violated. The same kind of detachment that occurred at certain other crisis points in my life. For instance, the time when I was ten years old and was (willfully) almost drowned by another Scout during a Boy Scout camping trip to Garner State Park in Texas. The time my girlfriend Cat stabbed another girl I was seeing and tried to nail me before I got the knife away from her. Outrunning the cops or engaging in a shootout with what you think are cops. Your mind remains oddly calm at moments like this. Go figure.

Unlike my drowning episode, I didn't struggle frantically or otherwise while I was being raped. I held about as still as I could, what with a Gillette Blue Blade, melted with a match into a toothbrush, held just below my Adam's apple with enough pressure that it slightly pierced the skin. It wasn't a time for movement, not if I wanted to stay alive. Or so I thought. Later, I wondered if a razor blade could have really cut deep enough to kill me. Just one of the things you think about in hindsight that lends to your guilt at not resisting.

And, yes; there's guilt. There's a support group set up for every kind of trauma there is except for men who have been raped by other men. I guess most of us aren't wild about going public with this kind of news. Besides, I hate to think what the twelve steps would be in recovery. I realize it's enormously difficult for a woman to admit she's been raped, but for a man, I think that it's darn near impossible. A raped woman can still get dates, but when a man is raped, there goes the ol' macho thing right out the window and that's what most of us figure is our chief attraction to the babes. Giving our "feminine side" the space to breathe is what the Seven Sisters of magazinedom would have us believe to be the wave of the present, but your average guy on the make still relies heavily on muscle-flexing and steely stares. Clint Eastwood movies shown on late night TV still get better Neilson numbers than Alan Alda vehicles. Telling a prospective bed partner you've been raped is likely to result in a circumspect tear, a hand on your arm...and a move on down the bar to the guy who looks like Steven Seagal. At best, if you happen to end up between the sheets after imparting this bit of your past, you can bet you're going to end up on bottom and leather will be involved.

How can I write about this? "Just tell it," my friend and MFA advisor said, her intelligent eyes sad. "Just the way you told me. Don't try to be literary. Just tell it the same way, as if we were back at Charlie O's, having beers together."

She added, "And leave me out of it, please. Don't put my name in your book." A common request, I discovered, as I began researching past events. Go figure.

It sounded easy then. I had thought forty years enough distance to be able to record the incident for others to see. It wasn't enough distance. Not nearly enough. I needed another forty years at least. Only thing is, by then, I'd be in my hundreds and with the way my body has been going south, I doubt if I'd have enough energy left to flip on the computer.

Besides, this has to come out. I've just told the first person in the universe what happened to me in jail that February morning. Not even my wife knew. A public person, if you will. Oh, I know my friend and advisor would never reveal my secret, but it's no longer a secret now that I've confided in her. It's out in the world, floating, exposed. And I *want* to write this. See if it's the kind of therapy folks claim it is.

First, though, let me tell you about the events that led up to that night in the South Bend jail when I was raped. Looking back, I can see now that I was headed for that moment from the git-go.

It took a lifetime, but now I understand at this later date that we create our own destinies.

Good or bad.

What I remember mostly after my amorous visitor and his wayward hormones had left is climbing back up onto the top bunk and lying there, his jizm oozing down between the inside of my legs, turning cold in the air. I didn't want to wipe it off. I didn't want my fingers touching it. It was bad enough that my legs had to. There was a sink out in the bullpen but I couldn't make myself go use it. I was convinced everyone in the cells lining the bullpen had heard what happened, were laughing at me, even though only the usual snoring and sleep-twitching sounds came from my fellow criminals in the other cells.

After Toles left my cell, I lay on my bunk and the oddest image entered my mind. James Baldwin. The inside book jacket photo of the black author of *Go Tell it on the Mountain*. I'd been on a Baldwin binge just prior to being arrested. I knew instantly why he came to mind, why his picture presented itself on the movie screen of my brain. The chief impression I'd always gotten after finishing one of his books was...semen. There was semen everywhere in the pages of his work. That he was a brilliant writer was evident to me after reading the first page of the first book of his I'd picked up, *Giovanni's Room.*

And he seemed to be a physically *little* black man, the same as Toles. I knew intellectually they were different kinds of men, had totally different sensibilities, but from that moment on, they were connected, as if they were twins or closer, different manifestations of the same person. It wasn't fair, but I couldn't help it. Before that day, Baldwin had been my favorite writer. I haven't read him since. I can't bear to even pick up one of his books, hold it in my hand. I can feel the semen oozing out from between the pages. It feels dirty. Since that day, I've felt that the kind of writing you describe as *powerful* is always dirty. There is always a kind of lust involved, usually sexual, that shines through whatever story the writer is telling. This was true of Baldwin and this seemed to be true of any author who influenced me. I read guys like Balzac, Victor Hugo, Dostoevsky when I was twelve and their stories seemed the same as Baldwin's and a few others. Dirty. Miserable creatures; ugly, misshapen, who lusted after something or someone and tried to hide those urges behind lyrically-elevated sentences about idealistic yearnings, usually political. But they weren't fooling me. All they really wanted was to release jizm.

I lay there on the bunk, on my side, my face to the wall, not even pulling my blanket over me. The only way I could deal with what had happened was to reduce it in my mind to solely a physical level. The emotional part, I shoved aside, pushed way back in my mind, kept it there until the present moment, some four decades later. That night, I compared what happened to a proctologist probing me with a gloved finger. Doctor Happy Hand. This is all it was, I think, amazed. It wasn't that bad. I'm not bleeding, at least I don't think I am. The pain wasn't that great. It hurts worse to get hit in the mouth, sometimes. Of course, a poke in the chops doesn't carry nearly the same social stigma.

While he was raping me, I remember being surprised. He wasn't that big. Much smaller than I was. Weren't black guys supposed to be hung? Somehow, that knowledge gave me a bit of perverse pride, helped me endure what was going on. Ego had been at the center of everything in my life; no reason to expect it to disappear in a little crisis like this.

Weird stuff went through my head during the rape. I worried I would like it and if that would make me a homosexual. I worried I would end up so traumatized I could never go to bed with a woman again. As it turned out, it would be three weeks before I masturbated again...nearly three years before I could test the Big Kahuna on a real-life opposite-sex human being. I was on my way to a two to five year sentence to be served out at Pendleton Reformatory, where comely maidens would be in short supply.

What may have saved my life and some of my sanity was the abruptness of it all. It was probably beneficial to my mental health that my attacker hadn't read any of those books on prolonging the sexual experience...Illiteracy is sometimes underrated.

Earlier that previous afternoon two black men approached me as I sat at one of the two picnic tables set up in the bullpen. Around the bullpen, which was just a big, square open space, were cells on two sides, the concrete wall of the building at the back, and open bars and the one entrance at the front. The cells contained two bunks, one above the other, and they swung down on steel bands from the wall. There were doors on the cells but they were never locked. One or two men were in each cell, depending on the current population. This particular area of the jail was for those already convicted of their crimes and awaiting transportation to either Pendleton or the Michigan City Prison. Back in 1966 there were only two adult maximum security prisons in Indiana. Pendleton was for felons under the age of thirty and Michigan City housed the older convicts and those on Death Row. Occasionally, younger inmates would be sent to Michigan City and older ones to Pendleton for safekeeping—guys that had been threatened at their original prison and asked to be moved. That usually didn't do them much good, as guys in both places had contacts in the other one and the hit was usually carried out eventually.

"Hey, man, 'sup?" asked the smaller of the two, a burglar I later learned was named Toles. The other, a huge, blue-black hued man named Cleaves, didn't say much. Toles was about an inch and a half shorter than I was, maybe five-eleven. Cleaves went about six-six and was built like a chunk of marble. I think he was in for armed robbery or killing his parents or his Sunday school teacher or something like that.

It never crossed my mind that I was being set up. I hadn't had much experience at that time with what went on in the joint and the rumors I'd heard were sketchy. Rape just never entered my mind. I was to become more suspicious and cynical in the future, but at that point I was in the rookie season of my criminal career. Nowadays with what's been revealed on documentaries on TV I would know, but in those days Ozzie and Harriet hardly ever talked about what went on in jails or if they did I missed that episode.

We started playing cards and I started smoking the squares Toles offered magnanimously. Nowadays, everyone who has been to a movie about prisons or who has read a book on the subject knows you don't accept gifts in jail. Oh sure, I'd heard guys joking about such things, but it didn't really register in my innocent mind. Besides, I fancied myself quite the barroom brawler and Toles just didn't seem the kind of guy who would put up much against my fearsome punch. His large amigo was a different story, but Cleaves never said but a word or two all afternoon. He just sat there with a surly look and I didn't pay him much attention.

I was cocky then, too. The cockiest guy around. Invincible, in my mind. I'd had so many fistfights, I thought there wasn't anybody who could whip me. Oh, I lost a great many of the fights I was in, probably more than I won, but the thing was, nobody *beat* me. No matter how badly I was whipped, I would always bounce back up and laugh like a hyena who enjoyed having his nose broken. I was as proud of my ability to take a punch as I was to deliver one. What I didn't realize was I had never been in a real fight. One in which you could be rendered room temperature.

The best way I can describe my general attitude at the time was that I was inflicted with the short man's disease. I never knew a little guy who wasn't always trying to prove himself. That was me, a short guy trapped in a tall man's body. I was six-foot and a half inch tall, but I acted like I was four-eight. I had to fight everybody. All the guys I ran around with, I ended up fighting. Even friends.

Danny was a good example. About two inches taller than me and maybe thirty pounds heavier, Danny McGowan was my best friend at the time. He was fearless, just as I was. We'd pull the craziest jobs, robbing and ripping. Always trying to top each other. That old schoolboy rivalry thing.

One winter night, we were having a party in our apartment. It was me, Danny and Rat and some girls we picked up down at the Bonnie Doone drive-in restaurant in South Bend. We three guys had rented the apartment a few days before. Dead broke, we had convinced the elderly landlady we had checks coming in from our new jobs at the Uniroyal plant in the neighboring town of Mishawaka, and she had let us move in on the condition we pay her as soon as we got paid. None of us had a job at Uniroyal or any place else. We figured we'd pull a burglary or an armed robbery, get the money that way. So far, nothing had materialized.

We'd been living on popcorn and beer and occasionally a steak we'd filch from the back of Walt's Restaurant on Highway 31. Walt's had an illegal pinball machine that the owner paid off in cash back by the meat reefers, and one of us would play the pinball while the other two stuffed their shirts with frozen T-bones whenever the coast was clear.

We were partying down and people kept coming in. Some of our friends had come by and brought girls with them and there must have been fifteen-twenty people in the apartment. Pretty soon, the noise level got up there and I told Danny to cool it. He was making the most noise and the landlady lived downstairs.

"We're gonna get kicked out," I told him. "Where the fuck we gonna go if that happens, Danny?" It was about ten degrees below zero out and snowing like it could go on for two or three days. Typical, miserable, Indiana weather.

Danny just laughed at me and got even louder. He was doing it on purpose. So I took a poke at him. Smacked him in the mouth. In a second, the other guys had us separated and then we were piling into cars and heading for the south end of town, off Highway 31 to a country road. Rat had come to his senses and organized the caravan. He didn't want to get kicked out any more than I did.

When we got outside of town, on this little country road, we all jumped out of the cars and Danny and I squared off. As much as I fought all the time, I wasn't really much of a boxer except in my own mind, where I was a legend. I usually depended on sucker-punching a guy or selling him a wolf ticket, in prison parlance, but Danny knew me and wouldn't buy into my bad-ass act. Two-three punches, and he had me down on the side of the road, straddled over me. "Give it up, Les," he said. "I don't want to hurt you." He always had a soft side to him.

"I'm done," I said, and he stepped aside and I got up. We were all pretty drunk but Danny was farther gone than any of us. He turned and I saw my opportunity and cold-cocked him up alongside his head. I caught him pretty good and he fell down into the little drainage ditch running alongside the road. Every time he tried to climb back up on his hands and knees, he kept sliding back in the snow. It didn't help that every time he got to the top I'd haul off and kick him in the face. There was blood everywhere. It was just too slick and he was too drunk to negotiate the incline with me practicing my field goal technique. Finally, a couple of guys came over and grabbed me and let Danny weave his way to the top. Get in the car, somebody said, and Danny stood there, his T-shirt torn and bloody and his face a mess and he told us all to go fuck ourselves, he'd walk back.

"Fuck him," I said. "He wants to walk, lettim." They asked a couple of more times, but Danny was a stubborn fuck, so we left him there, beside this deserted country road, nothing on but a ripped-up T-shirt and jeans and tennis shoes, no socks, blood everywhere and his nose puffed up. And it was freezing and spitting snow.

The next day, he still hadn't showed up at the apartment, so we drove back out to where we'd had the fight, thinking maybe he was frozen to death. We couldn't find him, even though we found the spot where we'd fought. It was easy to find—blood-soaked snow was clearly visible. I was starting to feel guilty about the whole thing by then.

He showed up three days after the night of the fight, with new threads and a story about how he'd hiked over to Highway 31 and a girl coming home from Ball State University had picked him up, taken him home with her and screwed his lights out. Her parents were in Florida, he said, and they had this big-ass house all to themselves and they did the horizontal bop in just about every room in the place. He told me he appreciated what I'd done—it was the best piece of ass he'd ever had. It sounded like a tall tale, but there he was, new duds and all that he claimed the girl had bought for him and he sure didn't look like he'd missed any meals. So there we were, friends again, like nothing ever happened. That was the way things went in those halcyon days.

That was the kind of cocky motherfucker I was then, what my general attitude was all about. The fight with Danny was maybe a month and a half before I ended up in jail with Toles and I didn't think anyone could whip my bad ass.

I had a lot to learn. Mr. Toles was about to "educate" me...

Lights went out at ten and I rolled over on my side, face to the wall and thought about a girl I had been dating: Cathy. Cathy worked for WSBT-TV, Channel 22, as some kind of news editor. She was a beautiful, tiny blonde with a fizzy personality—you know—all bubbly and smiling all the time. Great girl. She didn't have a clue what I was into until a piece of film she was editing showed me being brought into the station, whereupon, she told me later, she fainted.

I was just about to go to sleep, wondering how I was going

to square things with Cathy, knowing I wasn't, when all of a sudden somebody grabbed my hair and I felt something sharp at my throat. It was Toles.

"Get on down, white boy," he whispered, and I didn't know what else to do but "get on down." He walked me over to the side of the cell, against the wall, and when we got there, he reached around and unzipped my pants and pulled them and my underwear down to my ankles. Naturally, he kept the razor at my throat during all of this.

I remember thinking what my father would do if this had happened to him. My father was the most powerful man in the world to me. Is today, too, I guess, even though he's been dead twenty years. He never took shit from anyone in his life, except his mother-in-law, my grandma. I knew exactly what he would do if he ever found himself in the same situation I was in. "Cut my throat, punk," is what he would have said. "You better kill me, though, or I'll kill you." More probable, he wouldn't have said a word, would've just turned and broke the guy's neck. Even more likely, he would never have been selected for rape. He carried himself in such a way that I can't imagine something like this ever happening to him. This is exactly what I thought about the whole time Toles was raping me. What my dad would have done. Thinking I would never be the man my father was. I just didn't have it in me. I was too afraid of dying. I was weaker than my dad and that was the worst part of the whole deal, knowing that.

Other things go through your mind. Weird things. I was looking at the wall before me while Toles was penetrating me and wondering when the coat of gray paint had been applied and by whom. Inmates? Outside contractor? I thought of people driving by on the street outside, totally unaware of what was going on just a few feet from them. A million things go on at once, a hurricane of ideas, but at the center I was calm. All during the act, I concentrated on the razor blade at my neck, thinking that when he came, he would be so involved in physical ecstasy (it's very hard to write these words in this connection—*physical ecstasy*) that his hand would waver and I could turn and hit him. It never happened.

Instead, he was just gone and I was standing there. I stood there a moment, just listening, hearing nothing but the sound of my own breath.

I didn't cry and I kept thinking I should, but I just couldn't. My mind was simply numb. After a couple of minutes, I walked over to my bunk, the top one, and climbed up and lay down, facing the wall.

I lay like that for hours. I heard the first stirrings of prisoners, first the coughing, then the squeaks as men in the other cells swung their feet over the edges of their bunks, and then the plop of feet hitting the floor. Laughter, talking, the sounds of the one stool being flushed over and over, guys joking about different stuff, cursing. The guard coming around with the day-old rolls and the coffee in tin cups and the men bitching about how stale the rolls were as they formed a line at the front bars where they shoved the food through the opening designed for that purpose. A little later, the sounds of cards being shuffled, guys walking by my cell in pairs, talking. All the while, I just lay there, not moving, and then I began to think about what had happened. I had kept my mind away from what had gone down, but I let it back in.

For some odd reason, I didn't get mad. I remember thinking that I didn't deserve to get mad. After all, I had let Toles rape me and hadn't resisted in the least. By my non-action, I had surrendered the right to anger. What rose up, in the place of vengeance, was a weird kind of resolve. Feeling I had relinquished my manhood completely, and that surrender had rendered me dead in spirit, and I decided, without dwelling on it, I was going to kill Toles. Somehow, I knew that was the only chance I had of recovering myself, although I also felt even if I succeeded in killing him, I would still be less of a man forever. But I had to do it. The emotional climate I found myself in was that of floating (in my mind) around something big and that I didn't dare think about it directly. It was like plunging into a quarry—you know the water will be freezing and since you've never dived into that particular body of water, you could easily break your neck on something submerged and out of sight, a rock, perhaps, so you don't think about it, you just do it and you have to do it head-first, never feet-first. A macho thing.

And that's what I did. I walked out into the bullpen, saw a mop standing in the corner in the back and I walked over to it and picked it up. Toles and Cleaves were sitting at the picnic table at the front and I walked toward them with the mop. Just before I came up to them, I stopped, put the mop on the floor and put my foot on it, breaking off the mop head. I walked on up to the two and instead of going after Toles, I went after Cleaves, the bigger of the two. I cracked him across the face with the handle, coming from left to right and then came back the other way. I nailed him good. Blood flew from his nose the first time and then the side of his head on the second blow and he went down on the floor, a surprised look on his dull, churlish face. Toles just sat there, no doubt stunned by the suddenness and ferocity of my attack. I hit him next, a glancing blow alongside his ear and he stood up, rage in his face, and I took the handle and thrust it as hard as I could into his Adam's apple, like a spear. Cleaves was trying to get up, reaching for the edge of the table, when I hit him again. I went back and forth, just swinging methodically at both men like it was a job of work, and then there were three guards who came in the bullpen and grabbed me. Toles and Cleaves both lay on the floor, Toles silent but not knocked out, looking up with hatred in his eyes, and Cleaves sat there, legs splayed out in front of him, blood streaming from where I'd caught him across the front hairline and from his nose, just looking up at me like some cow that had been pole axed.

The thing was, I felt nothing. Completely dead, devoid of all emotion. It was like it was some job, a piece of work I had to do was all.

The guards didn't even ask me what had happened. They hustled me upstairs to a cell they used for solitary and pushed me in. I lay there all day. Nobody came by, not even to deliver a meal. Finally, about six o'clock, a guard came up and told me to come with him. He took me downstairs to another bullpen and told me to take a shower. I did and he tossed me a pair of orange coveralls and another guard came in with a tray of scrambled eggs and toast, which I sat and ate at one of the tables. The first guard sat across from me and didn't say anything. When I was done, he told me to grab one of the cells on the other side, and I went over and lay down and went to sleep almost immediately.

Three days later, I was transported to the Pendleton Reformatory. During those three days before I was led to the police bus to be driven to the joint, shackled by handcuffs and ankle chains, no one talked to me nor I to them. I ate my meals when they came and otherwise stayed in my cell except to go to the bathroom.

I concentrated very hard on not thinking about what had happened.

And that's what I've done for most of the forty years since I was raped. Concentrated very hard on not thinking about what had happened. Or tried to rearrange it in my mind so that somehow it became heroic. That *I* was somehow heroic in the fact that I survived the attack. That perhaps not resisting represented more an act of intelligence than anything else. But that's just not the way it was. I may have been acting out of a sense of self-preservation, but no matter how I cut it, I was a coward and I wish I hadn't been and I can't rewrite it to make it come out differently. It's taken three decades to realize this. It was just one of those horrible things that happen to people and it matters to me because I was the one it happened to. I wish it hadn't happened, but it did and I have to live with it. I know I can survive, because I have, but I also know what happened on that early morning in a dark cell has tainted my life ever since and will continue to do so in various ways. And knowing that I can endure with that memory, is, in a way, heroic I think. I have to think so.

I've also come finally to the realization that in the end, I wasn't a coward. True courage is doing something you're afraid of. If you're not afraid, it isn't really bravery. And I was scared when I went after them with the mop handle, until I got into it and then everything, all emotion just vanished.

One thing I've wondered about. Like I said, Toles didn't have much in the way of equipment. I wonder if that had something to do with him being a rapist. Has anyone ever done a study of the size of genitalia among rapists? Don't laugh—I think that's a legitimate source of study. I know I'm well-hung and have never considered raping anyone and I'm curious as to if Toles and others rape males and/or females because of feelings of inadequacy. It kind of makes sense that men who feel inadequate might counter that feeling by performing violence on their victims. I wish someone would address and study this. Maybe after years of being called names like "Needle-Dick the Nose Fucker" rape is just their way of assuaging their bruised feelings. Maybe this is why men are rapists and very few women are. Makes sense to me.

One positive thing that came out of that experience. Well, out of *this* experience—that of writing it down and exposing it to the world, to be precise. That I can now jump in and have my say when women get together and begin talking about rape. For years, I sat back when such a discussion would spring up at a party (sounds like some zippy party, doesn't it!). For a man to contribute anything to such a topic would surely bring withering scorn from the women present. "What would a *man* know about being raped?" they would surely say. No more. Now, I can leap into the fray. "You wanna talk about rape?" I'll begin with. "Now, let me tell you about…"

V
PENDLETON

On my first night in Pendleton, in quarantine, I laid on cold steel slats, no mattress. There had been a riot two days before our bunch got there and the inmates had burned everything combustible, including the mattresses. The pillows, too, were gone. They did give us a thin Army-blanket that you had to lay over you in a diamond shape if you were taller than five-ten. I beat that by two and a half inches.

When I woke the next morning, there was a dusting of snow on my blanket, down at my feet where the blanket had slipped off. My toes were white. Well, the tops were white. Underneath the snow, they were blue. The rioters had busted out the windows as well. Quarantine was in the only cellhouse that had windows to the outside. This was on the thirteenth of February and it also happened to be my birthday. Didn't look like there was going to be any cake or presents.

The superintendent announced to the inmates, "You people busted up everything and now you have to live in it. I'm not giving you anything and I'm not fixing the windows, et cetera."

He didn't either. It was one cold spring. A shitload of guys came down with pneumonia and worse. I don't know whether anybody died. There were rumors that some did, but then we didn't exactly have *The NY Times* to check to see what was really going on. In movies, somebody farts in prison and in six minutes the entire population has the details. In Pendleton, you could have a guy get exed three cells from you and you might not ever know about it for a month. Or ever.

One cool thing about quarantine. One of the hacks told me the cell I was in happened to have been John Dillinger's cell when he was imprisoned here.

Pendleton, at that time, was one of the baddest joints in the country. During the years I spent there, then-President Johnson had commissioned a study on penal institutions. One day, a bunch of us were sitting around watching the only TV in the cellhouse (black and white) on a rec night when Johnson came on to report their findings. He said the study had shown that Pendleton was "categorically, the single worst prison in the U.S." We all stood up and cheered like he was talking about our football team and we'd just won the Rose Bowl or something.

It *was* bad. During my stay, I lived through eight riots, not counting the one that had just ended when I arrived, but for which I paid for with snow on my toes and a few other discomforts.

I'd seen a lot of things before this, but there are things that happened in Pendleton that I'll never be able to talk about. There were some good things too. I made friendships that were stronger than any I've ever had before or since.

My first night out of quarantine was an early taste of what prison was like. The guy in the cell next to me, a black guy, had been slow-walking a debt of a carton of Camels to this guy. That night, the guy who was owed the cigarettes walked by his cell and threw a beaker of acid in the black guy's face. He'd gotten the acid from some inmate who worked in I.D.—Identification Department—where they printed and photographed all new inmates. It was some kind of acid they used to develop pictures.

The guy lay in his cell and screamed all night. We were on the second tier and just below us I could see the hack at his desk. He never moved or even looked up all night. Just kept sitting there, reading his comic book or whatever. Toward morning, the only sounds coming from my neighbor's cell were little tiny whimpers. When they let us out for breakfast they must have come and dragged his ass out, because he was gone when we came back to get ready for work.

A few weeks later, the black guy came back from the hospital. Obviously, he hadn't died. He might have wished he had. Half the skin on his face was turned a permanent blotchy pink, the color of bubblegum. He'd lost one eye completely and most of the sight in the other.

You could get just about anything in the joint you wanted except a girl. That was at a time when there weren't any female hacks, so it may be different these days. Although there were guys in there you'd swear they were girls and after you'd been in a while, that's the way you saw them. They went by women's names and you thought of and referred to them as "her" or "she." Any drug you wanted, long as you had money, you could score. Drugs were everywhere. And we ran (shot up) *everything*. I even knew guys who'd run aspirin and claimed you actually got a high from it.

One night, a couple of buddies told me they'd scored some embalming fluid. They swore it was the best high you could get. I figure they got it from some inmate who worked on the burial detail. If you died and nobody claimed your body, they had a little cemetery just outside the walls for your final resting place.

I was all set to shoot up with them, but we had a shakedown at my cellhouse when we were coming in from work and all of J Block was shut down until morning. These two guys from H got out to the gym, where they ran the shit. Killed both of them. That was one time I was happy to have been in a cellhouse shutdown.

I was lucky in another way. I came from South Bend and we had a large contingent of guys from there. That was the only thing that saved my ass. I saw lots of guys come in from small towns who didn't know anybody and they usually became (sex) punks in a few short weeks. Guys from larger towns—from South Bend and Naptown and Fort Wayne—they had friends who would look out for each other. Small-town guys were fucked. Literally.

Back in my first week in quarantine, I got hit on by a black guy coming back from noon chow. Guy said he was going to make me his kid. First thing I did was tell Paul Dover, a friend of mine from South Bend who was doing time for armed robbery, I think. Paul was one of the toughest S.O.B.'s I've ever known. He ended up as Pendleton's heavyweight boxing champ, in fact.

One time, before I got sentenced, a bunch of us were hanging around about three in the morning downtown South Bend at an all-night restaurant that was mostly a hangout for the town's hoods and outlaw element. Lots of cops hung out there, too. Some Mexican girl was giving Paul a hard time and my friends and I were in a booth a couple of booths back and laughing at this girl. It sounded like Paul had dumped her and she wasn't happy about it. When she started getting really loud about it, Paul took her out behind the restaurant. Everybody followed. The girl tried to slap him and he just grabbed her arm. He wasn't paying that much attention and she pulled a knife and stabbed at him. He ducked, but the knife caught him in the neck, down near the shoulder. Went all the way in, up to the hilt. Paul just reached up and plucked the knife out. Then, he stood there and laughed at the girl, blood running down and soaking his shirt. This bitch didn't know whether to shit or go blind. Finally, she just started laughing like a hyena and Paul went over and gave her back her knife. Ended up taking her home.

That was Paul.

I told him what this black guy said and he said he'd take care of it. When they let us out for evening chow, he had me point out the guy and he walked over to him. He said something to this guy and pointed to me where I was standing a few cells over. I couldn't hear what he said, but the black guy said something I figure was a smart-ass remark and started to turn away. He didn't make it. Paul just reached down with one hand on the guy's ankle and another on his arm and picked the guy up and dangled him over the side. We were three tiers up. He let go with one hand and stood there holding this guy by the ankle with one hand.

The black guy started copping major deuces. He was crying and pissing his pants at the same time. Urine was running down his face. A hack walked around the corner making his rounds, looked up and saw what was going on, shook his head, turned around and just walked away, out of sight.

The guy never fucked with me again. Nobody else did, either. If Paul Dover was your buddy, nobody fucked with you. I had the chance to do a similar favor about a year later to a guy who'd just come in from some bum-fuck town in southern Indiana. Tipton, I think it was. That turned out to be a wasted favor. A week after I'd saved this kid's butt, he was turned into a trick anyway. I guess he liked the lifestyle or something since he could've avoided it.

Another time, I was sitting in the chow hall, just minding my business and trying not to bite down on a rock. We were having beans for that meal and there were rocks in the beans all the time. If you weren't careful, you'd bust a tooth. Rocks were in these big sacks because and the company was paid by the weight. Most of the time, the seller put in a shovel of gravel to "help" out the weight and therefore the price. The inmate cooks never bothered to try to sort out the rocks, but just dumped everything into the big cooking pots they used. You just had to pay attention so you wouldn't bite down on one by mistake.

All of a sudden, it got real quiet. When it gets quiet in the joint, something's going down. And it was. One of the inmate cooks was walking toward one of the tables and he had a meat cleaver in his hand, swinging it like you'd swing a bucket of blueberries. He walked up to this guy and the guy stood up just as he got there and the cook caught the guy on the upswing. Just buried that cleaver in the other guy's stomach like it was a dance they'd choreographed together and walked away.

The guy should've been dead on the spot, but he wasn't. He

turned and walked out the door and toward the inmate hospital, bent over holding onto the cleaver handle. We got up and watched him as he walked all the way across the quad and up the steps of the hospital. He got halfway up before he collapsed and fell down and the cleaver and everything it was holding in came out. Blood and guts went everywhere. I still can't believe the guy made it that far with a meat cleaver in his stomach.

Anyway, distracted by this business, I bit down on a rock and busted a back tooth in half. Years later, I wrote a short story about it, that, although it was published as fiction, was almost a verbatim account of what happened. The story, titled "Toothache," was first published by the literary magazine *Kansas Quarterly/Arkansas Review* and they nominated it for the Pushcart Prize. It was later included in my story collection, *Monday's Meal*. A lot of the stories in that collection were based on things that happened during my outlaw days.

We found out later the guy who'd whacked him did it because the guy was slow-walking on paying back a pack of cigarettes. I guess they forgot to put that warning on the pack.

I was there about a month before I saw Toles, the guy who'd raped me back in the South Bend jail. I was going back to my cellhouse to get something and he was coming in, dressed in the orange coveralls you wore when they transported you from city or county jail. He looked at me but I don't know if he recognized me or not.

For the next year and a half I only ran across him once or twice and then a month before I came up for my parole hearing he ended up dead on the roof of the laundry with a bunch of holes in him somebody'd put there with a bent-out laundry pin during one of our riots. A laundry pin is a big brass pin that looks like Baby Huey's diaper pin they use to fasten the big canvass laundry bags, Straightened out, they're a mean killing weapon of about a foot long. There was a big to-do about it but they never pinned it on anybody. It looked like I might not get my parole since I was a suspect and was questioned several times. But it came through all right and the case was dropped for lack of evidence. That's all I'll ever say about this.

There was another incident about the same time that could have cost me my parole as well.

I was working in the barber shop one day and a black guy climbed in my chair. Normally, unless you were a punk, black guys didn't get in white guy's chairs for their haircut or shave. In fact, blacks and whites never mix and when they do, you know one's a punk. I started to walk away, thinking this guy had made a mistake, when he grabbed my arm and told me what he was going to do with me sexually. I didn't even stop to think, just grabbed my straight razor off the backbar behind me and went after the guy. The only thing on my mind was that I was going to kill him.

I'd just been paroled by the board. I knew I was going to lose it by going after him, and would end up doing not only the rest of my sentence, but a new one for attacking him. If I killed him, which was my intent, I knew I'd be looking at life, most likely. There was no way around it, though. I'd seen so many guys come back that I knew it was likely I'd be back some day as well. And, if I'd let this guy sell me a wolf ticket and I came back, my life would be over. I'd end up a punk and no one would help me nor should they if I couldn't carry my own water.

What I'd do if someone went after my booty. I'd decided a long time ago that I'd have to do something about it regardless of the penalty. I'd already prepared for the situation by being in that place in my mind where I wouldn't even think, but just kill the guy. Or get killed. Things like that can go either way.

The barber shop hack was a black guy named Jonesy. He was one of the good guys. A lot of the hacks weren't much better than the guys they guarded—they just hadn't been caught for their criminality. But Jonesy was different. He actually cared about the guys inside. Somehow, he grabbed me and shoved me into the instructor's office and locked the door behind us. Then, he talked to me. Talked me into giving up the razor in my hand.

Once I was disarmed and settled down, he went back out where everybody was gathered, watching, and sent the guy who'd hit on me back to his cellhouse. I realized I'd definitely blown my parole. I was certain Jonesy was going to write me up and that would be the end of any parole. I mean, there were two dozen witnesses. Only he didn't. He never said a word to anyone about the incident and a month later I got out on parole.

Jonesy really went out on a limb for me. If anyone in the administration had ever found out about his failure to report my actions, he not only would have lost his job but probably would have been prosecuted himself. To do what he did was just amazing.

That's when I began to change my mind about black people. Up until that moment, I had been as racist as anyone else and more so than most. For a black man to save my ass in that way was just the most remarkable thing I'd ever had happen to me. For the first time in my life, I started to understand that race had nothing to do with a man. It was what was on the inside that counted, not the color the person's skin happened to be.

Wherever Jonesy is, I hope he's a happy man and has achieved what he wanted out of life. I sure owe him mine. If I hadn't gained parole at that particular time, I have no doubt what would have happened. I would have ended up killing someone or someone would have killed me before much longer. There's no doubt in my mind that's what would have happened if I'd stayed any longer in Pendleton.

I managed to be lucky in another way, too, while I was there.

You can be smart as hell, but intelligence and two bucks will only get you a bad cup of cafe au lait. In Pendleton Reformatory, I was able to get into the barber school. The barber school was considered the best "lick" or job in the joint, and competition for the few spots was keen. You had to pay someone off. To make even the short list for a school slot set me back ten cartons of Camels with the understanding that if I actually got into school another ten cartons would be forthcoming. That represented a fortune since my only source of income was the state pay for my job, which at that time was six cents an hour, if I remember right. And no 401(k)s. When I first arrived, my parents would send me a few dollars here and there, but that stopped fairly early on within a few weeks, as did almost all communication with them. My one and only time to get an allowance and it took prison to get it...

I earned money by playing poker and shooting craps. Since my Navy days, I had become a pretty fair gambler, and even today, at my advanced age and long removed from those days, I can still roll sevens about fifty percent of the time, much to the amazement of my son Mike. When we play Monopoly we have the most fun trying to call our number before we roll and he's getting pretty good at controlling the cubes himself. I hope I'm not teaching him the wrong skills. His mother is convinced I am. Time will tell.

Three of us, myself, Joe Jared and Bud Palmer, set up a floating crap game and it was amazing how many so-called street-wise guys never caught on that you shouldn't roll dice on a blanket. Of course, Indiana wasn't New York City, which is where the guy hailed from who taught me the ivories when I was in the Navy, and where, according to him, everybody on his block was a hustler. He was a good teacher and I wish I could remember his name because the skills he taught me led to me being able to afford barber school which literally saved my life.

Barber school was great. I found that cutting hair is harder than it looks. I loved learning to shave with a straight razor. There was a test you had to pass before the instructor let you go to Indianapolis to take your state board. He lathered up a balloon and you had to shave it completely without busting it.

Taking the boards wasn't easy, mostly because each student had to furnish his own male model for a haircut and shave. Guys on the outside had no problem. They just grabbed their father, brother or a friend, but the guys in the joint usually didn't have anybody like that who would volunteer. Most of our families had kissed us off by that time. So, Mr. Bowden—the instructor—would take us to Indianapolis a couple of hours before the exam and we'd cruise the skid row part of town to try and find alkies who would be our models. He'd promise them a bottle if they'd let us give them a haircut and shave. He was a great guy, Mr. Bowden. I don't know how many bottles he bought for winos in the twenty-some years he was the barber school instructor at Pendleton, but it must have been a lot.

The guy I got for my test was in such an advanced state of alcoholism that all you had to do was barely touch his cheek with your finger and it blushed red. Paper-thin skin with hundreds of capillaries ready to burst. He was also shaking like he had St. Vitus Disease. Some fun. I doubt that any of the civilian guys could have shaved him without killing him, but then they weren't required to shave a balloon. Bowden had his reasons for making us pass that test.

In some states, a felon can't get a barber's license, but in Indiana you can get a license, no matter what your crime. I ended up working in a barber shop in South Bend with twin brothers who were both out on lifetime parole for murder.

We used to laugh about how many guys were cutting hair in barber shops in Indiana who had done time and how the straights never had a clue. I could walk into any five shops in any town in Indiana at random and end up seeing someone I knew from the joint in at least one of them. Straights were never aware of how many barbers had done time.

To get released on parole you had to have proof that there was a legitimate job waiting for you, and if you didn't have one, you weren't released until you got one, even if you'd been approved for parole. This was difficult to do unless you had people on the outside helping you. One of the many reasons why the commercial prisons they have today are a bad idea. They send inmates to other states to these places and any contact you might have had that could help you get a job before release is largely gone now for those guys. The other trades taught at Pendleton were useless. They had a machine shop, for instance, that had machines that were from the past century. Barbers coming out had a better situation, which made getting into the barber school very desirable. In the mid-sixties, it was well-known among the barbering fraternity that men who had received their training behind bars were the best in the state. There were two reasons for this reputation. One, the course of study in a traditional barber school on the bricks takes about ten months. Inside, the least time you spent in school was two years and many times up to ten years or longer before you were paroled. Two, while the average student on the outside might see five or six live "models" a week to practice on; we saw fifteen a day, five days a week. At that time, all inmates were required to get their hair cut every two weeks. We had a hundred times the experience. And no outside distractions for studying the textbook. There was always a waiting list of employers for our services when we made parole. It just showed what true rehabilitation could accomplish, but that makes too much sense for today's politicians and prison officials.

If I had to come up with one or two words that would describe my experience in prison, that would be easy. The word(s) would be: *Constant awareness.* Not for a single second in my two plus years inside the walls was I not on guard. It wasn't stomach-clenching, hands dripping with sweat fear, but more of a constant awareness that at any second you could lose your life if you dropped your guard. If you saw me at any time or any place during that time, you wouldn't guess for a minute that I was worried about anything at all. I walked with the cocky walk of the badass, curled my lip as good as any Hollywood actor, and moved like a gunslinger at all times. I wasn't worried—not in the usual sense of the word—but I was always alert.

There was just never a time when I wasn't totally aware of my situation and how quickly it could go south. I suspect the same holds true for most of us imprisoned. Most of us don't act or look as if we're nervous about anything, but I'm pretty sure we all are. The few that aren't are either too dumb or too naive.

The thing is, you learn very quickly that it doesn't matter an iota how big or how bad you are, or how many friends you have who assure you they have your back. None of that matters in the least. Not after you've seen too many little guys attack and shank guys twice or three times their size. Not after you've seen a guy you were just talking to about everyday matters and who seemed as calm as a retired priest, suddenly turn and hit another inmate in the face with a rock they've just picked up for no reason at all. Not when you've seen a six-foot-eight-inch mountain of a man cornered by eight other inmates in his cell and proceed to knock his brains out.

You find out very quickly that you have absolutely no control over anything that happens. That if an inmate doesn't suddenly go over the edge into madness, you might find yourself in a dark place with a guard or three who just naturally hate prisoners and aim to do them harm.

There were these two twin guards—the Huckeby's—who were good examples of that. The Huckeby's ran the hole—solitaire—and they had quite the reputation. Regularly, they'd roll out an inmate in there and take turns tuning him up. When they got tired of thumping on his noggin, they'd lay him down, one brother would hold him down and the other would pick up the end of one of those big heavy benches they have there in the corridors and drop it on his melon. Usually, several times.

One guy they'd reduced his brain to mush with their fun and games was a well-known inmate named Maggie. Maggie had lost so many of his marbles that you knew it was him coming from a block away. He kind of half-ran, half-walked, his arms all akimbo when he ran. He always had a goofy grin on his kisser. On Saturday mornings, he'd get on his hands and knees and go up and down the rows of men watching the weekly movie, trading blowjobs for tightrolls.

One of the guys who knew Maggie before he got messed up, said he was just a regular guy before all the head-bashing shit started.

Whenever you saw the Huckeby's you just did your best to vacate the area or, if you couldn't, try and become as invisible as possible. Over the years, lots of inmates had vowed to kill them when they got out and we heard stories once in a while that some ex-con had caught them in some bar in the town of Pendleton, but nothing much happened except some big-ass fight. Where usually the ex-con got his ass handed to him by the brothers.

You pick up habits inside that you can never get rid of. All tied to being situationally aware at all times.

If you stay alert you stay alive.

Until a few years ago, I went back down to Pendleton and spent the day with the guys in the barber school at least once a year. Some things are the same, but some things are very different.

The races, for one. When I was incarcerated, the majority of the population was white. Today, it's black. It all changed when drugs entered the equation…which is the other major change.

When I was doing my outlaw bit, drugs weren't much of a thing at all. Oh, there was weed and there was heroin and acid and even prescription pills but drugs just weren't a big part of anyone's life. Very few guys doing time for drug offenses. I know because I worked in I.D. when I first got out of quarantine and saw everybody's rap sheet and so knew everyone's offense and I doubt if there were more than say ten guys locked up for dealing or the like. Not only did drugs change the landscape of prisons, they changed the landscape of America.

In those days, we thought of guys selling drugs as mostly punks. Same with the guys caught on drugs while they pulled B&Es or armed robberies. Punk-asses who needed artificial courage to pull jobs. Most of us took pride that we weren't drunk or fucked up when we walked into a liquor store and held down on the citizen behind the counter or broke into a bar at 3:00 a.m. I can't ever remember pulling a job high or drunk. I would've felt like some kind of sissy. Afterwards, sure. I got drunk plenty of times after I did a job. But, hardly ever before or during one. I still think of outlaws that way. When we bragged about our crimes, we rarely brought up our dealing times.

I also thought of black guys as punks. It just seemed like they'd hardly ever fight you one on one, but they had all kinds of guts if they outnumbered you. When I was inside, white guys just never worried about blacks all that much. Nowadays, it's all gangs and that crap. I guess if I was inside nowadays, I'd probably do the same—join a white gang. Maybe not—I just never wanted to be part of anything like that. But I didn't have to think about it then. There just weren't any Crips or Aryan Nations or any of that business. I don't think there were any Mexicans at all when I was there. I don't remember a single one. Or Asians. Mostly white guys and maybe ten percent blacks. Whites stayed with their own kind and blacks did the same thing. In fact, the cellhouses and dorms were all segregated then. I don't know if they still are, but if they aren't they're making a big mistake.

When I was in K-Dorm, I was in the white dorm on the second floor and just across from us was the black dorm. Most of the weight-lifters were in our dorm. In the mornings, before they rolled the doors, a bunch of guys from our dorm would throw on white sheets and make the black guys across the hall go nuts. They'd all scream they were gonna mess us up, and then the doors would roll open. And, both sides would pile out to go to chow and the black guys would just put their heads down and not say a word and file on out silently. The blacks just had no power at all, in those days.

Different story today.

The thing was, the races didn't mix then and there was very little trouble.

Only the black guys were into male sex. Whites just didn't play that game. Well, some did, but only as punks. And, punks to black guys. You never saw the reverse. Most of us white guys always saw it as homosexual sex and wanted nothing to do with it. Black guys came from a different place, it seemed. To them, sex in the joint wasn't being homosexual—it was some kind of power thing. They seemed to believe it was a *macho* thing, somehow. Never made much sense to me, but…

There were a few whites who were punks and had black daddies. None of the other whites would have anything to do with them. One guy I knew from the street—Danny Brown—and had been friendly with on the bricks—was turned into a punk. Never spoke to him after that. I don't know any other white guys who did either, once he became the black guy's kid.

Things have really changed…I can't help it—I'm glad that I was in when men still acted like men for the most part. I don't have anything against homosexuals—in fact, there were a few bona fide homosexuals inside and those guys I'd talk to. That always seemed legit, even though it wasn't something I'd do. It was the guys who thought they were being macho by fucking other guys I didn't have much use for. I can't help it—if it quacks like a duck, walks like a duck, looks like a duck…it's most likely named Donald. A guy who has sex with another guy in the joint and doesn't on the outside is still a duck…Once you've seen 'em duck-paddling you can't unsee that…

VI
PAROLE

My future parole officer secured a job for me with a guy named Ray Smith, who owned a barber shop in Roseland, Indiana, a suburb north of South Bend, near the Michigan line and the town of Niles. That's when my real education began.

For nearly a year at Ray's, I struggled to build a business, adding a customer here, one there, until I had a good, solid clientele. Almost the very instant I achieved a full book, Ray hired twin brothers, both of whom were out on lifetime parole from Michigan City for murder, and gave them each half of my business. Ray had been a cellmate of one of them. I was back to ground zero.

The day that happened, I walked around in a blue funk all day. Finally, after a year of hard work I was beginning to see the fruit of my labors and he had yanked the rug from under me. The anger built up all day and that night after he put the "Closed" sign in the window and pulled the shade I walked up to him, called him an asshole and told him I was going to throw him through the window. Two of the other barbers ran over and grabbed me and hustled me out to the back parking lot.

"Look, kid," one of the guys said. "It's not right what Ray did, but he's the boss and you're on parole. You fuck him up and you'll go back inside. Be smart—walk away from this job and get you another one. I'll calm him down so he doesn't report you to your parole officer."

I took the guy's advice. What choice did I have?

From that job, I went to a barber shop out on the west end of South Bend. We were on a turn system, which turned out to be not as fair as I was led to believe. Half the time, when it was my turn and someone walked in the door, one of the co-owners Alvarez would say, "Oh, sit down, Les, that guy always waits for me." So I'd plunk my butt back down in the barber chair, he'd greet the guy and begin cutting his hair. This went on for months until one day my father-in-law—I'd gotten married to my third wife Sheila at that point—came in the door for me for the first time to give him a haircut and right away Alvarez said, "Oh, that guy always waits for me, Les." I gave him a look as the light bulb went on and then ignored him. When my father-in-law came in, I sat him down and cut his hair. The minute he left, I began packing my tools.

"What are you doing?" asked Alvarez.

"Don't fuck with me," I said. "Don't even talk to me, motherfucker. I'd love to have an excuse to bust your fat face." I walked out and never went back, didn't even come back to collect whatever meager pay I had coming. I was afraid of what I'd do.

That was the shop where one of the co-owners was a lush. When I first started, Alvarez had a partner. Jim drank vodka all day long, thinking nobody could smell it. He had bottles stashed all over the place, even one in the toilet tank in the bathroom. Whenever he wasn't busy, he'd go into the bathroom and sit there nipping.

One day, he'd been in the john for about an hour and one of his regulars came in. "Go get Jim," Alvarez told me. I went and knocked on the bathroom door and there was no answer. I started knocking and ended up pounding on the door and yelling, but there was just no answer.

"Motherfucker's drunk as a loon," Alvarez said. He looked all over for the key but couldn't find it, so we ended up busting the door down. Jim was in there, all right. Dead. Sitting on the stool, slumped over, an empty vodka bottle on the floor where he'd dropped it. It turned out he'd drunk more than his heart could stand and it gave out. Alvarez didn't think I saw, but he went through his partner's pockets before he called the police, and dug out his money and stuck it in his own pocket. I just stood there watching, shaking my head.

From there, I went to Lakeville to a shop owned by a guy I'd met. Dean, the owner, had business up the kazoo and had only a part-time barber, a Welshman from Mishawaka named Roger, who was a really good guy. Roger only worked Saturdays. Just about the time I got a good clientele established, Dean hired the kid of some woman he was romancing and there went my business again.

There was only one thing to do. Open my own shop. This was illegal, since I didn't yet have my time as an apprentice in to qualify for my Master Barber's license which was required by state law for shop ownership, but I found an old retired guy and bribed him for twenty bucks a month to hang up his license and put his name down as the owner and opened up a shop in River Park in Mishawaka. The guy lived a few blocks away and the plan was that if the barber inspector came by I'd say Mr. Hughes had just gone home for a minute. I'd then—if this happened, which it never did—call Mr. Hughes and tell him the inspector was there and he'd come down in a hurry and pretend to be working there. I kept a chair and a set of tools next to mine for just that purpose.

I'd started taking classes at the South Bend regional Indiana University campus at this same time and my third wife Sheila was pregnant with our first daughter, Britney. Business boomed, almost as soon as I opened the doors and I was humping, working full-time, taking a full load at IUSB, and trying to spend time with my family. It was one of the best times of my life. I was out of prison, about to get off parole, going to school, had a nice wife and a child on the way and life was looking up.

I was beginning to change my outlook on life. I was married to a sweet, wonderful girl and the birth of Britney caused me to begin looking at things differently. I started thinking about what kind of a father she was getting and I wasn't very proud of the image. It would take a few more years and the birth of two more children before it really sank in fully what a crumbbum I was, but it was looking in on Britney's sweet little baby face at night that began the process.

I was getting back to my writing then, as well, and the stories were flowing. I had written stories for as long as I can remember, all the way back in grade school, but I hadn't written much during my stint in the Navy and while in prison. Now, I was just full of ideas and the stories began pouring out.

One would probably think that the first thing someone just released from prison would want would be sex or booze. Maybe drugs, if that was your "thing" on the bricks before you were incarcerated. That's the scenario most often seen in movies and books.

Not this parolee! The one thing I wanted more than anything else was to soak in a bathtub. For two years, the only time water hit my body was in a shower with a hundred other guys, half of whom were looking at the other half's asses. I craved luxuriating in a hot tub. And a razor I could use only once and throw away. *That's* true riches.

The other thing I wanted was silence. There is not a minute of your existence in the joint where there isn't noise. It's one of the things everybody hates but which you never see portrayed in fiction or films. Even late at night, there would be guys sobbing for their mothers or screaming because six guys were poking them in the ass. I can't remember a single second of blessed silence the entire time I spent inside. It seemed like just about every day somebody was crying and moaning all night because he'd just come in and somebody had just busted out all their teeth that day. That's the first thing they did when they made you a punk. Bust all your front teeth out. Made for a smoother blow job.

The first purchase I made when I got out was a carton of Camels. That was a fantastic feeling, to have that many cigarettes I could actually smoke all by myself.

Sex was in my thoughts when I got out, but curiously, it wasn't really that big of a deal. For one thing, I entered freedom with a gigantic inferiority complex. It felt almost as if there was a huge letter imprinted on my forehead that screamed "ex-con" to everyone. I was sure there wasn't a girl on earth who would want anything to do with scum like me. I sure didn't think I could rap with a girl the way I had before I got sent up. My confidence was pretty much shot. I figured there was no way a decent girl would go out with me. There was also the specter of that rape hanging over me.

Anyone who saw me then probably wouldn't have realized any of that. I acted cocksure, but that's all it was. An act.

I was mostly scared I'd mess up and get sent back to finish my sentence. There were all kinds of horror stories circulated in the joint about how P.O.s—Parole Officers—would violate you for looking cross-eyed at them. There were lots of guys who turned down parole to finish their time. The way they told it, it was better not to have to report to anyone when you were released. They'd rather do another two years behind bars than to have to report to a P.O. Under some P.O.s, it was supposedly worse than being in the joint itself. That never made any sense to me, as I figured even a limited kind of freedom was better than being inside, but there were plenty of guys who didn't see it that way. As it turned out, there were some P.O.s like that, but I was fortunate. The guy I drew turned out to be a prince. Walter helped me in so many ways and in every way was the best kind of P.O. a guy could draw. He helped me get a job, was understanding when I wanted to change employment, gave me permission to do just about anything I wanted, including getting married, enrolling in college and opening my own business. If it hadn't been for his support and help, I doubt if I would have made it.

I was lucky, drawing Walter. The day I reported in, there were two of us there to meet our P.O.s. I'd gotten to the office first, so went in first and drew Walter. They all worked in an open space in cubicles and right after I sat down, the other guy came in and sat in front of the other P.O. and the first thing that guy said was, "I can't wait to send you back, asshole." Yowza. Turned out, he did, too. Violated him within the week. I just got very, very lucky in drawing a good guy and not an asshole.

Another thing that was nice was not having to wear blue denims. It was several years before I could even wear blue jeans and I was almost thirty before I purchased my first blue denim shirt. At least the one I did end up buying didn't have #49028 stamped over the pocket!

My first couple of meals were a bit awkward. For two years, I'd only had a soup spoon to eat with. No knives or forks. Everything was eaten with that spoon, which you carried with you all the time. They also served as a weapon since you'd file down the handle on the floor of your cell. If you got caught with one filed down, you were in trouble, but I never got caught.

Nowadays, I hear all this crap about inmates being mollycoddled. They may have a few more amenities than we did, but it's still not the "country club" life some would have straights think. Nowadays, they're allowed to have a TV in their cell if they have the means to purchase one, and radios, stuff like that, and that's a lot better than when I was there, but even so, it's no day at the beach.

Our "entertainment" in those days consisted of being let out of our cells in the evening from six to eight. On alternate days, each cellhouse would be allowed to go to the gym or out in the yard, depending on the weather, and the alternate day our cell doors would stay open after evening chow and on those days, we were allowed to go to the other side of the cellhouse where they had rows of chairs set up for those who wanted to watch television on a black and white set. Or we could walk around, bullshit with each other, play cards, stuff like that. Shoot craps. That was my game and how I made most of my money. That was it, entertainment-wise. The library was a joke. Mostly Zane Grey novels and not much else.

Every other Saturday morning, we got to go to the theater and watch a movie. Usually, the movie was at least ten years old and usually much older and not too violent. The administration didn't want to get anybody stirred up. But, as bad as these movies were—usually Rock Hudson/Debbie Reynolds dry-hump romps—they were the highlight of our week on the week we were allowed to go.

One night, while watching TV in the cellhouse, I watched an inmate get whacked out ten feet from me. I was in the fifth row, watching *I Love Lucy* and this guy was sitting a bit to my right and two rows ahead. An inmate came up behind him and proceeded to hit him at least ten times with a claw hammer. He just kept burying that sucker in the guy's melon...and that's exactly what it sounded like. Somebody smacking a watermelon. There were maybe twenty inmates sitting there, watching the tube and not a one of us moved. Just kept watching ol' Lucy. We all got sprayed with blood and bits of bone and brain matter. After the guy got done whacking this poor slob's brains out, he disappeared and in a few minutes the hack on duty came around the corner making his rounds and found the body. All of us who had been sitting there were pulled in for hours of questioning but none of us had seen a thing.

Some guys thrive in prison. Some come from such wretched environments that three squares a day and a steel cot represent something better than they ever had on the outside.

And a few loved being in prison for the sex. There were just some guys who enjoyed getting fucked in the ass or giving blow jobs. Some of these "queens" would actually become women in every aspect except their equipment. They dressed like women, spoke like women, acted like the opposite sex. Those inmates were actually thought of as women by the rest of the population and referred to as "she" or "her" and that's the way we thought of them. They actually became women in our minds. I never had a problem with those guys. They were up front about who and what they were. And, there weren't all that many of them in my day.

After I was there about a year, I lay in my bunk one night and tried to see if I could get sexually aroused in my mind over the image of a young guy who had just been brought in as one of the murderers in the Sylvia Lykens case, a big deal at that time. This kid was sixteen and was beyond handsome—he was downright *pretty*. But, try as I could, I just couldn't make myself become turned on over him or any other man. That's when I knew beyond a shadow of a doubt, that even though I had been raped, and had been behind bars for a long time, there was no chance of becoming gay.

An inmate "girl" named Susie was a huge black "girl," who wore wigs, makeup, the whole schmear. She was quite a sight! She was six-foot-eight and the wigs she wore added another couple of inches to her height. Susie had a cute little trick. When the Saturday morning movie ended and five hundred inmates streamed out and back to their cellhouses, Susie would catch some poor chump out of sight of the hacks and thump him on the top of his head, knocking the unlucky victim out. She hit down with her fist, like you'd pound on a desk. She'd drag him over behind a bush and rape him while he was unconscious. Usually the poor guy would be somebody who'd just gotten released into population and hadn't yet learned of her trick. The rest of us avoided her like Dean Martin avoided Jerry Lewis after the split.

The Sylvia Lykens case was a big one at the time. Sylvia Lykens was a little girl whose mother worked in a circus or carnival and had left her with an Indianapolis family while she was on the road. The family, which consisted of the boy I knew in Pendleton—he ended up being our "receptionist" in the barber school—his sister and their mother. They tortured Sylvia, who was around fourteen, I believe, over the course of the entire summer before they finally killed her. Had her tied up to a bed in their basement. All three family members took part in the torture and killing. They found her body covered with cigarette burns and other scars from the family's tortures. The mother and daughter ended up doing life in the Indiana Women's Prison and the son was sent to Pendleton for the same sentence. If you saw him on the street, you'd think this was a kid your baby sister could whip.

His first day in population, some big guy hit on him when he was walking out in the quad and this kid just turned around and stabbed the guy in the throat. He had to jump up to reach the guy's throat. The dude bled out in about two minutes. That ended guys hitting on him. For a while, at least.

After I was released from Pendleton, my fighting career took a sharp nose-dive. Pendleton gave me a dose of reality. Before, I never realized how easy it was to get killed in a fight. I always figured at the worst, you might get a few stitches, a black eye or maybe a broken nose or a cracked rib or two. Before Pendleton, I was also under the impression that if a guy was smaller than I was or close to the same size, there wasn't any way he could whip me, much less kill me. When I left there, I knew better. Anyone, anywhere is capable of killing another man in a fight, fair or otherwise. I still had fights now and then, especially a few years later when I went to New Orleans, but my days of looking for a fight every time I turned around were over.

Prison taught me one thing: That it wasn't a place I ever wanted to return to.

VII
COLLEGE AND MARRIAGE

I attended Indiana University at South Bend during the late sixties up through the early seventies. I took my first classes right after being paroled from Pendleton. I'd been nervous about college, believing all the hokum that it was hard and you really had to have brains to succeed. That's just a myth college graduates perpetuate for those who don't get to go. College was infinitely easier than high school, which was ridiculously simple.

As an education major, I was required to take eighteen credit hours of what they called "Professional Studies." This was stuff like the history of education, method classes and the like. All I remember from those classes was that Horace Mann was some kind of big name in the business. Mostly, you went to class and said things like, "Golly gee, I sure want to be a teacher and influence little lives," collected your A and went on to your next inane class. One of our classes was led by this young, hip professor—in *his* mind—who had all of us call him by his first name (the hippie movement was in full swing and old institutions were tumbling down). This guy had a wife and six kids, one per year since they'd been married. He also had an eye for cute coeds and ended up divorcing his wife and marrying this eighteen-year-old girl in our class. I wonder if they're still together. No doubt.

There was a campus population explosion at the time and this guy's class was held in a trailer they put up on a side lawn. All we did the entire semester were little "feely-trust" exercises.

A typical one is where he'd turn the lights out and we'd all get in a circle and one by one, stand in the center and when he gave the signal, we were supposed to fall back and "trust" our classmates to catch us. Intellectual crap like that. The eighteen-year-olds ate it up. I went to the dean after about four weeks of this. "Look," I said, "I'm not a kid and I've got all my marbles. This class is a joke and the prof is a clown. I'm paying for this myself, not Mommy or Daddy and I'm being cheated." I was mad, Jack.

The dean tried to explain to me how valuable these little trust exercises were to us, but after about ten minutes of this idiot I just walked out. All of the education classes were like this, as well as a lot of the others. A couple were good, mostly in literature and psychology. There was a psych professor we all idolized, Dr. Henry Corte, but he proved too popular and the school got rid of him, despite protests and marches on his behalf by the students. This was typical of the times. Henry taught behaviorism and showed us where Freudian and clinical psychology were bullshit and the department chairman, being a Freudian, despised him. And she had a lot of clout. Her husband was the head of the psych department at Notre Dame and that made her Mrs. God in the eyes of the I.U. folks. Just a little bit of a university inferiority complex going on, I suspect. Students quit taking her classes to take Henry's and the school couldn't have that.

Henry made another mistake that became the excuse to fire him. He had the idea that the present grading system, based on the curve, was fucked. His opinion was that it took some people longer than others to master a subject and what was important was that they mastered it within a reasonable period of time. His analogy was in the form of a question. "Would you rather fly with a pilot that got a C+ in Landings, or would you rather be on a plane with a pilot that got A's, even if it took him longer to learn than some of the other pilots?" His theory made sense to us, which also meant that it was a doomed theory, according to the university lights.

That was the third time I learned that institutions are basically anti-logical. The first was in the Navy and the second was Pendleton.

Corte instituted an ingenious system for the times he called "programmed classes." His classes, like most others, met twice a week. You got reading material for each week and at the Monday session you got a lecture over the material, then on Thursday another lecture and then a quiz over that week's material. If you received a grade lower than an A, you had the option of retaking the quiz—different questions but over the same material—at the end of the next Monday's class. You could also get tutored by "proctors" over the material to help you understand it. Proctors were students who had taken the course previously and earned high marks—kind of T.A.s. I was chosen to be a proctor. We got a grade for our efforts and a letter in our records attesting to our snazzy tutoring. Henry didn't care if the entire class earned A's; in fact, that was his goal. The administration didn't like this because he totally ignored the curve, which is sacrosanct in higher education. It didn't matter that his students ended up with a better knowledge of psychology than some of the profs walking around—THE CURVE IS HOLY!

So he got fired, and dozens of students transferred to other schools, such as Western Michigan University, Georgia Tech and Kansas University, schools that emphasized behaviorism and thought the way Henry did. The department chairman got some students to take her classes again—since she was the only game in town—and everybody except the students was insanely happy.

There were some other good teachers there too. Elaine Hemley taught creative writing and was the first great writing teacher I'd ever had, although much of what I learned from her was outside of the formal class structure. She formed a writing group with five or six of her best students and we'd meet at her home in the evenings. I learned more from those classes in what amounted to a workshop than I did anywhere else. She was just a marvelous educator. Up until a few years ago, I kept in touch with her. Her son, Robin Hemley, who is today an educator himself and a wonderful writer, used to sit in our group and hold forth with the adults. He was twelve, if I remember correctly. Last I heard, he'd taken his mother to where he lived at the time, in eastern Washington, and had her placed in a nursing home. That's when I lost contact with Elaine.

A couple of other teachers stand out in my mind. Dr. Tom Vanderven, a marvelous Shakespearean scholar and playwright was tough, but fair, and you actually learned from his class, as you did from Gloria Shapiro and Paul Parrish. There were a couple of others who epitomized what education should be about. The guy (I forget his name) who taught biology was excellent. I got one of my two C's from him but I treasured it more than most of my A's. I *earned* that C.

By and large, however, higher education was a joke. I think it used to be better, when they restricted who got to attend college. Now, the level of student ability is so low they've lowered the standards accordingly and what we have these days is not education but diploma mills. It's not just college—high schools have lowered their standards a great deal since the sixties and it's getting worse.

While attending IUSB, I became involved in student politics. As a sophomore year I was elected as a senator to the student council. The next year, I became student body vice president and then in my senior year, I was voted student body president. Not bad for a guy just out of prison, I thought. I had a lot of pride in those elections, even if they weren't possibly the cleanest campaigns ever waged.

During the campaign for student body president in my senior year, our party defaced all of our own posters the night before the election. We got the idea from the folks who worked for Congressman John Brademas. Our party chairman, John Felabom, had witnessed Brademas' workers doing the same to *their* guy's posters.

When the students came in the next day and saw the nasty things scribbled on our posters, we collected an enormous sympathy vote. Our entire slate was voted into office, all sixteen of us. No one else was elected except for one senator's slot where we hadn't slated a candidate.

I resigned a few weeks after I won the election. I'd just wanted to show I could win the thing. My vice president, Fred Sulok, knew I was going to resign and turn it over to him. It was just something I could put on a resume. I'd already had two years of student government and it was mostly a bunch of b.s.

Being in student government in those days was big-time stuff to most students. A former student had drawn up the student government constitution, which the administration had signed, making it legal. They hadn't read it too well, thinking, probably, that this was just some student. The problem was (for the administration), the guy who drew it up was a prelaw student who knew his stuff. According to our constitution, which was legally binding since the administration had signed it, the student government had carte blanche authority over the student activity fees, which were in six figures. Mondo bucks for those days. The administration had no control over them—they were ours to spend as we pleased. Every year, the chancellor tried to wrest control back, but was powerless to do so.

We were all paid. As Vice President, I earned a salary each semester of six hundred dollars and when I became President it went to nine hundred per semester. During my senior year, I made money going to school. I had about two hundred and fifty a month from the G.I. Bill, nine hundred for being Student Body President—for a short time, since I resigned, but I was in office long enough to draw the first check—six hundred for being the sports editor of *The Preface*, some work-study money, and I was making a lot of money as a hairstylist at Michael's. This was the early seventies and the least I ever made at Michael's was five hundred a week and usually a lot more, many weeks a thousand or more. That was good money in those days.

Briefly, I thought about becoming a lawyer and perhaps going into "real" politics, but there was the matter of my criminal record. I had a lawyer doing the paperwork that would give me a full pardon and erase my record but it took so long I dropped it. My sister Jo had married Indiana Governor Bowen's nephew Jim and I figured that was a good time to apply for a pardon, but then Governor Bowen retired and was appointed Health, Education and Welfare Secretary by the President, and my "in" was gone.

There were some things I wouldn't have put on my pardon application. I'd joined Students for a Democratic Society (SDS), which was your basic subversive organization—I *know* it's a bit incongruent to be a member of SDS and College Republicans at the same time, but the main reason I joined SDS was for the girls. Same reason I'd joined the College Republicans. I quit SDS when I was invited to a Weatherman meeting and they began talking about blowing up the South Bend post office. Just a tad too political for my tastes. I was protesting against the Vietnam War and I was a Navy veteran of the war period. Lots of inconsistencies in my lifestyle!

Also, during that period, the student council had authorized and paid for Gus Hall, the perennial Communist Party presidential candidate to appear on campus and no hotel or motel in town would let him stay there, so, as student body president, I invited him to stay in our house. On the day he spoke, before a tiny crowd of perhaps twenty students and faculty, there were three beefy ex-football types in the back of the room in suits who carried tape recorders and made notes as he spoke after I introduced him. I'm sure there's a dossier on me somewhere in Washington! A week later, I was on the dais with Governor Bowen to dedicate a new building at IUSB and I made a dedicating speech that was reprinted in the *Tribune*. Lots of inconsistencies.

There were a few more activities I was involved in that I didn't have my lawyer put on my pardon appeal form.

I was womanizing big-time. As one of the most popular people on campus and in the beginning of the sexual revolution, I took full advantage of it. At this later date, I'm heavily ashamed of what I was doing. I was married to a wonderful girl whom I constantly betrayed. During my years at IUSB I went to bed with just under three hundred different girls. I kept a list. Being a hairstylist didn't hurt, either. Every good-looking woman that sat in my chair got hit on and it was amazing how many wanted sex with the guy who cut their hair.

I remember times when a new customer would come in for her appointment and we'd end up a half hour later in my car with her giving me a blow job and I couldn't remember her last name. Sometimes not even her first name...Sex was everywhere.

It almost cost me a heart attack one time. This was early on at IUSB, when I still had my shop in River Park. I was fucking this married lady and a few of my buddies knew about it. She was an absolute knockout and married to a hillbilly.

One morning, I'm cutting a lady's hair and one of my friends from school, Bob Wensits, was sitting on the waiting couch when the phone rang. I answered it and this voice with a southern accent said, "I know you're screwing my wife."

"No, sir," I said, trying to keep the lady whose hair I was cutting from knowing what the conversation was about. "I believe you've got the wrong number."

The guy on the other end became violent, saying he was going to drive by and shoot me through the window and general stuff like that. I kept denying I was the guy, couching my language so the client wouldn't know what I was talking about and then he hung up after telling me he was on his way over... with his gun.

Immediately after I hung up the phone, I swung the lady in the chair around so that she was between me and the window. Bob Wensits busted out laughing so hard he fell off onto the floor. I couldn't figure out what was so funny. I hurried the lady's haircut up, collected her money, and as soon as she went out the door, I ran over, locked it, turned off all the lights and put up the "Closed" sign. Bob was still laughing and then he told me what he was laughing about. It seems it wasn't the girl's husband that had just called after all. It was Fred Sulok, another friend, and he had set me up. Bob was in on it and had come in just to see my reaction.

"I can't believe what you did!" he chortled, tears coming up in his eyes. "You got that woman between you and the street. You made her a shield!"

Yes I did. Nothing wrong with my I.Q.

The person responsible for me even attempting college was a petite blonde I'd met named Sheila. We ended up getting married and she gave me two beautiful little girls, Britney and Sienna. Sienna married Jason Cox and they gave me a grandson, the cute-as-hell Logan. They live in Edwardsburg, Michigan, these days. Britney graduated from Purdue University and lives with her husband, Ray Robinson, in Louisville, Kentucky, where she works in the computer industry. Sheila's raised them pretty much on her own and she did a fantastic job.

I met Sheila while cruising downtown South Bend at the drive-ins. Bonnie Doone's and Azars sat a block apart and were the hot spot for teenagers at the time. Dozens and dozens of cars full of kids just cruised back and forth between the two. I was with a buddy and we started talking to these two girls in a car next to us. Immediately, I liked the tiny one, Sheila, and it ended up we made a date for the following week. Yeah, a *date*. I was back in Indiana...

I was maybe four months out of Pendleton at the time, on parole, and my confidence with girls was at an all-time low. I just knew that they could all tell I was an ex-con and that no "nice" girl would ever have anything to do with me. I went out with Sheila a couple of times and decided to take the plunge and tell her about my past. Well, some of it. The Pendleton part. I figured as soon as I told her that would be the end of us as a couple. But, I was really attracted to her and knew that if I didn't tell her pretty soon, it would only get worse the longer I saw her. Eventually, I knew she would learn the truth.

She totally surprised me.

While she didn't condone what I'd done, she told me her parents had always taught her that a person should forgive and forget, if someone had done something bad, just as long as they had truly repented and had changed their ways.

When she reacted in that way, I felt more gratitude than I've ever felt in my life. Sheila made me feel like there was some hope, that maybe I wasn't a complete loser.

We ended up getting engaged and then married. For me, it was for all the wrong reasons. I loved her, but I wasn't "in love" with her. It wasn't fair for me to marry someone in that situation, but then being fair wasn't something I was ever notorious for anyway.

She would have been much better off if she'd married someone halfway normal. That sure wasn't me.

At first, everything was fine. As time went by, my self-confidence slowly returned and in a few months I was almost as cocky and full of myself as ever. We developed a problem that got bigger and bigger. Sex was just not fun for her. It was physically painful. It wasn't her fault. She went to the doctor and he told her she had a tipped uterus, a physical condition that made sex painful for her, at least with me and my oversized organ. I said I understood and was sympathetic, but after months of not much of a sex life I began to cheat on her.

The honorable thing to have done would have been to get divorced. She could have found someone who was more compatible and ended up with a decent life. I was a totally out of control womanizer. I screwed everything in sight and justified it by saying that I was too young to end up a monk, especially after two and a half years in the joint.

The more we went on, the more we both slipped into our

own decades. Me, I was trying to recover my lost 1960s—lost from four years in the Navy and two-plus years in the joint; Sheila, in the decade we were actually in, the seventies.

I was going to bed with quite a few women, but then I decided to give college a try and once I was in school I went crazy, screwing everybody in sight. After my first year in college, I decided to open my own shop in River Park in Mishawaka, the twin city with South Bend. I'd had that open about a year when Michael Murray, the most successful hairstylist in the state talked to me about going to work with him. I closed the shop and joined his staff.

Months after I joined, he entered me in the state hairstyling competition along with a couple of other guys from the shop. Michael himself had won state styling competitions and even the national competition and urged all of us to get involved with it. It was a huge deal in those days.

My first effort came in a year when they had a tri-state competition between Indiana, Michigan and Ohio. There were over 600 stylists vying for the honors. To my surprise, I won a second place and a third. Nobody could believe it. Michael had just suggested I enter to gain experience, figuring I'd have to be in three or four before I had a realistic chance of winning.

I went ballistic. In the party in the hotel after my victory, the whole shop was there and Sheila asked me how it felt to win two trophies.

"It's better than sex," I said and it was. It was wonderful!

Over the next few years, I managed to win sixteen state titles in Indiana, Illinois and Michigan, but none were sweeter than the first. Nor were any of the hairstyling honors that followed any better. These are some of the honors and awards that came my way during my thirty-year styling career:

1. Sixteen-time State Hairstyling Champion, Indiana, Illinois & Michigan.
2. Platform artist for Clairol.
3. Featured on TV's *PM Magazine* for color expertise.

4. Featured on fashion show on Cox Cable Television in New Orleans, hosted by Paul Cimino.
5. Associate Editor for *Cosmetology Today*.
6. Quarterly columnist for *Nails Magazine*.
7. Author of *You and Your Clients*, Milady Publishing, *Managing Your Business*, *Milady's Guide to the Salon*, Milady Publishing, and *Milady's Guide to Becoming a Financially Solvent Salon*, Milady Publishing. Contributed chapter to last edition of *Milady's Standard Textbook of Cosmetology*. *You and Your Clients* and *Managing Your Business* were selected to be the first books on audio-tape for Milady's SalonOvations.
8. Wrote articles for *Bride's Magazine, Bridal Trends Magazine, The National Beauty School Journal, Cosmetology Today* and *Hair and Beauty News*.
9. Photos of my styles published in *Touts* and *Gambit*, many as the covers.
10. Featured in stories in many newspapers, including the *New Orleans Times-Picayune, The Ft. Wayne Journal-Gazette, The Warsaw Times-Union* and *The South Bend Tribune*.
11. Former Artistic Director for Snobs Salons, New Orleans, Stylist for such renowned salons as Busta at the Fairmont, New Orleans, The Crop Shop, New Orleans, Kenneth's, New Orleans, Corey's, New Orleans; Manager, Michael & Company, South Bend, Nu-Tech, Ft. Wayne, and others. Was the co-owner (with wife, Mary) of Bold Strokes Hair Designers, Inc. in Ft. Wayne, and former owner of The Prime Time Hair Designers and Hairport, Ltd.
12. One of the stylists for the models' hair at the 1986 Liz Claiborne Spring Show in New Orleans.
13. Designer of Bold Strokes Designers product line.
14. Hair designing technical articles published in *Barbers, Beauticians and Cosmetologists Magazine*.

15. Interviewed, upon invitation, for the position of Acquisitions Editor for Milady Publishing's new salon line of books and magazines, *SalonOvations.*

There have been many rewards in my hairstyling career, but none meant more than those first two trophies.

Unfortunately, that gave me an even bigger head and I became even more out of control. Sheila didn't deserve any of that. Her only crime was to marry an asshole.

Besides screwing everything I could get my hands on, I was doing drugs heavily. Who wasn't in those years? One time, over at Michael's apartment, he brought out some liquid hash. Stuff sold for ten bucks a drop back then, which was salty. He fired it up under a glass and I took a hit. Then another. Then another. They told me to slow up, it was powerful stuff, but did I listen?

Driving home was the worst experience I'd ever had on drugs. It was like a bad acid trip, only much worse. The houses all seemed to be breathing, expanding to double their size and then deflating as they let their "breath" out. I kept zoning out and then coming to and finding myself, miraculously, still steering down the street. Half a mile from my house was a railroad crossing and I pulled up three cars from the front. Worried that I'd space out and crash into the car ahead of me, I put the car in park.

I don't know how long I was out, but when I came to, there were probably fifteen cars behind me, nothing in front of me, and everybody honking. There was a guy at my window, beating it with his fist. Somehow, I managed to get home and went inside. I was freaking big-time by then, seeing all kinds of stuff. For some reason, I brushed by Sheila, went into our bedroom and crawled underneath the bed. I was sweating like a reporter at a Bob Knight news conference after he's asked a stupid question. Sheila got really worried and was going to call an ambulance.

"No!" I said. "Just leave me alone. If I look like I'm going to die, then call them, but not until then." Actually, I thought I *was* going to die. All I could think of was that if she called an ambulance, the cops wouldn't be far behind and I'd end up going to jail. I'd almost rather die than go to prison again. I passed out and spent the night on the floor under our bed.

There was a funny incident that took place about that same time. One afternoon, I was on my way home from work and decided to stop at the Mishawaka Bonnie Doone to pick up a sandwich. Sheila worked later than I did and I figured I'd just save her fixing supper. I pulled in at the drive-through and there was one car ahead of me, at the window. I waited behind what looked like one guy in the car and waited some more. I saw that he was talking to the girl at the window and figured he was trying to romance her. No big deal—we've all done that shit. But, then more time went by. Finally, I laid on the horn and whipped around him. Just as I went around his car, a guy sat up in the passenger seat that I hadn't seen. He gave me the finger as I went around and I pulled out on the street and over to the curb.

He came running up and I figured we were going to get it on. Except, he threw his leg up on my passenger side window and reached into his boot and pulled out a hunting knife. Well, that was an easy call. He still had his foot up on my door and I just hit the gas and dumped him on his ass.

I thought that was the end of it and turned right at the next street which was my street and was just tooling home. Actually, I'd already forgotten the incident. About a quarter mile later, I noticed this old beater barreling down the street after me. It was the car from Bonnie Doone's. I just laughed and punched the gas. I had a new Challenger and there was no way that piece of crap could catch me. I pulled away like they were standing still and then had a thought. I had a gun under the seat. I hit the brakes, whipped over to the side and jumped out into the street with my piece and began firing at them while standing in the road. I saw a bullet hit their windshield and then it got really funny. The driver stood on the brakes and there was all this smoke and screeching and they got it stopped and whipped around and took back off the way we'd just come.

I got back in my car, a big shit-eating grin on my face and I actually said it out loud. "Don't bring a knife to a gunfight, you dumb shit."

Then, I went home.

I can't believe all the crap Sheila put up with.

I quit doing drugs for the most part after that episode. I never liked weed so that was easy. Mostly, I'd just get nauseated and the high I got was lousy. I figured out that I was only doing it because everyone else was and thinking about it that way made me see that was a pretty lousy reason. Plus, I always felt guilty whenever I did any drugs, remembering my opinion about those who did as being weak. Mostly, I quit because I didn't like the feeling of not being in control of myself.

The absolute worst crap I laid on Sheila came from when I went to the national hairstyling convention and competition which was held in Chicago that year. I was on the four-man state styling team and we won the nationals, except they stripped us of our title when it was discovered one of our members had cheated. The thing was, he didn't have to, but it cost all of us the national title.

During the convention, I was screwing young hairdressers left and right. I was a big name in the business so it wasn't any problem to score. For years, hairstylist conventions were the best place in the world to get laid. I took a friend of mine one year, a guy whose dad owned a chain of funeral homes and who had all the money in the world. After that first convention with me, he quit going to Acapulco and Cancun and took his vacation at the nationals for years after that. An average day at a five-day convention would get you laid at least five to six times with different girls if you had a good rap and were in shape.

This year, I ended up with the third girl of the day—a hairdresser from Milwaukee—and we went up to my hotel room. After we were done, she started sobering up and bawling that she was getting married in a week and wanted to kill herself for cheating on her fiancée. She actually went to my window and tried to get it open. We were on the fifth floor.

"Go to your own room if you want to kill yourself," I told her, grabbing her and shoving her out into the hall. "I can't stand the publicity." I don't know if she ended up killing herself or not, but I didn't see her around for the rest of the convention.

Another time, my undertaker friend and I picked up a couple of girls at one of the bars at the convention center at McCormick Place and hustled them up to their hotel room. Each of us was fucking a girl in the twin beds when the door opened and this lady came charging in, screaming at the top of her lungs. The girl I was with was her daughter. We grabbed our clothes and ran out into the hall, laughing and trying to get our pants on.

On the last day I ended up with a gorgeous little redhead. Problem was, she was from Elkhart. This was the Midwest Beauty Convention, one of the biggest in the country. It drew 35,000-plus hairdressers from all over the country. And I end up with someone six miles from my house!

She was great in bed and we had a terrific time. About a week later I got a phone call at work from this girl. She was crying. It turned out she just discovered she had a case of gonorrhea. From a guy she'd been seeing at home before the convention, she said. She was sorry, but she figured the right thing to do was call me and let me know. In a way, it was decent of her.

I went down to South Bend's free VD clinic and got tested and sure enough, I had a dose. That's when it got hairy. I had to tell Sheila she was probably infected too since we'd had relations after I'd returned home.

I wrote her a long letter, telling her what had happened. At the end of the letter, I said I was going to leave her with the letter and while she read it I was going to go have a couple of beers. After I returned, if she wanted me to leave, she could leave me a note and I'd understand and pack my stuff. This was in case she didn't want to see my sorry ass.

I went down and had about four beers and finally got up the

nerve go to home. When I walked in, she was sitting on the couch. It was plain she had been crying but she was more mad at that point than anything. I didn't know what to expect. All she did was look up at me and say, "You got caught this time, asshole. All I have to say is that you better not get caught ever again or I'm out of here. You just used up all your strikes."

That was just one of a thousand times I didn't deserve this girl. I knew this in my heart, but I still couldn't seem to keep from fucking up, over and over.

What made the whole thing even worse, was that I'm allergic to penicillin and so they didn't give me a shot but only made me take a sulfa pill, but when Sheila went down and got tested and found she was positive too, they made her get a shot.

"I didn't do a damn thing!" she said, really pissed now, "And I have to be the only one who gets a shot! All you had to do was take a damn pill!"

Over and over, I kept screwing up the one decent person in my life. I can't believe that after all I put her through she doesn't hate my guts, but Sheila has never been anything but a lady.

After working for Michael for a couple of years, I was approached at the national convention by Lloyd Lejeune of Baton Rouge, who had won the national individual styling title the year before. Lloyd wanted me to move to Louisiana and work for him.

Initially, I turned him down, but the more I thought about it, the more the idea appealed to me.

Finally, I decided to take his offer. Sheila was great about leaving her family and the place that had been her home all her life.

By the time I decided to take Lloyd up on his offer, he'd already filled his position. I was full of disappointment after I talked to him and he told me the bad news. But, he said, he had a friend who could use someone. He'd make a call and see if the guy wanted to talk to me. His friend was Bobby Savoy, the Louisiana state Roffler dealer.

Lloyd connected us and we began to speak over the phone. Bobby was one of the most successful dealers in the U.S. He operated his state-wide franchise out of Opelousas, Louisiana, the same town the world-famous chef Paul Prudhomme hailed from. Opelousas was a true Cajun town. Most everybody in town spoke French and was a coonass.

Bobby had a small shop but it was barely going. He was so busy he hadn't spent any time in it in years and business was nil. He had a woman stylist working, but she wasn't doing much.

He shot me a deal. Come down, he said, and get his shop going again and he'd pay me a salary. I would also travel for the Roffler organization, talking barbers and beauticians into Roffler training and individual franchises (you had to have a franchise to obtain their products). Every time I sold a franchise I'd get a healthy commission.

It sounded great. We sold our house to Bob Wensits, a good friend of mine from IUSB, packed our stuff in a U-Haul and took off for Louisiana.

At first, everything was great. While there wasn't much business, Bobby was at least paying me a decent salary and I was working for one of the biggest dealers in the nation. Bobby was a prince to me.

On the first week, he sent me to some godforsaken town out in the middle of the swamps to talk to some barber who had expressed an interest in Roffler training. This place wasn't even on the map! It sat fifteen miles from the nearest paved road. I drove into town and thought I'd been transported back to the Old West. The main street through town was a dirt road. The "town" consisted of maybe half a dozen businesses on each side of a single street. An old-time gas station right out of Edward Hopper, a cafe that I swear was called "Mom's," this guy's barber shop and a couple of other ratty-assed businesses. All the buildings were slanting at precarious angles, about ready to fall down. The weirdest thing though was the sidewalks. The sidewalks were *wooden*! I swear to God...wooden-fucking sidewalks!

I clumped up on the pine to this guy's shop and walked in. I had no more than introduced myself, when this redneck says, "You a Yankee?"

Well, half and half, I said. I grew up in Texas but have lived in the North, too. With that admission, this asshole just turned his back and said to get out. He wasn't talking to any Yankees. He and my grandmother would have gotten along famously.

Cool, I said, and went back out to my car. When I had arrived, there wasn't a single car on the street. When I went back out to get in my car, there were now three. My car and two pickup trucks. One of each parked in front and behind my car. There were two men in each pickup and clearly visible were rifles slung in their back windows. There was less than twelve inches between my bumpers and each truck.

It wasn't the summer heat that made me break out into a sweat.

I started up my car and it took me ten-fifteen minutes to jockey my way out from between the trucks. I was pretty sure it wouldn't be a good idea to tap either of their bumpers. My guess was it wouldn't take much of an excuse for the occupants to jump out and thump on the head of the guy in the car with Indiana plates.

Finally, I made it out and started back out of town. As soon as it was clear I was going to make it out of the parking space, the lead truck pulled out and when I followed the truck behind me pulled out as well. I was the middle of the Oreo. We drove like that all the way back to the main highway, about fifteen miles away. Nothing but swamp on either side of us. If I sped up to go around the truck in front he sped up so I couldn't. If I slowed down to let the truck behind me around, they slowed up as well.

I was as sure as I'd ever been of anything in my life I was going to end up in that swamp. I figured the gators were already licking their chops.

I'll never know how close I came to buying the farm, but I honestly don't think I was far from it. It was tense. At last I reached the highway and went around the front truck. As I pulled onto the state road, I heard both trucks honk and looked back and they were standing outside their trucks, guns in hand, all four of them waving just as friendly as could be.

As soon as I hit Opelousas, I headed straight for Bobby's house. "Don't you ever send me someplace like that ever again," I said, the minute I saw him. I told him what had gone down and he laughed. But he never sent me to any shop out in Deliverance country again. Not that I would have gone without an Uzi.

One Monday, Bobby asked me to deliver some products to a shop in New Orleans. The woman stylist—Wanda—who'd been working there before I'd come down asked if she could come along since she had no appointments on the book and I said sure. Halfway to New Orleans, I pulled off at a roadside tavern to get some coffee. I pulled up and parked in front of a huge plate glass window. There were at least three tables in the window, all full of people eating and drinking. We weren't six feet from them and each of us could see the others clearly. I turned off the ignition and reached for the door when Wanda, out of the blue, reached down and unzipped my pants. In two seconds, she had my cock out and was blowing me. We ended up with her bent over the back of the front seat and me putting the wood to her. When I finally turned around, there must have been twenty people all bunched up at the tables looking out at us. I waved, pulled my pants up and took off.

We got coffee a little further down the road.

Wanda decided she was in love. From that incident, every time I turned around she wanted to screw. Not that I resisted. She was a knockout with a serious set of knockers. But I knew sooner or later Sheila would find out. Wanda was getting more and more brazen. That situation, coupled with the fact that the business just wasn't growing in the shop at all, convinced me it was time to move on. By that time, I'd met quite a few stylists around the state, so I made a few phone calls and we ended up packing up and moving to Lake Charles to work for a couple of really great guys, Sam and Pete.

Lake Charles was wonderful. As it turned out, we never built up enough of a business to live on and ended up heading back to Indiana, but while we were there both of us loved it. It was an outdoorsman's paradise. Sam and Pete took me fishing back in the bayous and I swear the bream and bass would bite at a bare hook. Wildlife was everywhere. Lake Charles was at the funnel point of the geese and duck flyway and when they migrated you couldn't see the sky for the fowl.

Sheila, Britney—she was just an infant then—and I drove down on weekends down to Calcasieu Bayou where it empties into the Gulf to fish. There was a canal that ran alongside the road we took and one time, in a ten-mile stretch, from our speeding car, we counted over a hundred alligators seen just from the car. We fished and crabbed at the end of the bayou, with the Gulf two hundred feet away. Alligators were always stealing your bait and you'd hook one once in a while. The best thing to do was jerk back on your rod, snap the line and leave your hook in their mouths. Sheila would usually watch the crab lines while I fished.

One time, she pulled up a crab line slowly, thinking there was a crab on the end, only it wasn't. It was a medium-sized gator, about four feet long. He came right up to the bank, his snout resting on the mud. We had our camera and I begged Sheila to put her foot on his snout so I could get a picture, but she wouldn't do it.

Another time, she really got mad at me. A water moccasin came up out of the water, straight toward us. I grabbed up the only thing in sight, Britney's folded-up aluminum stroller and beat it to death. Only problem was, the stroller was destroyed by the time I was through. That really got Sheila frosty.

There was a girl working for my bosses and we had a brief fling, usually going out to catch a nooner a few times a week. One day, Nancy pulled out a joint and shared it with me. It must have been laced with something because I've never been that high before or since with just weed. When we came back, there was an old guy sitting in my chair, waiting for me. I got the haircloth around him and picked up my comb and scissors. He was chattering a mile a minute. Then, I started spacing. It took over an hour and a half to cut this guy's hair in what should have been a ten-minute job. I'd space out and then come back to earth, minutes later, and this guy would be in front of me and I didn't even know what planet I was on. Every time I'd finally achieve reality, I'd see Nancy around the corner at her chair and she was cracking up. She was the only one knew what was going on. And this guy never stopped talking the whole time. Somehow, I finished his haircut, but the next time she offered me a joint I vehemently backed off.

Shortly after that, we moved back to Indiana. Instead of going back to work at Michael's or another job in South Bend, I decided to try opening a shop in Warsaw, Indiana. Neither of us had even been through the town, but it looked like a nice place to live when we drove down. There were exactly a hundred lakes in the county and I wanted to be around water if I had to be in Indiana.

Sheila's father Harold graciously loaned us $2,500 and with that I put together a shop.

Without knowing a single person in the town, the day I opened my business I was booked ahead a week and a half and shortly thereafter was never booked less than six to eight weeks ahead during the whole time we were there.

I just opened up smart.

***

Warsaw, Indiana was a terrific place to live. One of the many regrets in my life is that I didn't stay there. We ended up living in a great two-story house on Chapman Lake and there have been few places in my life that I enjoyed living at more than there.

Even for the early seventies, $2,500 wasn't a lot of money to start a business, but I figured out ways to do it cheaply. I scoured the countryside until I found an old barn under construction. They sold me planking for next to nothing and from those I made backbar shelving. At a railroad salvage yard, I found brand-new nail kegs I was able to get for a nickel apiece. Those I filled with sand and placed products in them for retail. A department store in South Bend had just gone out of business and I was able to get huge mirrors from them for the taking. I contacted a beauty shop in South Bend that had gone bankrupt and purchased three styling chairs. The frames were in perfect shape and I had each reupholstered for fifty bucks apiece, which gave me brand-new chairs. All in all, I completely furnished the salon with all the equipment and decorations I needed for under $1,500 and the rest was spent on utility deposits, phone and a bit of advertising.

If I was creative in the physical part of the shop, I got really creative in advertising and that was the key to the shop's instant success. I'd named the shop "Hairport, Ltd." I only ran two newspaper ads, but the second ad caused the phone to ring off the hook.

In the first one, I ran a pretty standard ad. It gave my name, some qualifications—state championships, etc.—and when and where we were opening. In the second, I had to fight with the newspaper salesman to get what I wanted. They wanted to sell me the same, tired ad everybody else in the hair business traditionally ran. I didn't want that crap, I told them, but they still argued. Look, I finally said, it's my money and I want to spend it like I want to, even if you think I'm an idiot. In the end, they gave in. They really had no choice.

I wanted a full page. In the middle of the full page I wanted only one line of text. No pictures, nothing. Just one sentence. And, I wanted it in the smallest print size they had. I wanted a print size that if you had 20-20 vision you'd have to hold it up to your nose to read, I told them. The sentence?

Your lucky number is (and it had the shop's phone number). That's all. That was it, the entire ad.

The minute the ad came out, the phone started ringing. And, even though it only ran one day, the phone calls it spurred lasted more than a month.

People would call and sound almost embarrassed. "Uh, what's this lucky number thing?" they'd ask. I had a twenty-second canned message I answered with. Briefly, I said I was new in town, had just opened a new hairstyling salon, and that if they took a chance and let me do their hair, I thought they'd agree it had been, their "lucky day."

It worked. I was booked solid for almost a week at the end of the first day. Folks figured if I was that creative in my ad, maybe I was creative with hair. It also helped that Warsaw was a small town. Word got around quickly.

I'd done a few more things that were different. Before opening, I'd researched the highest priced salons in town and set my prices at least double the highest prices of anyone else. I took all kinds of chances, but I figured what the fuck? The most I can lose is $2,500 and as it turned out, the salon was a huge success. I also didn't cut a single head of hair for the first week I was "officially" open. Everyone that called in for an appointment was told I couldn't get them in for at least a week as I was booked solid. I sprinkled hair all around my chair so that if anyone happened to walk in, I could tell them, "I'm sorry. I'm booked up until next week. I haven't even had time to sweep up after my last client. I'm getting a no-show, looks like, but there's not enough time before my next one to cut your hair." I'd show them my book, filled with phony names. The word got out quickly around town that even though I was brand-new, I was booked solid. When I did start cutting hair, I was.

I'd never take people right away the whole time I was there. If they called and wanted in on a Wednesday, even if I had an opening, I'd tell them I couldn't get them in until Thursday. Sometimes, I'd call one back, tell her I just had a cancellation near the time she'd wanted if I sensed I might lose her. I quickly got the reputation that I was hard to get an appointment with and it made me look that much better.

I got a unlisted phone number. It was on my card and that was the only way you could get it. I also had an 800 number, to my knowledge the first or one of the first times a hair salon had done that. I never again ran ads in the local paper but I did run ads in the Indianapolis and South Bend papers. And got lots of clients from both towns, even though South Bend was an hour away and Indy three hours away.

What a lot of haircutters never understood was that getting a haircut wasn't a necessity or a need—it was a desire. You had to create the desire. When I stopped cutting hair my price was a hundred dollars a haircut and when I'd begun it had been a buck. For basically the same thing.

Years later, Gary Wordinger, the top beauty product salesman in the state was still telling people that I'd "turned the town of Warsaw around."

I ended up writing three books for Milady Publishing on how to build a business and they're still selling well. Each fall I still get a royalty check for a couple of thousand bucks and it's been years and years since they were published.

I was making money hand over fist. I had a terrific wife and a beautiful little girl. Did that make me content?

Not this genius. I was screwing as many girls as I could, gambling like crazy and it was a rare moment when I wasn't high. It was during this time that I fell in love with a local schoolteacher. Our affair was widely known and the cause célèbre of town. Although it certainly wasn't the only one going on in town. There was more adultery in that town than any I've ever lived in, I think.

The teacher with whom I had the hot affair (I'll call her "Isolde") taught art at the middle school. We first became friends when she came in to have her hair done and from the minute you met her you knew you were in the presence of a truly free spirit. She was married to a hugely-talented artist and we all became friends, her and I, her husband (I'll call him "Todd") and Sheila. We lived close to each other on Chapman Lake and were at one another's houses constantly.

As our affair heated up, a teacher friend of hers joined our little tryst briefly, and when the teachers got out for lunchtime, I'd close the shop and all three of us would hop in bed for a three-way nooner.

Isolde was one of the great personalities of my life. We had an affair for the longest time and while the sex was fantastic, what made our relationship even better was that we were great friends, had the same cynical take on life. And she was an artist. If I were going to list all the attributes my perfect wife would have, Isolde would have scored tens in all the categories. I would have married her in a New York second, but when we were together we were both married and then when we both got divorced, we were states apart and each seeing someone else. There was one other element missing. Even though we both enjoyed sex with each other and had the utmost respect for each other as artists, romantic love never reared its head. Because of that, we probably could have had a terrific and long-lasting marriage, but we never did.

We lived the equivalent of two blocks apart on Chapman Lake near Warsaw, Indiana. She didn't have the kind of features one would normally call beautiful; a more apt description of her features would be "exotic." She was unusual-looking, much in the same way Barbara Streisand has a striking appearance (I don't mean by that that the two looked similar) and therefore beautiful because of her singular appearance. It's hard to find the right words to describe Isolde physically. A slight woman, all angles in her limbs, and her face was elfin, large,

Clark Gable ears, large, luminous eyes and skin the softest I've ever touched.

But it was her mind that captured me. She absolutely hated hypocrisy only she hated it in a forgiving way. Hate the hypocrisy, love the hypocrite.

For example, one time a student of hers gave her a Christmas present of a twelve-foot penis sculpted in rusted iron. She proudly displayed it in her front lawn. The neighbors loved this so much they circulated petitions to have it removed.

Isolde's husband Todd was so incensed at the narrow-mindedness of the petitioners that he took his chain saw and sculpted a willow tree that grew at an angle out over the lake in their front yard into a gigantic cock. "Now, they've got something to talk about," he said.

Another time, she was having a cocktail party at her house with twenty-plus guests and she excused herself to go to the bathroom. Passing her bedroom, she saw Noriko Nishi, a fashion designer friend of hers from Chicago, trying on some of Isolde's antique clothing collection, presumably planning to enter the room where we all were in a few minutes and surprise us. Isolde hurried back to where we were all sitting and told us what Noriko was doing and said we ought to turn the tables on her, surprise Noriko. At her insistence, every one of us took off our clothes, every stitch, and stuffed them into hiding places under couches, chairs and wherever we could hide them. When Noriko walked out in an Elizabethan costume, her mouth dropped as she viewed twenty-some adults, all buck naked, just sitting around chatting and drinking our cocktails.

Todd was a terrific guy. He got this great idea to have some fun with the retired guys who spent their days fishing on the lake. He bought these gawdy-ass bright yellow plastic fish with black polka dots from Stoner's Magic Shop in Fort Wayne and told me his idea.

One of us would get in our scuba gear and slip underwater with the plastic fish—they were about the size of an eight-pound flounder—and the other one would drift by the targeted fisherman in a boat. Armed with a camera. The underwater team member would locate the fisherman's line and hook and attach a polka dotted fish to it and tug on the line.

We got some great photos when the old coots hauled in their "catch."

Another great idea of Todd's came when he was driving home from high school and saw a crew taking down an old telephone pole. He stopped and asked if he could have it. Permission granted, he then hired a dredging company to come and get it, cut it in half, and then erect it in the middle of Chapman Lake in a submerged sandbar that everyone used to party on. Todd then attached an old-time crank telephone on it and rigged it up so he could ring it via remote control.

He and I would then float near it on his Hobie Cat and wait until somebody came by in their boat. When they drew near, he'd ring the phone...and they'd go up and answer it!

The best one was when he bought an electronic bullhorn that could be heard for miles. He and Isolde would invite twenty or so friends to a backyard cocktail party and wait until twilight. The lake would be filled with pontoons, fishing boats and skiers. He'd stand out on his bank and turn on the bullhorn.

"This is the U.S. Coast Guard," he'd bellow. "A Russian sub has been spotted on Chapman Lake. Everybody must return to shore immediately."

And people would comply. They'd race to get off the lake, never stopping to figure out how a Russian sub could travel to a landlocked lake in Indiana...or why on earth they'd *want* to do such a thing. They'd just get off the lake. I don't want to imply that the good folks who lived on Chapman Lake were gullible or anything, but...

And then, like all things of that sort, it wore itself out. I had maxed out the potential for the salon and I had screwed what seemed like was half the population of the town. Things were just boring. That was when I decided to sell the shop to an employee for a dollar and move to Fort Wayne.

Most of the time spent in Fort Wayne was boring beyond endurance and eventually I was able to escape. I put in what became quickly a very successful salon in a private racquetball club on Trier Road I named the "Prime Time Hair Designers," and it was there that I met a girl I'll call "Patty" and who ended up working for me and becoming the reason I left Sheila and my daughters, Britney and Sienna. Sienna had come along right after we moved to Fort Wayne and we were living in the nearby little town of Leo.

VIII
DIVORCE

Although there have been well over a thousand women sexually in my life—one-nighters, for the most part—there have been less than a handful that I had serious feelings about. For the longest time, I thought I was incapable of loving anyone, that the capacity to love was a blank spot in my DNA code. Always, there was a detachment from every girl I was with, including at least some of the ones I married. One thing; I never lied to any of them or told them I loved them. The only girls I ever told I loved were the ones I married, even if I didn't. A guy who told a woman he loved her to get in her pants has always seemed like a punk to me. Definitely not a player.

Patty was an exception. Looking back, I'm not sure now if love was what I felt or if the feelings I experienced toward her weren't just intense lust. She was the sexiest woman I had ever been involved with up to that time.

When I met Patty, I was married to Sheila and we had just had our second daughter, Sienna. I had just opened a hairstyling salon in the Summit City Court Club on Trier Road in Fort Wayne. The Summit was a private racquetball club, and so I named the shop Prime Time Hair Design. When Patty came into my life, we'd been living in Fort Wayne for about a year.

I had more business than I could handle, turning away dozens of people each week and one day this drop-dead gorgeous-looking blonde walked in and asked for a job. I hired her immediately.

I maintained a strictly professional relationship with Patty at first. I'd had affairs with women who'd worked for me before and the last one had turned out to be very sticky. Sheila hadn't found out, but it had been close.

At the time, I was involved in hairstyling competitions, and a few months after hiring Patty, the annual state competition came around in Indianapolis. I had one model lined up but needed another and so I asked Patty if she would be my model and she agreed. The model I already had was a former client from Warsaw, a young girl named JoAnn Prout and JoAnn had arranged for us to all stay at the apartment of a guy she knew in Indianapolis, rather than pop for a hotel.

When we got to Naptown, we all went out partying and did a lot of coke and weed and drank our asses off. I hadn't sworn off drugs completely and mostly did them when I went on a trip or to a convention or something like that. When we got to the apartment of JoAnn's friend Jim, we were all wasted, so JoAnn and Jim went off to his bedroom and Patty and I curled up on the floor on a makeshift bed JoAnn had made up, of cushions and blankets. I fell asleep almost immediately, as did, I assume, Patty. I hadn't yet made a move on her, although I'd thought about it. Earlier, while we were out, I flirted a little, but no more than that.

Sometime during the middle of the night, I awoke to see JoAnn hovering over both of us, pouring something over both of our bodies. While asleep, the covers had fallen off and it turned out we both liked to sleep in the nude. Patty had taken her clothes off under the covers as had I and we were both naked and being drenched with warm oil by a giggling JoAnn. JoAnn said, "I thought I'd help you guys out," and then she disappeared, laughing, back into the bedroom.

I reached for Patty and we began kissing and fondling each other and ended up making love and then again. And then again. Three times that night we made love. She was the sexiest woman I'd ever known in my life. From then on, that was all we did. Sex. Morning, noon and night. I couldn't get enough of her.

The problem I had with Patty was that she was as promiscuous as I was. That wasn't a problem with most of the other girls I dated or had sex with...but then I wasn't in love with them. Being in love brought along the baggage of jealousy. Maybe love isn't the best way to describe what I felt for Patty. Obsession would better describe what I felt. The trouble was, I didn't trust her at all. And for good reason. She was exactly like me. If she had a chance to get laid, she took it. Does it sound like I held a double standard? Most certainly!

After we got back from Indianapolis, our "affair" took off with a burning intensity. I couldn't keep my hands off her and she was the same with me. I had rarely been this turned on by a woman before. All I could think about, day and night, was sex. We were doing it at least twice a day and sometimes three and four and even five times. I was in heaven.

And hell.

The sex was fantastic but it came at the price of enormous guilt. At home, I had a wonderful wife and two beautiful daughters. Sheila was everything a man could ask for in a mate, except for one area. Sex. She was loving, warm, compassionate, bright, and a terrific mother to our children. She kept a clean home and was a fabulous cook.

In every room of the house save one, Sheila was the perfect wife. In the bedroom however, it all fell apart.

Nothing we tried could keep sex from being painful for her. That was always the excuse I used on myself when I had affairs. I wasn't getting much at home. Like I needed an excuse.

Patty and I were doomed from the start. Both of us were intensely jealous of the other. Probably because we knew intimately of the other's libidinous nature. Even though I was "in love" with her, I was still chasing plenty of other women when I could get away with it. Now, I had two women to keep my "affairs" secret from. My wife and my girlfriend.

I was doing a lot of drugs and some drinking at the time, although not as much drinking as Sheila thought I was.

We were near the end of our marriage—even Sheila was beginning refusing to ignore my asshole antics—and I agreed to go to marriage counseling with her. This needs a little setting up. Before, when I'd roll in at two or three in the morning and Sheila would be waiting up and ask where I was, I'd say, "Oh, I was out with a blonde." Or a brunette. Or a redhead. Then, she'd say, "No, *really*, where were you?" I'd say, "With a blonde *and* a brunette." Which was where I was, out with some woman. She'd persist and finally I'd say, "Okay, I was out with the guys, drinking." She'd accept that.

Well, the first thing Sheila told the counselor was that the reason our marriage wasn't working was that I was always out drinking with the guys. The counselor insisted I join Alcoholics Anonymous, which I did. Before that, I had a drink occasionally, but was in no way an alcoholic. AA damn near made me into one, though.

I made arrangements for a couple of guys to pick me up for the AA meetings, which were held in Fort Wayne at Parkview Hospital's South Unit (the wing for the alkies and mentally-challenged). These guys were twin brothers, both Amish, who the court had ordered to attend AA because of frequent DUI's. These two guys would pick me up and already be toking from a bottle of vodka when they hit my house in Leo. All the way to the meeting we'd drink as fast as we could from the bottle. During the meeting, at the break, we'd sneak out and hit it again. There was a liquor store across from the hospital on State Street and we'd get our butts over there as soon as we were released from the meeting. You had to get there fast as there'd always be a long line of customers from the AA meeting that had just gotten out. We'd buy another bottle there and have it killed by the time they dropped me off at home. The most intense drinking I ever did in my life was when I was attending those AA meetings! If I ever open a liquor store, I'll make sure to locate it near to an AA meeting...

My marriage was on the skids. I'd rented an apartment under Patty's name for our love nest and one day I just packed up and moved there permanently and that was the end of our marriage. Stupidest thing I ever did. Smartest thing Sheila ever did, getting rid of me.

The single hardest thing I've ever had to do in my life was tell my oldest daughter Britney that I was divorcing her mother and leaving. I still can see us, walking down the road in front of our house in Leo and trying to explain to an eight-year-old angel why her daddy felt compelled to break up her family and leave her and her mother and baby sister. I just about ruined hers and her sister's life over my selfishness and just downright stupidity. Sienna was an infant, so I couldn't talk to her. I just went in, bent over and kissed her in her crib and walked out of the house for the last time.

I stayed drunk for a week. I mean, *drunk*. It was the only way I could keep from killing myself. All I could see was the tears in my daughter's eyes, the accusation that was there. If I'd been any kind of a person, I think I probably should have killed myself and rid the world of the scum I'd become. There has never been a lower moment in my life and I can't imagine how there could be.

Once I moved out, things went rapidly downhill. Out of guilt, I paid Sheila separate maintenance of $250 a week until the divorce went through. The salon was still cooking, but I was starting to fall behind. Since we were all but living together, I quit taking out a commission from Patty's earnings each week and let her keep everything she made. It was coming to the place where I was going to have to do something and the idea of New Orleans was starting to brew in my mind. When Sheila and I had left Lake Charles, I'd wanted to give New Orleans a shot, but decided not to and we came back to Indiana instead. I'd never given up the idea though.

My relationship with Patty grew stormier. Our days were spent in either screwing each other's brains out or having screaming fights or both.

When I first left Sheila, Patty told me to just stay with her at her house. At the time, my understanding was that she was divorced.

Turned out I was misinformed.

The morning after the first night I spent with her, we got up in the morning and after the kids left for school, jumped in my car to go to work.

I'd just put the car in reverse to back out of her driveway, when out of nowhere a Jeep drove up and blocked the driveway. It was Pete, her husband.

I'd never met him but knew of him. He was a legend in Ft. Wayne. After an illustrious career at Bishop Dwenger High School as a star basketball and football player, he played college basketball for Xavier. He'd quit football after high school to concentrate on basketball, but he was such a great athlete that the Dallas Cowboys drafted him to be on their taxi squad. At six-eight, he was simply a force.

Even though I'd never seen him until that moment, I knew instantly it was Pete who came striding up the driveway. I was trapped and pretty sure I only had a few minutes left to live. It was then that Patty told me she wasn't quite divorced yet...

I looked around for a weapon to defend myself with and all I could find was a small Phillips screwdriver lying on the console. I picked it up and then quickly reconsidered. It seemed likely he'd just make me eat that, so I dropped it back on the floor.

He strode up to the car on her side and she rolled down the window. He bent over and fixed me with a killer glare. "I don't care what you do with her," he said, meaning Patty, "but don't do it in my house."

My only thought was that I was going to die and I knew I

wanted to go out on a high note. I remember thinking, What would Woody Allen do? I looked at him, smiled, and said, "Pete. Do you mind if I call you Pete?"

He just snorted, straightened up, and strode back to his Jeep and left.

That was the only time I ever saw him in person, but I had one more experience with him during my time with Patty. A few months later, Patty and I had a big fight and she stormed out of our apartment we'd then gotten together. I was sure she was going to find Pete and grudge-fuck him to get even with me. I was half in the bag, and kept getting madder and madder. Finally, I decided to find him and fight him. There have been times in my life when I lacked what is usually called "common sense" and this was definitely one of them.

I went to all the places where I knew they'd used to hang out, and I took my pocketknife with me. Hunting bear. The last place I looked was a place Patty had told me once was his favorite hangout, the Acme Bar on State Street. If I found him there, my plan was to carve him up.

Luckily, he wasn't there. When I left there, my mad was cooling down considerably, and I decided not to look any more for him and went home and slept it off.

And that was our only two encounters, even though he hadn't been present in the flesh for the second one.

To my good luck...

Sometime later, I was talking to a friend of his and he convinced me Pete was actually a pretty cool guy. And, that it was probably fortunate that I hadn't found him that night. I agreed completely.

From that first night, Patty decided to rent an apartment under her own name for me and for her whenever she moved out of her house. I paid for it, but she got the lease under her name.

A couple of weeks after I left Sheila and the girls, Patty was off for the day and I got a phone call from her at work. There'd been a fire at the apartment. There wasn't much to burn. I had a mattress on the floor and that was the extent of the furniture. Somehow, it had gotten up next to the wall heater and caught on fire. The firemen's eyes must have popped out at what they saw. There was a smoldering mattress and blanket and around it were the following items: a huge jar of Vaseline, a *Hustler* magazine, a top hat of the kind Fred Astaire wore in one of his movies, a tube of KY...and a riding crop. Nothing else in the apartment, except some clothes in the closet.

They'd notified Patty since it was her name on the lease. They'd sent two firemen to her house to have her fill out a form. She was mortified, when they told her about the items. She knew right away it didn't take two firemen to come to her place to get the form filled out. They just wanted to see what the woman who owned these "furnishings" looked like!

I laughed so hard I had tears in my eyes, but she didn't think it was that funny.

Over the next few months, our relationship got rockier and rockier. One time, I had just picked her up at her house and we had gone to one of our regular drinking spots, the Phoenician Restaurant in Georgetown. It was winter and we'd just sat down at the bar and ordered a drink and all of a sudden I didn't want to be there. I excused myself to go to the bathroom and once out of sight, raced around to the pay phone and called a girl I'd been seeing on the sly. Dana said, sure, she'd come pick me up, so I slipped out the side door. She showed up in a couple of minutes and we drove down to Columbia City and partied at a place called The Hotel and then had sex out in the car. Afterwards, Dana drove me back to the Phoenician and I sat in her car for a minute deciding what to do. My leather winter coat was still inside where I'd left it. Just then, a van pulled up beside us and Patty's two best friends—a couple—got out. I didn't think Patty was still inside but I ducked down anyway. A few seconds later, Patty came out and ran straight for the car. Her friends must have seen me. She ran to the passenger side where I was locking the door and frantically rolling up the window. I almost got it up, but her fingers hooked into the glass.

"What should I do?" Dana said.

"Just start driving," I said. "She'll let go."

Only she didn't. Dana drove in a little circle around the parking lot and Patty just hung on with her fingers and ran alongside the car. Dana stopped the car and Patty let go of the window and leaped up on the hood, banging on the glass.

Dana had a lot of balls herself, so she just tromped on the gas and then hit the brakes, hoping to knock Patty off. It didn't work. She tried it two or three more times and Patty just hung on. By now there was a crowd gathering in front of the restaurant watching our drama.

"Fuck it," I said. "I'll take care of her," I told Dana.

"You sure?" she said.

"Yeah."

"Okay," she said. "Call me tomorrow, okay? If you're still alive!"

We laughed and I opened the door and got out. Patty was screaming at me, but I walked up to the door of the restaurant talking to her along the way. I always had the confidence I could talk anyone into anything if I wanted and sure enough, in ten minutes I had her believing I'd just had this incredible dumb-ass attack and that I loved her more than anything. We ended up back at the bar, kissing each other.

There were numerous incidents like that.

I finally moved out of the apartment and into a friend of mine's apartment downtown in the West Central section. Wendell had worked for me in Warsaw a couple of years before and we'd stayed friends. He was gay and at one time when he worked for me was going to get a sex-change operation. In fact, he and Isolde and I had made a pact one night when we sat on the floor and killed a bottle of Southern Comfort between us. She was going to be his last fuck before the operation and I was going to be his first after he became a woman. He backed out eventually, when his boyfriend who was going to finance the operation, changed his mind and decided he liked Wendell as a guy but wouldn't as a woman.

Anyway, Wendell said it would be fine to crash at his place in the West Central section of Ft. Wayne and I could sleep in a little loft he had over his living room.

One Sunday, I had just come back from South Bend after seeing my daughters and I called up Patty at her house to see if she wanted to come over. No, she said. She was low on gas and didn't have any money so she'd just stay home. That was fine, I said. I was tired and going to bed.

As soon as she hung up, I called Dana and she came over and picked me up and we went out, had some fun, screwed and then she brought me back to Wendell's. We were in the alley behind his house, kissing, when all of a sudden Patty emerged from the darkness and started screaming at us. After calling me everything she could think of, she stalked back to her car and disappeared. I told Dana goodnight and went in the house.

I must have been a little high because I forgot to lock the door. About an hour later around three in the morning, I woke up and Patty was at the top of the ladder you had to crawl up to get to the loft and she was grabbing for my cock. She was also screaming. "If I can't have it, nobody will!" This was way before Lorena Bobbit and if Patty had succeeded in her mission, Bobbit's little trick would have been old hat by then.

I grabbed her hands while she was trying to yank out my trouser worm by the roots and she scratched the hell out of my face. Just raked it the full length. There was so much blood I was having trouble seeing. The whole time she was doing this, she was screaming curse words at me at the top of her lungs. The whole house was up by now. I saw Wendell come around the corner from his bedroom with his boyfriend and through the windows I could see lights popping on all up and down the street. I just started talking to her, telling her I loved her and didn't know why I'd been such a chump as to cheat on her but that I really did love her and would never do it again.

Little by little, I got her calmed down and backed down the ladder and little by little got her to the side door, sweet-talking her all the way. She was almost all the way calmed down and outside on the stoop and everything was fine when I couldn't resist it. I looked down on her smiling face and said, "Uh, Patty...does this mean we're not going to the prom together?" Don't ask me why I did that—I was always doing stuff like that. That started her all over again. She got this crazed look on her face and jumped for the door but I slammed it shut and locked her out and went back inside, ignoring her new tirade. Eventually, she left and just as eventually a few days later, she forgave me and took me back.

Looking back, it seemed I acted like that in every relationship. I always had to "test" women, make them "prove" they loved me. I'd do everything in the world to them I could to make them leave, just to see if they would and then I'd see if I could get them back. It was this huge, sick game I played all the time.

Our relationship continued like this for several more months and then I must have finally gone over the edge in her mind and she left me. I was convinced it was for good and severe depression set in. In my self-pity, and with my thoroughly sick mind I looked at my situation and thought, hell, I left my family for her and now she's left me. There was nothing to live for anymore, I was convinced. I drove out to Coliseum Boulevard and rented a room at a Motel 6 and holed up with a couple of bottles of Jack Daniels. For three days, all I did was drink Jack and nibble on some chocolate donuts I'd bought. When I was as drunk as I could get, I got out my Norelco razor and poked back a ceiling tile and found a pipe and tied one end of the cord to it. I brought a chair over, stood on it and tied the other end around my neck.

Then, I kicked the chair out from underneath me.

***

The damn cord broke.

I crashed to the floor and just lay there. All kinds of stupid things were going through my mind. I thought about going to a store and buying a rope but remembered that I was broke and I'd have to drive back to Wendell's to get my billfold which was on top of a dresser. It was going to be a chore to kill myself. Something that at first seemed like it'd be a simple thing to do was fast becoming complicated.

A ray of sanity must have entered my sick-ass brain. I started laughing at the ludicrousness of the situation. I must have laughed for ten minutes solid, choking and sputtering and half-crying. When I was done, I picked my sorry ass up and got the hell out of there. I knew exactly what I was going to do.

IX
BACK TO HEDONISM
IN A BIG WAY

I got on the phone and called my best friend from Pendleton, Bud Palmer. Bud was working in some little barber shop in Fort Wayne and we'd been out drinking together a few times.

"Wanna go with me?" I asked as soon as I heard his voice.

"Where?" he said.

"I don't know," I said. "I'm just heading south, see where I end up. Get out of this fucking snow."

On the way over to pick him up, I stopped at a convenience store to pick up some butts and ended up holding up the joint on a whim. It'd been a long time since I'd done something like that, but it felt good. I got into a little argument with a lady and her bratty kid that I eventually wrote a short story about. I also wrote a novel titled *Just Like That* about some of our adventures on this trip.

Bud was like me, ready to drop everything at the slightest urging and in half an hour after leaving the store I was at his house and he was packing up. First, he went through the house and grabbed everything he could find of value that we could pawn. It was his girlfriend Tammy's house.

Once we were in the car, he told me to stop by Parkview Hospital where Tammy worked in the kitchen.

I waited while he went inside and shook her down for what cash she had on her and he came out and we were on our way, stopping only to stock up with beer.

We ended up partying all along the way and nailed women in every state between Indiana and New Orleans. Once there, we found ourselves stone broke and he called Tammy and she wired him some money. He loaned me some and caught the Greyhound home. That was the last time I saw Bud until a few years later when I spotted him at the Three Rivers Festival back in Ft. Wayne and we talked for a little bit. He was always a true friend, ready to drop everything and take off with me. In the joint, he was one of the guys who kept me from getting nailed by others. Bud is a true bad ass and would kill for a friend in a nanosecond.

I stuck it out in New Orleans after Bud left for a few weeks, getting by with some minor hustling, shooting pool, stuff like that. One time, I watched a woman make a drug deal outside a bar on Jefferson, and when she went back inside, I went up to where she was sitting at the bar, grabbed her purse and ran. She had over two hundred bucks in it and six grams of coke in it all packaged up, and that kept me going to a long time. I was sleeping on the banks of the Mississippi behind the Café du Monde. Sometimes, I'd eat at one of the missions and sleep in one of the many flop houses, one in particular over on Camp Street. One night I got into a fight with a guy who tried to steal the piece of plastic I used to cover up with at night and the guy cut my arm pretty good. I kicked his butt and the cops showed up and took us both off to jail. A nurse stitched me up and it wasn't that big of a deal. In the morning they kicked me out and I went back to where I'd been sleeping behind the Café du Monde and found my sheet of plastic where I'd left it. Finally, I saw this wasn't working and picked up enough money to get a bus ticket back to Indiana.

A special friend of mine, Jim Teusch, gave me a job in his shop and I got together a stake. As soon as my poke was healthy, I headed back down to New Orleans.

The second time I moved to New Orleans I played it a little

smarter. From Jim's shop in Fort Wayne, I called Lloyd Lejeune, the guy I'd met at the Midwest Beauty Show before to see if he might know of a job available in the Big Easy.

He did. He had a friend in New Orleans who he thought needed a stylist. He called back a few minutes later and I had a job in New Orleans, out in Metairie. Donald Brouchard—not his real name—even offered to let me stay in his house with him and his wife Brenda, once I explained I was low on cash. Sight unseen, strictly on Lloyd's recommendation the guy did that. He was a prince.

The next day, I was on a bus rolling south.

Two days after I started working for Don. I saved someone's life. I was walking back to Don's house along about four in the morning from a blood 'n guts place named Polly's, ready to call it a night. As I stepped across Jefferson Highway, I saw a white Lincoln parked in front of Don's salon—which was on the way to his house, a block behind it—and a middle-aged Oriental couple standing in the street beside it. The man was bent over and the woman was patting him politely on the back.

I walked up to them. There wasn't a single car going by and no one on the street at all, except for us three.

"Is he choking?" I asked the woman, who was standing there, patting who I assumed was her husband, timidly on the back. She nodded yes. She obviously couldn't speak English. This guy was in serious distress. Even in the dark you could see he was turning an ashy color and his eyes were bulging out and he was making little pawing motions with his hands.

"Mind if I try?" I asked the woman and she gave a combination shrug and nod of her head, her eyes huge and luminous. I stepped behind the man and put my arms around his middle, clasping my hands together at his stomach and squeezed hard. Nothing. Just the week before I'd read an article about the Heimlich Maneuver and it said in the article that sometimes you had to break ribs when you did it. It was better to break ribs than let the person choke to death, the article had said. So I tried it again and I cranked the guy as hard as I could. I was actually trying to break a rib. I figured that was the secret, from reading the article. I'd never seen the Heimlich done but had a rough idea from reading about it.

Wham! Out flew something about the size of my fist, white and gooey. A hunk of white chocolate, as it turned out.

The guy stood there gasping for about five minutes while his wife and I stood there watching him. She went back to her pitty-pat routine on his back, but you could see he was going to be all right. Then, they started bowing to me, these little jerky half bows that looked like those birds you buy and set in motion over a water glass. I pointed to the hairstyling shop we were standing in front of and said "I work there," but I don't know if they understood me. They kept smiling and bobbing up and down, bowing, and then they got back in their Lincoln and drove off. I could see the guy's arm waving at me out the window.

I walked on to my boss's house and went into my room and went to sleep. *Where were the fucking newspaper reporters and TV stations?* I thought just before I dropped off. *I'm a fucking hero and no one knows it!*

The next day at work, I told everybody what had happened, but they all just laughed and said, "Sure, Les, sure." Nobody believed me. Pissed me off.

Two days later, I walked back in the shop after going to lunch, and there's this young Oriental guy sitting on the stairs talking to Don. Turned out it was the guy's son, the one I saved. He spoke English.

It seems his parents told him what happened and they'd understood what I was telling them, that I worked there, but they'd looked up and down Jefferson for two days without recognizing where they'd been. Their son had then just started going down the road, stopping in each shop he saw until he got to Don's. When he'd told Don what he was doing, Don told him he had the right place and I was gone to lunch.

The son thanked me on behalf of his parents and we talked a little bit, but I had a customer and had to go take care of her. After a while, the Oriental guy stuck his head in my booth, shook my hand and left. Never saw him or his parents again.

Never saw anything in the papers either.

X
CAT

A few days after I moved back to New Orleans, Patty started calling me and we began talking and she decided to fly down to see if we might reconcile. Her planned week with me turned into a shorter visit of three days after we soon figured out it was truly over. We weren't through the second day of her visit before we started fighting again, screaming at each other. The next day I sent her in a cab to the airport.

Two days after Patty left, I met Cat.

I was still without a car at the time and mostly hanging out at Polly's—not the real name—which was within walking distance.

It was there I met my Cajun princess.

Polly's was quite the place. It never closed, even for Christmas Day. Even on Christmas, drunks needed their booze and that's who hung out at Polly's. Drunks and outlaws. They had a series of country-western bands that played there, almost continually, and the only thing they had in common was that they all played off-key. It was a great pick-up place though. Polly told me one time, that, "There's not even a padlock on the door. I couldn't close even if I wanted to." Polly's had the biggest cockroaches I've ever seen. Two of them could—and would—carry off your bottle of beer, if you didn't keep an eye on it.

The first night I went to Polly's was memorable. There was a tiny bar right by the bandstand itself with two stools. It looked like it had been set up there so the band member's wives or girlfriends could sit there, close to their husband or boyfriend while they played.

There was a washed-out bottle blonde sitting there who was so anemic that today she'd be suspected of being a meth addict. She sat there, head cupped in her hands while she stared dreamily at the lead singer and guitar player while he worked. The band was godawful—playing country western songs totally off-key, but most people were so drunk they didn't notice. Another woman, a brunette, was on the dance floor, gyrating by herself, but with her eyes also glued on the lead singer and performing dance moves you usually see on a stage at a strip club. Moves clearly choreographed to send this guy into a state of sexual frenzy.

All of a sudden, the blonde at the mini-bar launched herself off her stool toward the dancer and the two began to mix it up. The brunette got in a good lick and smacked the blonde in the chops and something flew from the blonde's face toward me like a heat-seeking missile. It hit me in the forehead and dropped down. I climbed down off my stool and picked up the object. It was a glass eye!

I stood there holding the orb, not quite realizing what had just happened, and the blonde ran over to me, and took her eye back and stuck it back in her eyehole. "Thank you," she said. "I really appreciate this. I can't afford a new one."

All the fight went out of her and she went back to her stool and the other woman left. I eventually learned that this was an almost-nightly occurrence. The guy in the band was her boyfriend and she came to sit in the same spot every night when he played and almost always some other woman would begin flirting and the fight would be on. I don't know if she ever lost her eye that way again, but it wouldn't surprise me if she had.

Oh, yeah. She bought me a beer for saving her eye.

Polly's had become my nightly hangout after Patty went back to Ft. Wayne. It was about one in the morning a couple of days after she'd left and I was sitting at the bar when this girl walked in. She was drop-dead gorgeous. Coal black hair and the greenest eyes I'd ever seen without colored contacts. And boobs. She had a set of hooters that'd put your eye out if she turned too quickly. I went over and sat down beside her at the bar and began running my game.

We ended up back at her place in the Houma House Apartments over off Veteran's Highway in Fat City and the next morning she asked me to move in with her, be her boyfriend. By this time, I'd learned her life history and the fact that a high-class call girl thought enough of my love-making talents to invite me to move in was a heavy-duty stroke to my always-needy ego. I considered it for about a nanosecond before I said okay. She was gorgeous, the second-best I'd ever had in bed, and she liked my "meat." That's what she always referred to it as. Her meat.

Your meat's in Indiana, Cat.

It turns out Cat was sold by her mom to Carlos Marcello, the head of the New Orleans Mafia when she was ten years old. When she told me that, I said, "You must have been an extraordinary ten-year-old," but that wasn't it, she said. Carlos just liked his "women" young.

"What'd he pay for you?" I asked. What else do you say when someone lays something like that on you?

"About a hundred dollars, I think," is what Cat said. "Actually, he just gave her some dope for me and I think it was worth about a hundred bucks. She probably threw in a blow job. She was a hooker."

My guess is it was worth a whole lot less. After all, the guy got it wholesale. The dope, I mean.

It further seems that this romancer of young girls usually got tired of them when they made the mistake of attaining the ripe old age of twelve or so and threw them out onto the street. Most died, Cat said. Drugs, smacked too many times by a pimp, rough sex with tricks, things like that. She, Cat, was one of the survivors. Like most of the others, she'd gone on down into the Quarter and became a prostitute, doing well. When I met her, she was well past that period of her life. She was twenty-five, working as a waitress in a classy restaurant, the Lil' Cajun Cuisine, in Metairie just off Veterans Highway and made money on the side as a call girl. Her words, not mine. She had five or six wealthy businessmen she serviced once or twice a month.

One of them was a politically prominent man whose son became even more well-known than his dad, in the entertainment business. If I said the name, you'd know it instantly. Even if you don't watch much TV. I won't use his name, not so much for fear of a lawsuit as I'm more afraid I'll end up in a swamp as alligator bait somewhere if I ever return to New Orleans. This guy has that kind of power.

This citizen was an interesting trick. He would hire Cat, me, and a black prostitute friend of Cat's named Jackie. He'd send a city limo for Cat and me at our apartment and then we'd drive over to Jackie's shotgun house in the Ninth Ward and pick her up. He'd have a suite rented at one of the classy hotels downtown, the Fairmont or Intercontinental and we'd truck on up and he'd already be lying on the floor buck-naked. The girls would undress and get into their high heels. Cat had a special pair of black high heels she wore only for this trick. *Client.* I'm sorry. She called them "clients." They were only about an inch and a half heels. I'd take a seat at the wet bar and start mixing all of us drinks and cutting coke lines. Then, the girls would take turns walking up and down on his back and whipping him with these little crops they both had. We'd all cuss him out the entire time of our "session," call him the worst things we could think of, scream at him. His driver/bodyguard would sit out in an outer room, reading *True Romance* and eating Girl Scout Thin Mints cookies, which he loved and had an unending supply of. Trouble is, you'd think there'd be a bunch of ways you can cuss a person out, but there aren't that many. Only about seven or eight good ones. It was all kind of boring. After about an hour of this stuff, he'd get his nut. He and the girls would shower down and get dressed and then he'd take us out in the limo to a really nice restaurant like Arnaud's or Gallatoire's. Then it was back into the limo, envelopes all around and we'd be whisked home. In the envelopes would be two hundred fifty for each of the girls and fifty for me. And I never had to lay a glove on him. Easiest money I ever made. Plus the booze we got to drink was always top shelf and the meal he treated us to was first-rate as well. The coke wasn't stepped on, either.

About a month after I moved in with Cat, she said, "I'm going to give up being a prostie."

We were sitting on the couch, drinking wine and watching the tube. We had just finished screwing for the third time. One of those times wasn't regular sex; it was one of the golden showers Cat favored, so I probably shouldn't count that as one of the three times, except that she got off quicker with that than she did with regular sex, proving the brain—or lack of one—is the biggest and most important organ involved in sex. Come to think of it, I don't know as you could classify what we did in bed as "regular sex" as Cat liked me to smack her while we were doing the nasty, so it wasn't exactly Ozzie and Harriet sex. She liked to be smacked *hard*—we're not talking about a little spanking on the po-po—she dug being smacked in the jaw with a fist. "Harder, harder," she'd hiss. "Don't be a pussy, Les." Must have been something from her idyllic childhood, I figured.

"Don't go crazy on me," I said, alarmed somewhat at her proclamation that she was going to quit hooking. "I know you love me, babe. You don't have to do something like that."

I could just see our coke money going out the window. I guess we just loved each other in different ways.

By that time, I was working at Snobs close to our apartment in Metry. We lived at Houma House Apartments a block away from her day job at the Lil Cajun Cuisine restaurant and about six blocks away from Snobs on Arnoldt.

Cat was always after me to go down to the Quarter with her

and her girlfriend Jackie. Jackie was also a hooker, a beautiful black girl. She still worked on the street, although Cat had given that part of the business up, taking care of a few businessmen only these days. Usually on a Sunday or Saturday night, she would say, "Someone's coming over," and I would go out for a couple of hours and drink beer at a bar while she did her "business."

I went with the girls a couple of times. They would solicit sailors and tourists and give them blow jobs in secluded doorways in the Quarter. They wanted me along for what they called "protection," but that was a laugh. Neither of these girls needed protection. I should have been there to help out the sailors.

They enjoyed was getting some poor sucker off a Norwegian or Russian oil tanker back in one of the gardens that are all over the place in the French Quarter and then mug him. Stick him up with a pistol or knife and take his money. Cat had a little Raven .25 caliber she kept in her purse for those occasions.

"Sailors always keep their stash in their socks," Cat told me. She was right. It was where I'd kept my money when I was in the Navy.

The last time I went with them, they tricked some Russian guy off a tanker back into the space next to Pat O'Brien's where it goes on back to the Dungeon. Halfway back, instead of a blow job, he got a knife held to his stomach.

"Fuck you," he said in perfect English. He'd been acting like he didn't understand us.

"Okay," Cat went. "Then, fuck *you*." And she pushed her knife into his stomach. It was a *big*-ass knife. He just crumpled at the knees and I felt like doing the same. In a flash, both girls were rolling off his black shoes and sure enough, there were bills in each of his socks. They got his billfold too, but there wasn't much in there. Maybe five bucks and some Russian funny money. No credit cards.

She was always doing Ludes and she'd go off like that in a nanosecond. You never knew which Cat you'd get—nice Cat or I'll cut your dick off, Cat.

The next week, Cat said, "Let's go down to the Quarter, honey. I'll call up Jackie."

I just laughed. I never went with them again after that. Too fucking dangerous. I'd been in the New Orleans jail and that was bad enough. I sure as shit didn't want to end up in Angola at the Farm. I'd seen that movie and it didn't have a good ending.

We checked the *Times-Picayune* for a few days after Cat had stabbed the Russian but there wasn't anything we could find. Maybe he hadn't died like we thought. It's hard to tell in New Orleans. Lots of stuff like that doesn't make the paper.

The reason Cat and I broke up was her jealousy. *She* was the whore, but she was jealous of *me*. And I never did anything to provoke it. Well, I did, but nothing she knew about or could prove, anyway. She was just naturally suspicious of men, I guess. Probably came from her occupation, most of the tricks being married men with kids and a lawn and a monthly luncheon down at the Rotary Club. And a wife who charged a higher price for her booty than women like Cat did.

We'd gone to Florida for the weekend, down to Pensacola Island, where we rented a condo. Everything was great, the sex, the weather, the booze, the food. We talked about getting jobs and moving there.

On the way back to New Orleans, just on the other side of the bridge connecting the island to the mainland, I pulled up to a liquor store to get a six-pack for the drive home. A man and woman waited on us, and we could tell they were married when one of them said something to the other about their kids. As I was paying for the beer, I said to the woman, "I really like your haircut. Who does it?" I explained that I was a hairstylist myself, worked in a salon in New Orleans called Snobs. Cat had gone in with me and she complimented the lady, too.

As soon as we got back out to the car, Cat began unloading on me. "You son of a bitch. Everywhere we go, you have to flirt. You were trying to fuck that girl back there."

My jaw literally dropped. "Cat," I said, "I was just paying the lady a compliment. Christ! Her husband was standing right there. You think if I was going to hit on someone I'd do it with her husband there?" It was nuts, her ragging on me. She kept it up, but I just shut my mouth and drove. It was just Cat being Cat.

After a while, I had to take a piss, so I just pulled off the highway and walked over to a stand of trees. Just as I was whipping out my trouser worm to drain the main vein, I heard the car tires screech and when I looked back, Cat was pulling away, leaving me there.

My billfold was in the glove compartment and I was left standing there with nothing but my T-shirt, shorts and flip-flops. Not a dime on me or any I.D. I didn't even bother to wait to see if she would come back for me, just walked back up to the highway and stuck out my thumb. The second car by stopped and gave me a ride all the way back to New Orleans, two blocks from our apartment. We must have passed Cat on the way, or else she'd stopped off somewhere, because she wasn't there when I got walked up to the second floor where our apartment was, overlooking the pool. I got the spare key we kept under the mat and let myself in and started throwing my things into my suitcase.

About twenty minutes later, Cat walked in and did a double-take at seeing me there.

"I was going back to get you," she said, as soon as she recovered from the surprise of me being there.

"Fuck you, Cat," I said. "It's a two-hour drive back to Pensacola and you haven't even started yet. At the best, I'd be waiting by the side of the road for four hours. You're a liar. You weren't about to come back for me, bitch. I'm outta here." I finished tossing the last few things in my suitcase and lugged it to the door. Just as I got there, I heard her fire her pistol. I whipped around and there she stood, her gun pointing at me. She'd shot at me!

I ran as hard and fast as I could to the bedroom where she was and tackled her, going for the gun. I got it from her and smacked her in the chops as hard as I could. This wasn't a funtime sex smack. I was trying my best to knock her out but all I did was bloody her nose and make her madder. I took the clip out of the gun and ejected the shell that was in the chamber and threw it in the living room. Then I got up, went to the front room and called a cab, leaving Cat lying on the bedroom floor where she stayed, staring daggers at me and snarling. As soon as I got a cab on the way, I went downstairs to the parking lot and got my billfold from her car. *Her* car! I'd just given her every dime I had the week before, for the down payment. It was a brand-new Mercury, and she didn't have a nickel of her own money in it yet, only the two thousand bucks I'd given her for the down payment. It was supposed to be "our" car, but I'd told her to just get it in her name. The only money I had in the entire world was twenty-two bucks and change and I figured I'd go to Snobs, about a mile away, spend the night there and then figure out what to do next.

I'd just got back up to the apartment, to pick up my suitcase and go down and wait for the cab, when just behind me two cops came charging into the room with their guns out and yelled at me to lie down on the floor. In the few minutes I'd been gone, Cat had called the cops, told them I was beating her up, and they must have had a unit in the neighborhood because it only took a minute or so to get there.

They took me to the Orleans Parish jail. I don't go with her to roll drunks to avoid this kind of happy horseshit, and I'm just minding my business when I end up there. Some justice in life, sometimes. I could have told them Cat had fired her gun at me, but I thought about it and the fact she didn't have a permit, and for some stupid reason, I didn't. "Bail me out," I said as they were leading me downstairs, handcuffed. I didn't think there was any real hope of that, even after I didn't get her in trouble for having the gun, and I was right. I lay in jail all night, in the drunk tank with a bunch of fucking perverts, but nobody fucked with me. They must have seen I was in a mood.

The next day they released me, telling me Cat had refused to press charges. That was big of her.

After the shooting incident and my release from the New Orleans Parish jail, I went to Cat's apartment, grabbed my suitcase and called a cab. Cat was at work when I got to her apartment, which was undoubtedly a good thing. The jail was pretty full when I left. I had the cab take me to Snobs on Arnoldt Street in Fat City where I worked as the artistic director. After paying and tipping the driver, I walked upstairs with less than ten bucks to my name.

For the next two weeks, I slept on the table in the massage room at night. I'd take Marine showers in the shampoo sinks, washing myself with a shampoo towel. I used the salon washer and dryer to do my laundry. I made enough in tips to eat on, and at the end of the two weeks, had enough in my paycheck to get an apartment just down the street.

If I hadn't just given Cat two thousand dollars—virtually every cent I had at the time—for the down payment on her new Mercury, I would've been sitting pretty good. Just bad timing on my part, I guess. I was out of luck.

A couple of days after I "moved in" to the salon, Anthony Jones, the English owner, asked me if I'd been sleeping there.

He didn't have a problem with that, provided none of the clients found out. Snobs was one of the toniest hair salons in New Orleans, and it wouldn't look right. Anthony was a real-life prince. Not only didn't he pitch a bitch about my crashing in his place of business, he co-signed a loan so I could buy a '77 Monte Carlo, my dream car, a few months later. I repaid him by fleeing to Los Angeles and abandoning the car alongside Airline Highway. He had to pay off the loan. I'm guessing that's what he did—I've never gotten back in touch with him.

He reads this, my guess is I'm going to get a bill. Or a visit. I hope it's just a bill.

I moved into a run-down two-story apartment complex a couple of blocks away and started getting my life in order. It was an outlaw complex, filled mostly with drug dealers, prostitutes and off-shore oil workers who liked to party when they were off the rigs. Rough little dump. All the "apartments" were one-room efficiencies. It did have a nice pool in the center that was kept clean. At least it looked clean. Most of us who lived there just called it "Drug Central."

I'd been in the apartment maybe a week before I saw Cat again. Snobs was on the top floor of a two-story building which housed various other businesses. Lawyers, a Lebanese restaurant, some other small businesses, mostly offices. Each night, I'd eat supper at the Lebanese joint. Great food, and I knew everyone there.

One night, I was sitting at the bar when Cat walked in. The restaurant had been one of my hangouts before we split up, so it was no great trick of detection to find me there. She was dressed to the nines, wearing a gorgeous, form-fitting red dress and matching heels. With her raven's hair, brilliant green eyes, and a pair of knockers most Hollywood actresses had to put on their platinum card, she was a traffic stopper.

"Hi, baby," she said, squirming her beautiful butt up onto the stool next to mine.

I started to get up, but she put her hand on my arm.

"Don't get excited," she said, laughing. "I just want to have a drink with you."

I relaxed, and she ordered me a Jack and water. That was easy—it's all I ever drink.

"I miss you," she said, after some small talk. You know—"How ya been—How's your hammer hangin'"—chit-chat like that.

I hated to admit it, but I missed her, too. What I missed was holding those perfect boobs in my hands, getting a mouthful of nipple. I'd been laid a few times since we parted company, but none them were half as good in the sack as Cat was. Of course, they weren't pros and she was.

"Let's go dancing!" she said, suddenly, her eyes bright. "I love dancing with you, Les."

I started to beg off, even though I was still wanting her. We were oil and water together and I tried to remember that.

"Oh, come on," she insisted. "Just dancing. Just have some fun like we used to." We *did* have a lot of good times, I recalled. It wasn't all hot lead bouncing around the apartment.

"We'll just go dancing," she said, continuing her sales spiel. "Nothing else. No sex, none of that shit. You go home to your place and I'll go home to mine. Let's just have some fun, sugar."

Will power wasn't necessarily a trait I possessed in abundance. Especially not with the woody that had popped up when she put her hand on my thigh and gave a little squeeze. Despite what she was saying, I knew that if we went out, we'd end up in the sack together. Not the worst way to end an evening, I thought. I did have enough resolve that I'd made my mind up that no matter what happened, I wouldn't move back in with her. Probably...

I expected we'd take off right then, but she said, no, she had to go back to her apartment and change. I couldn't imagine what she was going to change into that looked better than what she had on, but she said if she was going dancing, she wanted to get rid of her heels, get into something more comfortable. She'd be back in half an hour, she said, and left.

Sure enough, half an hour later she was back, wearing a pair of tight-ass shorts and a halter top that barely covered her breasts. Looking hot. Looked like she wanted to stay in Fat City and not hit any of the downtown hotels, way she was dressed. I had just started a new drink and she slid up on the stool beside me.

"Order me one," she said, smiling. "Wine."

I ordered her a glass of Chablis and John, the owner who was bartending, brought it over. She looked at the drink, her smile still on...and she picked up the drink and threw it at me, glass and all. As used to her mood changes as I was, it still shocked me. I just sat there like a dumbass.

"You fucking bastard," she screamed. It was unreal. Like Jekyll and Hyde. There had been absolutely no warning at all for her change of personality. Later, I figured she had dropped a 'lude or two. She loved Quaaludes, and in the past when she'd done them, her personality would flip-flop between every extreme you could imagine in the time it takes to pick up a prostitute in an Airline Highway bar.

The noise level in the restaurant dropped instantly and John came running around from behind the bar. He'd seen Cat in operation several times before, when we'd had arguments in the restaurant.

As John came around, Cat just started screaming at me. Every foul word you can imagine. I was still in shock, I guess, but then John grabbed her and I tried to help. He was going to hustle her outside before she chased away every customer in the place.

Together, somehow we got her outside. She was kicking, scratching—at me—and hollering the whole time. Once outside in the parking lot, John backed off, but I still had hold of her arms. Just to protect myself. She was kicking with her leg, trying to nail me, and digging her nails into my arms and drawing blood as I tried to just keep her from doing damage to my face, which was her intended target. From out of nowhere, two cops came running up and grabbed her. It took the both of them to get cuffs on her.

They'd seen the whole thing, one of them said, from across the street at the Godfather (Mafia nightclub which Carlos owned—lots of parallels going on in this matrix) parking lot. John gave his version, which dovetailed with mine, and the other cop said they would run her in.

"Oh, man, no," I said, knowing what that would mean. "You'll just make her madder. You wanna get me killed? Have a heart, man."

In the end, after much discussion, the cops let her go, first making her promise that she'd leave and wouldn't come back or bother me anymore. She calmed down, agreed, and they escorted her to her car. Coming back, the policemen suggested I take out a peace bond on her.

Once the excitement died down, I went back inside and apologized to John.

"Forget it," he said. "It's not your fault, Les. We know she's nuts." He bought me a drink and brought me a clean bar rag and I tried to clean the wine off my face and arms. My clothes were soaked. My arms were also bleeding from where she'd scratched me. It was still early, around midnight, and I'd planned on going out that night, so I decided to walk down to my apartment, shower, get fresh clothes on and go out and run the traps.

I said goodbye to John and the others, who wished me well with the "crazy lady," and walked out of the restaurant. Just as I stepped off the curb to cross the street, a black Mercury came out of nowhere, trying to run me down. I saw it coming at literally the last possible second and sprinted for the other sidewalk and dove behind a cement post like a halfback going over the goal line. The Mercury bounced off the post. It was Cat.

The street was full of party animals. This was Fat City, the locals' party area. Thirty-some nightclubs and bars within a three-block radius. Many owned by the Mafia. There were hundreds, if not thousands, of people in the street and on the sidewalks.

I got up, dusted myself off, and began walking fast down the sidewalk to my apartment a couple of blocks away. Cat kept pace in her car, following me every step of the way, yelling curse words at me out her window. People looked at me like I was the Boston Strangler, probably figuring I'd done something horrible to this beautiful girl who was pursuing me down Arnoldt. I could see girls with their dates looking at me out of the corner of their eyes. I imagined them thinking... *interesting guy— must be pretty hot to have that babe chasing him...* Well, they probably weren't thinking that, but I imagined they were. I just kept moving, trying to ignore Cat and the scene she was causing. Half a block from the complex, she turned off on a side street and I walked the rest of the way in peace.

By the time I'd finished my shower and started to dress, the previous events had faded from my mind. I'd just laid out my clothes and was trying to decide where I was going, when the doorbell rang. Like a contrived plot point in a bad novel, I walked over and opened it.

It was Cat. And she had a knife in her hand. A big-ass switchblade. One I'd given her as a present a couple of months ago. One she'd stuck in a Russian sailor one fine weekend day. A knife with a history.

She didn't say a word, just stepped in and tried to gut me. I ducked and ran back to my bed, looking for something to defend myself with, a jacket or sweater or...*anything*. She ran after me and all I could see to grab was a shoe. She made another stab at me and I brought up the shoe and the knife sliced through and stuck in the shoe and I broke her grip and stood there with the shoe and knife in my hand. All of this happened in nanoseconds. I took the shoe—the knife embedded in it—and threw it out the open door onto the landing. She hissed *Bastard!* at me and ran out after the knife. I ran behind her and slammed the door shut and locked it. I didn't have a phone, so I couldn't call the cops, so I just sat and waited for about half an hour. I finished getting dressed and had to dig out another pair of shoes to wear.

All of this may sound strange to those who don't operate day-to-day in the outlaw culture, but these kinds of things happened all the time and I didn't give much thought to it, other than to be pissed that I'd lost a shoe, which lowers the value of the remaining one considerably. Especially since these were my one pair of Stacey-Adams and kicks I really liked.

After I figured enough time had passed, cautiously I opened the door a crack and then wider. Cat was nowhere in sight.

Neither was my shoe or the knife. I left my door unlocked—in case I needed to get back inside in a hurry—and went downstairs to the payphone on the outside wall by the parking lot. There was no sign of either Cat or her wheels.

I dialed the police and told the lady cop who answered what had happened. She seemed pretty bored with the whole thing and didn't want to send anyone out on what she figured was a wild goose chase. This kind of thing was pretty low-priority for a New Orleans Saturday night. I started to say "Fuck you" but thought better of it. For something as heinous as cussing her out, she probably would have scared up a SWAT team.

I hung up, went back, locked my door, and headed down the street to the Godfather. After a drink or two, I forgot all about it.

After that episode, I didn't see hair one of Cat for about a month. I didn't have much time to think about ex-girlfriends, as I was getting laid on a more-than-regular basis, by two or three different girls each night. There were many days when I'd have a nooner or two as well. Being a hairdresser at a toney salon like Snobs meant women were coming on to you all the time. New Orleans was definitely my kind of town. Everybody there was there for the sole purpose of partying and wearing out their sexual parts, it seemed. At least in the circles I ran in.

I partied so much, I decided to give it a rest one day. I hadn't missed a day without screwing for weeks and weeks. My body was worn out. I made up my mind that on Sunday, I wasn't going anywhere. I was going to relax by the pool with the nine pounds of the Sunday *Times-Picayune* and a cold brew and fuck the world. Read all the lies about how the Saints were only a player or two away from the Super Bowl.

It started out like that, anyway. At nine in the morning, I slipped into a bathing suit, grabbed the paper, and went down to the pool. At nine-oh-five, I had just turned the front page of the sports section when one of the girls I'd slept with a week or so before walked through the breezeway that led to one of the parking lots—there was one on both sides of the complex—and over to me.

"Hi, Sandra," I said, offering her one of the beers in the cooler I'd brought down with me. She sat down and popped a top.

"Let's do something, babe," she said.

"Well," I started. "I was just going to—"

"Go with me to a movie," she said. "There's that new one with Dudley Moore I've been dying to see. *Arthur.*"

There went my resolution to stay home. She checked the paper to see the nearest place it was showing—no problem, since New Orleans is filled with multiplexes that show movies twenty-four hours a day—and we decided to go to one at a shopping center a couple of blocks away. We threw some cold beers in her purse and off we went.

After the movie, which *was* great—I laughed until I cried at parts—we came back to the apartment and screwed. She didn't stick around, but left, and I gathered up my paper and beer and headed back down to the pool.

I hadn't even broken a sweat from the sun yet, when another girl came by. Nanette.

Guess what Nanette wanted to do.

Yep. Same movie. That was one hot movie.

This time, I laughed at the funny parts, but didn't crack any ribs.

Guess what Nanette wanted to do after the movie.

Yep.

Now, this is where it gets into hard-to-believe territory, but after Nanette left, I went back to the pool with my newspaper and beer. I got to maybe page three of the sports section, when yet another girl I'd been seeing showed up. By now, it was mid-afternoon.

"Hi, Brenda," I said. By this time, I had the routine down.

I was right.

This time, it was all I could do to work up a smile at the funny parts. More like a pained grimace.

And when we got back to my apartment, it was even harder to work up Mr. Happy. But I did, we did, and Brenda put it in the wind.

By now, it was early evening. I poured a glass of wine and was just starting to return to the pool when the doorbell rang.

Pam.

Movie.

Screw.

Truth is stranger than fiction. I swear by all that's holy, that's exactly how my "day off" from girls and sex went. Four girls came by, all with the same mission. See the same movie and screw Les. If you weren't around when *Arthur* came out, let me tell you, it was one hot movie. At least that's what my own informal poll showed. These days whenever it comes on the tube, I can't change the channel fast enough and Mr. Happy goes underground into deep cover.

Along about eleven-thirty, Pam left. I hit the sheets, totally exhausted. Just as I was dropping off, the doorbell rang. Oh. I almost forgot. When Pam and I were sitting in the theater, she turned to me and said, "You've seen this, haven't you?" I guess I wasn't hiding my moans too well. I admitted I had and she got pissed. "Why didn't you just tell me?" she said. "We could have seen something else."

"Nah," I said. "I've just about got it memorized. If they ever make this into a play, I'll know all the lines for all the parts and I'll nail the audition."

I got up and went to the door.

It was Cat.

No knife this time. Just a smile. And those great boobs, half hanging out of her blouse.

"I need to talk to you, Les," she said. "It's important."

I figured she just wanted to get laid. For some reason, her past efforts to decapitate me didn't even register. I was too tired, probably.

"Cat," I said. "We're over, sugar. Go home. By the way, if

you say you want to see *Arthur*, I'm taking a bottle of pills. *Two* bottles."

"I just want to talk," she said. She made it plain she wasn't leaving.

"Cat," I said, trying to keep my "sleep" edge. "I don't wanna argue. I'm just about asleep and if I don't go back and lie down right now, I'll be up all night. I've had a hard day. Too many movies."

"That's okay," she said, pushing in. "Just let me come in and we can talk in the morning."

Fuck it, I thought, closing the door behind her.

"Do what you want, Cat," I said, shuffling back to bed. "I mean it, though. We're not going to screw. I'm going to sleep."

I lay down on my side and closed my eyes. Cat shucked her clothes and crawled in beside me. Although she was naked, she didn't try to put a move on. I guess she believed me.

I was just about asleep again when the doorbell rang once more.

"Fuck," I muttered, getting up and going to see who it was. "They move the bus station here?" I muttered, talking to myself.

Outside, on the walkway, stood Rachelle, a girl I'd dated a few times.

"Hi, Rachelle," I said. "Look, I've got company."

"Oh," she said. "That's okay. I just wanted to talk to you, but it'll wait. I'll come over tomorrow."

We both said goodbye and she turned and began walking down the walk.

I went back in and Cat was up.

"Who was that!" she demanded, her voice angry.

"Just a friend," I said. "She's gone."

Cat ran to the door and stuck her head out. She slammed the door and came back to me and said, "You're screwin' that bitch, aren't you!"

I was thunderstruck. "No, I'm not (I was)," I said, getting more than a little pissed at her presumptiveness. "But if I was, it's none of your business. You and I are ancient history."

She stormed around, putting her clothes on, cussing up a blue storm. Once dressed, she stood at the door, her hand on the knob and screamed, "I never want to see you again."

"That's the whole idea," I said, worn out with the whole thing—her violent mood changes and unreasonableness. "Seeyalaterbye," I said, my standard one run-on word goodbye.

She slammed the door shut behind her and I went back to lie down. I'd just shut my eyes, trying to regain that sleep "edge," when I heard voices outside. I stumbled to the door and opened it and over the railing saw Rachelle, sitting in one of the lawn chairs by the pool...and Cat, standing in front of her, screaming at Rachelle, who didn't have a clue who this person was or what she was yelling about.

I took quick action. I'd just about had enough of Cat.

"Cat!" I yelled down. Both women looked up.

"Cat, if you don't get your ass out of here in three seconds, I'm calling the cops!"

Both stood up and started to walk toward the parking lots. As I said, there was a lot on each side of the complex and each headed for the side they normally parked in. I watched to make sure they were heading to different sides and then went back inside. For a second, I was tempted to call after Rachelle and explain what was happening, why this strange girl was getting in her shit, but I figured that Rachelle had a good head on her shoulders and would be cool about this and that I'd explain everything to her the next day. It occurred to me that if I had told Rachelle to come up, Cat would've gotten the wrong idea and a major fight would have broken out.

I went back inside the apartment and lay down for a second and then thought that maybe I ought to check to be sure Cat had really left. I just didn't trust her. I threw on a pair of skivvies and went to the door.

Sure enough, Rachelle was just disappearing around the corner of the breezeway to where her car was parked...and Cat was right on her tail, yapping something to her. I ran down the walkway to where there was an opening you could look out on the lot and by the time I got there, I saw Cat waving her arms and Rachelle just standing there, stupefied.

Rachelle was so tiny I knew she wasn't any match for Cat. If Rachelle topped the scales at ninety pounds I'd be surprised. I ran back to the stairs, took them two at a time and flew around the corner of the building to the lot. Just as I came around the corner, I saw Cat raise her arm and smack Rachelle, who ducked, catching the blow on her back.

I ran as fast as I could, arriving there just as Cat was raising her arm to strike again and that was when I saw she had the switchblade in her hand. She'd already stabbed her once but neither Rachelle nor I realized that at this point. As Cat was coming down with the knife, I grabbed her wrist with one hand and Rachelle with the other and shoved them apart as hard as I could. Cat went down on her hands and knees, then snarled and lunged at me, trying to catch me in my stomach with the knife. I ducked and at the same time grabbed her hand as it was coming across and smashed it as hard as I could on my knee, which made her lose control and the knife clattered to the pavement. My first thought was to find the knife before she did, that without it she couldn't do much damage. It was pitch-black so it took a few seconds before I felt it with my foot.

When Cat saw I had the knife in my hand, she snarled and took off running for the other parking lot, cutting back through the pool area. I stood there with the knife in my hand until I heard her car start and squeal out of the lot. I tried to fold it, but the blade was bent in two places and wouldn't close.

I walked over to Rachelle who was standing up against her car. She looked all right, but I wanted to be sure.

"You okay?" I said.

"I think so," she said. Just then, I noticed tiny speckles of bright crimson all over her white silk blouse. It looked like sprinkles of Tabasco sauce.

"Oh, man," I said. "She hit you in the nose. You've got a nose bleed."

I'm standing there, the knife in my hand, I've just seen Cat hit her with it the instant before I could get there, Cat had tried to disembowel me...and it still didn't dawn on me that she'd stabbed Rachelle. It hadn't dawned on Rachelle either. It just all happened too fast and I'd guess we were both in shock.

"No," she said. "She didn't hit me in the nose. I ducked and she hit me in the back."

"Turn around," I said.

The entire back of her blouse was solid red and a crimson stain was spreading down her white pants.

"Jesus," I said. "You've been stabbed."

"I have?" Rachelle said.

"Yeah. Can you walk?"

She could. We walked over to the pool area which was better lit. I slipped down her blouse a little to see the puncture. Blood had quit running except for little dribbles that came out when she moved, kind of bubbly stuff.

"You need to go to the hospital," I said.

"No," she said. "I'll be all right. I'll just go home and have my mom look at it. I don't think it's that bad."

Just then, a guy came through the breezeway from the opposite parking lot. I called out to him.

"Hey! I've got a girl here who's been stabbed. You know if there's a doctor in the complex?" That was a stupid question. I lived in Drug Central, home of drug dealers and prostitutes and house creepers. And me.

He came over.

"Man!" he said, when he saw all the blood. "I think the lady that lives there is a nurse," he said. He pointed to a ground-floor apartment on the other side of the pool from where we stood. I left Rachelle and ran over and knocked and knocked but no one came to the door. I went back to Rachelle, and she said, "I'm starting to feel a little dizzy. Let's go up to your room where the light's good so you can take a better look at it."

I held her elbow and we walked up the stairs and down the walk to my apartment and once inside I removed her blouse. Not much blood was coming out by now. It was just bubbling a little when her muscles flexed, but her entire back was covered with sticky-tacky, drying blood.

"Stay here," I ordered and ran down to the corner apartment where I knew an electrician lived. I banged on his door and he opened it, all sleepy-eyed. I told him what had happened and asked if he had any tape I could use to bandage her up. He went back inside and came out with a roll of black electrician's tape and both of us went back to my apartment. Rachelle was still standing where I'd left her. I went in the bathroom, got a towel and placed it on her back and the electrician and I wrapped tape around to hold it in place. It started bleeding again and we could see the blood start to seep through the towel which was folded in half.

"You got to go to the hospital," I said. "I don't think it's that bad, but let's not take any chances." My thinking was that the knife had hit the shoulder bone, bending the blade. "I don't think it went any deeper than an inch or two," I told her and she nodded. "That's what bent the blade." It all made sense then and it was only the next morning that we found out how wrong I'd been.

"Okay," she said, at last agreeing to go to the hospital. "Only I'm going in my car. I don't want my car left here. God knows what that bitch would do to it." Meaning Cat. It didn't dawn on me that Cat wouldn't have a clue what Rachelle's car looked like, having never met her before now. I found out later Rachelle didn't want to leave her car because she had six jumbo-sized garbage bags stuffed full of marijuana she'd just brought back from Houston and she was afraid that the cops would find it if she left it there in our lot.

So we walked down the stairs to the lot, got in her car, and I drove Rachelle to East Jefferson Hospital, about two miles away. During the whole drive there, she was alert, even making jokes about how she'd better not miss any work because of this shit or she was going to send Cat a bill for her missed pay. As for myself, I knew I should be thinking about her and her knife wound, but all I could think about was that I was dead tired and was going to be exhausted at work.

When I wheeled up to the emergency entrance, a rent-a-cop came out and I jumped out and explained what had happened. He ran back in and got a nurse and she came running out with a wheelchair for Rachelle. She waved goodbye as they took her in and that was the last I saw of her until two days later.

I went inside and told the rent-a-cop the story of what happened and gave him the knife which I'd brought along. About twenty minutes later, a real cop showed up and I repeated the story and the rent-a-cop gave him the knife. I told him some of the places where he might be able to find Cat. I figured she'd probably headed over to the Godfather.

"How bad was the girl hurt?" the cop said.

"I don't know for sure," I said. "I don't think too bad. I think the knife hit the shoulder bone and that's why the knife's bent. But, you need to check with the doctor."

Even after all that, all the blood and everything that had happened, I still had it in my mind that Rachelle wasn't hurt that bad. I'd seen lots of people cut before, with razors and knives, but in most of those cases they'd been sliced, not stabbed. I knew a body could bleed a whole hell of a lot, even from a small wound. All I'd seen when I looked at her wound was the entry mark, a straight line the width of the knife, about an inch and a half wide. I had no way of knowing how deeply it had entered her, honestly feeling it had done no more than put a shallow hole in her, maybe chipped a bone.

The cop left, not bothering to check with the doctor as I'd suggested, which later on led to even more trouble, taking it on faith that I'd described the extent of Rachelle's injury accurately. It was much worse than I could have ever imagined.

It must have been an off-night for violence in our part of New Orleans that night, since I didn't see anyone else from the time we arrived, until the next morning when I finally left the hospital waiting room.

Except two others.

Rachelle's mom and a gentleman friend of her mom's.

About forty-five minutes after I'd brought Rachelle in, a man and woman entered the emergency room, talked to the nurse at the desk for a few minutes and then came into the waiting room where I was. The woman walked right up to me and said, "If she dies, you die."

Well...hello! I assumed—correctly—that this was Rachelle's mom.

"Mrs. Raglun," I stammered. "I didn't stab your daughter. This other girl did. I saved her, most likely. I was the one brought her in."

Mrs. Raglun had the coldest eyes I think I ever looked at. She didn't raise her voice, just talked in this low, even tone that let me know she wasn't kidding around.

"I know what happened. They told me. It's your fault, mister. If it wasn't for you, my little girl wouldn't have been stabbed. You better hope she pulls through because if she doesn't, you're dead, and this guy will be the one to do it." She nodded her head at her companion. Years later, when the TV show *Miami Vice* came on, the first time I saw it I almost had a heart attack. The guy who played Sonny Crockett's lieutenant was a dead ringer for the man with Rachelle's mom. I never did get his name. He didn't say a word the whole time we sat in the waiting room, which was roughly between the hours of 2:00 a.m. and 7:30 a.m. in the morning.

Nobody said anything after that initial exchange. We each picked out a corner of the room and I pretended to read magazines. I had no doubt that I would be killed if Rachelle died. No doubt at all. In fact, a couple of times I visited the bathroom, which was just out of sight of the waiting room, and each time

I remember thinking, should I just go ahead and cut out, head for Mexico or Canada? I was thoroughly convinced what would happen if Rachelle didn't pull through. Luckily, I still didn't know the seriousness of her wound. If I had, I think I'd still be running.

Later on, it turned out that the man with Rachelle was connected with the mob, had performed wet work for them, and would have done exactly what Mrs. Raglun promised me he'd do. I never did know his name, but I'd see him from time to time across the street from the Snobs salon I worked at in Fat City in the ensuing months. At a nightclub called, appropriately, "The Godfather." Owned by the real godfather...

Along about six thirty in the morning, a young guy came out, introduced himself as the doctor in charge of Rachelle's case, and told us what had happened.

I was as wrong as you could be on her injury. The knife had struck a bone, it seemed, but it didn't slow it down much. It was bent because of the force with which it had struck the bone, but all that had done was deflect it in a slightly different direction. The knife had gone clear up to the hilt in her.

"From here to here," the doctor said, using his hand for demonstration, pointing from his wrist to the tip of his middle finger. About seven inches.

Both Rachelle's mom and I had asked the nurse at the desk several times while waiting for news on Rachelle but she had told us each time that she didn't know, that the doctor would be out eventually and tell us.

"I'd have let you know something before this," the doctor continued, "but we didn't know ourselves. She died on us twice and we had to bring her back. She's had six units of whole blood. The problem was, if the knife had pricked her lung even slightly, we couldn't have saved her. Her lungs would have filled with blood and she would have drowned. It wasn't until just a few minutes ago that the blood finally clotted up and moved away enough that we could get a clear picture. It missed the lung but by only this much." He held his fingers up to show the distance and you couldn't have put a sheet of paper in between them.

"She's going to be all right, I think," he said. "She'll be plenty sore, but I feel confident she's going to make it."

He left soon after that.

I was getting ready to walk out and catch a cab back to the apartment, when Mrs. Raglun came up to me. I'd given her the keys to Rachelle's car when we first met. She put her finger on my chest. "You're still not off the hook, mister," she said. "My daughter's still not out of the woods. I promise you, if she dies, you die."

With those encouraging words, I left. I went home, showered, shaved and went to work where I was a zombie, sleepwalking through my clients. At noon, Anthony called me over and told me to pack it in for the day. I didn't argue. I went back to my apartment and fell into bed, fully-dressed, and didn't wake up until the following morning. I walked down to Morning Call and had a couple of cups of cafe au lait and a beignet, picked up the *Times Picayune*, walked back home where I got undressed and got back into bed and slept until around three in the afternoon, then got up and finished reading the newspaper.

One odd note that I didn't think about until later, was when I went into Morning Call, Carlos Marcellos was sitting at his usual table. I nodded at him and it wasn't until later that it dawned on me how curious it was that I'd just saved a girl who, as it turned out, worked for one of his business partners, a guy named Ray—Rachelle and her mother—from one of his former playmates—Cat—and the whole weirdness of those connections was just that...weird.

Nothing in the paper about Rachelle. Or Cat. A big article about some flower show in Lafrenure Park

* * *

Rachelle didn't die and her mother and I actually became friends. Of a sort. I'd always watch my back around her.

"Les," she tried to explain, a few weeks later. "You've got to understand. Rachelle is my only child. It wasn't anything personal. Hell, I didn't even know you! I would have done the same no matter who it had been." That made me feel lots better, I can tell you.

Rachelle and I had been casual friends before that, fucking each other a time or two, but after that incident, we hooked up pretty hot and heavy for a short time. Three days after she was released from the hospital, we made love and that was weird. She was still in pain and I was worried she'd start bleeding again, so our roll in the hay was kind of tentative, at least on my part.

I hadn't known much about Rachelle before the knifing. Afterward, I got to know all kinds of interesting things.

The reason why she hadn't wanted to leave her car at my apartment, for instance.

Turns out, that when Rachelle was about thirteen or fourteen, she began working for Ray, her mother's boss. One of his many enterprises was an escort service for older, wealthy women. I met him a few weeks later, and he hired me to work as one of his escorts. Those were interesting times...

He had another business, which Mrs. Raglun was involved in. Ray had a cottage industry manufacturing fishing leaders and hooks and other similar angling paraphernalia. He hired mostly women, to put them together at a piece rate, in their homes. This was actually a big business, as he sold his products to national retailers like Kmart and Sears. To "grease" these deals, he gave large quantities of cocaine and marijuana to the national buyers, and for this favor he ended up with his products coast-to-coast. He also had a fairly large regular drug business. Ray was a man of many interests and talents.

Rachelle came into the picture with the drug business. Ray was a smart cookie. His modus operandi was to sweet-talk underage girls into picking up the drugs in Houston for him. They were all intensely loyal to him—read: in love—and the way it worked was that if any of the girls got busted transporting drugs back to New Orleans, they kept Ray out of the picture. Being underage, the most they would get would be probation. Once a girl was busted, Ray wouldn't use her any more. At least for the drug runs. He also dabbled in prostitution, both the male and female variety. Quite the entrepreneur, Ray was.

Usually, once a girl reached eighteen, Ray "retired" her from the drug transportation business. Rachelle was twenty-one, but still made runs for him. One, she hadn't ever been busted and figured probation was still the most they'd do to her if caught, and two, she had this intense loyalty to Ray and wanted to help the old boy out. Plus, he paid well.

She told me the reason she had stopped by to see me was that even though we'd only gone out a couple of times, she'd always felt that she could talk to me and when she'd returned from Houston that evening, her mother had told her that her grandmother had unexpectedly died. Rachelle was very close to her grandmother, closer to her even than to her mother. She'd come over to my place, she said, to talk. That was it. She just wanted to talk to someone who she felt had a sympathetic ear... and that happened to be lucky me. She'd planned to chat and then go home. When she'd left my door, she said she just went to sit by the pool and collect her thoughts. That was when Cat came down and started screaming in her face. The rest, as we say, is history.

I remember the first time I visited Rachelle in her hospital room and explained who Cat was and why she was trying to render her room temperature. "She's nuts!" she said. "Yeah," I agreed, and added, "I guess she doesn't like me anymore."

I made a run once with Rachelle to the drug warehouse in Houston and it was right out of the movies. It was a huge Quonset hut and marijuana was in bales. They had it all stacked on pallets. There was so much, they used forklifts to move it around. Rachelle would bag several bales from raw stock for Ray and her "pay" was what she could gather up from spillage on the floor. That was usually enough to fill at least one large garbage bag and sometimes two. She sold her share back in New Orleans at half the going rate for a lid. If I remember, right, a lid went for a hundred back then and she only charged fifty. For making that trip with her, she split her "sweepings" and I ended up with half a garbage bag full. I charged full boat when I sold my share.

We all became thick as thieves, Rachelle, Mrs. Raglun and myself, and soon I was introduced to Ray. It wasn't long before I was recruited into his escort service.

As escorts, our job was simple. Wealthy, older women would call Ray's service and he'd call one of his "workers" and we'd show up and take them places. Restaurants, usually. The best restaurants in town. Commander's Palace, Arnaud's, Gallatoire's, places like that. Afterward, we were expected to take them home or to their hotel or wherever and have sex with them. Each "job" paid us two hundred, which we split with Ray. Plus we got a great meal and most of the women tipped in addition. Sometimes, we made more on tips than on our fee. Sometimes, a woman would want more than just a one-night stand. One woman—the heir to the Ponchartrain Hotel fortune, a gal in her nineties—took me with her and her girlfriend (of similar age and I forget who she was or her name) to Puerta Vaherta. She rented the same villa Richard Burton and Liz Taylor used to own. It was an interesting trip. Before we left for Mexico, she decided my wardrobe wasn't good enough for Puerta Vaherta, so she took me down to Maisson Blanche and spent over a thousand bucks on some new threads for me.

It was hard work. Most of these women were in their sixties and seventies, minimum, and some were lots older. Their bodies might have been gone, but not their imaginations. This was definitely a young man's game. Some, you could get it up for, especially with the help of a little coke, but usually you'd just perform oral sex. Sometimes they enjoyed vibrators or other mechanical toys. Many were outright kinky. Golden showers, whipping, bondage, you name it, these ladies went for it. One "client" would cram this string with beads on it up her ass and a bowl of ice water beside the bed. Then, you spread-eagled and handcuffed her to her big four-poster bed. You'd go down on her and start pulling the string of beads out while you ate her, working her toward climax. When she got off, you had to reach over and dump the ice water on her at the exact moment she got her nut. More like work than sex. At least it paid well.

They did end up arresting Cat, but the cop who'd taken my statement at the hospital that night didn't check with the doctor as I'd suggested, just put down that Rachelle wasn't hurt that bad. When they found and arrested her the next morning, they charged her with simple assault.

I found this out as soon as I reached home after leaving the hospital. I called the hospital from the pay phone at the complex and they wouldn't let me talk to Rachelle, so I looked up her mother's number in the book and called her, and she told me what she knew, which was that Cat had been arrested but not for attempted murder or anything like that. She was pissed. Immediately, I began calling the jail to find out what had happened. They told me she had been arrested but said they couldn't give me any more information.

I called back three more times, hoping to get someone who would be more helpful, but got stonewalled each time. Finally, talking to a female cop, I lost it. I started screaming over the phone, "This is nuts! This motherfucking bitch almost killed this girl and tried to kill me. And you can't tell me anything? What kind of fucked-up police department do you have there?" The lady cop must have felt sorry for me because right away she started apologizing, saying it was against department rules to provide such information, but that she would. She said Cat had been picked up early that morning and was being held for a measly thousand- dollar bond. A hundred bucks would spring her. They'd charged her with what basically amounted to a misdemeanor because the cop had been too lazy to check with the doctor to find out the real extent of Rachelle's injuries. The lady copy didn't tell me that, but I pieced that together from what she did tell me. The cop told me that Cat's bond hearing was in about an hour. I knew from that she'd be walking free.

I called the district attorney's office and got some guy there and ran down the whole scene to him. "I'm sorry," he said, "but there's nothing we can do about it now. When she comes up for trial, we'll raise the charges to what they should be." I blew up again and he hung up.

That's exactly what happened. She called a client of hers, I found out later—an oil company executive—and he came down and bailed her out. Nothing I could do about it.

About a week after the stabbing, Rachelle called me and her voice was trembling. Cat had her brother call Rachelle and threaten her if she testified against her. Her brother had already done time for one murder and was pretty well known around town as an insane motherfucker who would kill you for a beer. Big, crazy coonass, who spent most of his time in a drug and liquor haze. When he wasn't maiming somebody.

Rachelle wanted to know what to do.

"*I'm* testifying," I said, "but I can't tell you what to do, honey. Do you really want this bitch to walk after what she did to you, though?"

She decided to go ahead and testify. That day. The next day she called again, saying she'd been threatened again.

This went on for days on end. First, she'd testify, then, there was no way.

Then, Cat called me. At work.

"I drive by every day," she said. "I see you at the window and you know I have a gun. One of these days I'm going to shoot you as I drive by." That gave me a warm and fuzzy feeling.

She called again.

"The reason I came over that night," she said, "was that I

was pregnant with your baby. I wanted to talk about it, see what you wanted to do. Guess what, asshole? I had it killed!" Meaning, she had an abortion.

Along about the same time, one of the girls I was screwing was a tall redhead named Pam. Pam was in love. Or so she said. She wanted to us to get married or at least live together. I wasn't at all ready to give up my freedom. We continued to see each other, but she became more and more miserable when she saw the parade of girls that I was screwing. Along about this time, I nearly got killed by some offshore oil riggers who lived in my complex and I ended up attacking my partner Tony and it was Pam who kept me from slicing him up in an incident that took place a week or so after the thing with Rachelle. I'll talk more about that in a bit.

Finally, Pam said she couldn't live in the same town as I did, not with all the girls I went out with. She was moving to California, get a job as a dog groomer, which was her trade.

My life was getting complex. Cat and her bad-ass brother were calling both me and Rachelle daily, threatening us with extinction if we testified against her. It didn't look like it was going to do much good, even if we did. The district attorney still hadn't changed the charges from simple assault to what they should have been—attempted murder—and it didn't look likely that he would.

I discovered from a coworker of Cat's—one of the waitresses at Lil Cajun Cuisine—that she was regularly going to Houston on the weekends with the guy who had bailed her out. I knew the guy—a nerdy little engineer who worked downtown in the CBD in the oil business. Cat used to make fun of him all the time after her "dates" with him, but I guess she liked him well enough to let him post bond for her and take her on little jaunts to Houston. Folks out on bond aren't supposed to leave the parish, much less the state, without permission. When I called the D.A. to tell him what she was doing, it seemed that he couldn't care less.

"Well," he said, "we have to actually catch her doing that before we can do anything."

Pam had moved to Huntington Beach, California and got a job as a dog groomer, working for Jack Kelly's wife, who owned a pet store in the Huntington Mall. Jack Kelly was an old-time actor who had played the part of Bart in the old *Maverick* TV series but was now the mayor of Huntington Beach. His wife had let Pam move in with them until she saved enough money to get her own place.

Nightly, Pam would call me, telling me how much she loved me and couldn't live without me. Ego-tripping stuff like that. It started out with short, five-minute calls and quickly evolved into hour-long talk-a-thons. I'd finally gotten my own phone and made the mistake of giving the number to her. There were times she called that I'd bed in bed with another girl and would just keep screwing and trying to keep me and the girl with me from laughing as I talked to Pam. She kept begging me to come out. I wouldn't even have to work, she said. She'd support us. She said some crazy things. Like, if I lived with her, I could even screw other girls, just as long as I came home to her at night.

Things were heating up in New Orleans with Cat and her brother, the threats becoming more vicious as the summer months rolled on and fall approached. Rachelle had made a final decision not to testify and she was adamant about it. She was scared shitless, just wanted to get on with her life and forget the whole thing. I couldn't really blame her for backing out. She'd been through a lot already, having almost lost her life. I wondered why her mom didn't sic the same guy on Cat she had on me, but Rachel didn't know why. I guess because Cat wasn't really after Rachel; just me. We weren't seeing each other much anymore and I had quit working for Ray. I began to realize that the only reason Rachel and I had hooked up on a regular basis was our shared experience with Cat and once the excitement over reliving that episode began to die down, so did our relationship.

It looked fairly certain that Cat was going to walk on the charges, and as nuts as I knew she was, I figured it was only a matter of time before she carried through on her promise to shoot me.

Snobs Salon was probably the toniest salon I worked in during my thirty-five years in the hairstyling game. We charged fifty dollars for a haircut, which wasn't the most I got—at Busta's at the Fairmont and at Albert Brown, The Salon my haircut price was a hundred (remember, this was the early eighties)—but for pure toniness, Snobs was it. The owner, Anthony Jones, was an Englishman, who'd borrowed the name Snobs from a classy clothing joint in London. Clients loved telling their friends they got their hair done at a place called Snobs.

My first day on the job set the tone for the rest of the time I was there. My first client, sales manager at New Orleans most popular rock station, handed me a fifty-dollar bill for her haircut and then tipped me with a rolled-up ten-dollar bill.

I didn't realize why she'd rolled up the bill until I unraveled it and about a quarter gram of coke fell out onto the floor by the front desk. Anthony was standing behind the desk when the white powder began falling onto the carpet.

"Are you an idiot, Les!" he screamed. Turns out, that's the way patrons tipped. Rolled up coke in a bill. In seconds, we were all down on the floor with straws.

After that, I was careful with my tips.

Snobs had a great decor. Forty-foot ceiling, the interior stark with light gray walls and an enormous Roy Lichtenstein painting. Anthony had three of the biggest corn plants I'd ever seen, by each of the three stations which were out in the middle of the main room. These suckers were more than twice my height. There were two small rooms off the main room, one we used for manicures and the other for massages. The bathroom was painted in black with makeup lights around the mirror and handcuffs on the walls. We were on the second floor of an office building, with the obligatory New Orleans balcony, where, sometimes in the summer, we'd take clients out and cut their hair in the sunshine.

I started a new service, cutting women's bushes into various designs like hearts. Got a lot of lays that way.

Anthony was about the coolest guy I ever worked for. The 1984 World's Fair was in town while I worked for him, and we all wanted to go, but tickets were pricey. I don't remember how much season tickets were, but I seem to recall they were at least a couple of hundred bucks. Anthony solved the problem for us. He had a printer friend print up counterfeit passes for us. Later, I learned that it was the only World's Fair to go bankrupt during its run, and I guess we contributed to that situation.

The first day we went, it was Anthony and myself and two of our stylists, Joyce and Nadja from his Tchoupitoulas Street Salon. Joyce had been there the week before—on a legitimate day pass—and led us around to the back to the service entrance where the high school and college bands and bartenders and other workers came in at. We were just going through the gate when a black guy in a rent-a-cop uni came hustling out of a little guard shack they had there, clipboard in hand, and yelled at us to stop. *Shit*, I thought. We're busted and are all going to jail. We whipped out our counterfeit passes but the guy barely looked at them. "You can't come in here," he said. "This is for workers only."

Then, Joyce blew us all away. She reached into her purse and whipped out some kind of badge, which she flashed at the guy. Later, I found out her father was a retired cop and she belonged to the Police Auxiliary and that's what the badge was for. "Narcotics," she said, and I remember my stomach caving in. The rent-a-cop stopped, obviously confused. "Names?" he said, and Joyce said, pointing to each of us in turn, "I'm Dorothy Sayers and this is Sam Spade (me), Phillip Marlowe (Anthony), and Charlie Chan (Nadja)." I've told this story many times, and people think I'm making it up, but I'm not. The guy never caught on as to the names, which was unbelievable. But, he began checking some kind of list he had. Turns out our "names" weren't on there. I guess he should have looked in *Books in Print*. "You're not on here," he said, and Joyce cursed, then said, "The lieutenant was supposed to call."

The guy stood there a minute, as if deciding something, and then told us, "Well, I'm not supposed to let you in if your names aren't on the list, but I will this time. Be sure and have your lieutenant call down next time." Joyce assured him we would, thanked him, and we entered the gates.

As soon as we were out of sight, we collapsed on the ground in a combination of eye-watering laughter and relief and then set out on what Anthony called "a pub crawl" where we tried to visit as many different country's bars as possible. I wrote a short story using this for a setting years later. After that, we returned many times, using our counterfeit tickets and never once were stopped or questioned. We always went in at one of the main entrances after that, though. Never again the service entrance!

The best bar by far was at the Australian exhibit. When we left there, we were on a true "crawl."

Around this time Snobs was hired by Liz Claiborne to do the hair of the models in her spring release show in New Orleans. We were one of the most prominent salons in town. I'd been asked to do the covers of the two fashion magazines—*Touts* and *Gambit*—and we did a number of local and national celebrities' hair.

It turned out to be a horrible experience. From the minute we began working, Ms. Claiborne was literally screaming at us, using the foulest language I'd heard outside of the joint. Actually, even in the joint no one went off like she did. After the second or third time she'd screamed at me, I went to Anthony and told him I was going to quit. "You can't," he said. "You quit and you'll never get a gig like this again." Like that was some kind of threat.

The next time she began to cuss at me, I looked at her and told her to get the fuck out of my face before she got hurt. That slowed her down for about two seconds and then she started up again. "Fuck you, you cunt," I said and walked off the set.

Later, Anthony told me that the instant the show was over, she completely trans-formed. He said she had what he called her "bum boy"—kind of a butler or a gopher—break out these solid silver serving trays, dump mounds of coke on them, and pass them around. He said she turned into this pussy cat and the models told him she was like this every time—a raging lunatic during the show and then a sweetheart afterward. I told Anthony that was fine, but I would never let anyone talk to me like that.

A couple of months later, she was on the Oprah Winfrey show and underwent a melt-down and lost her marbles and entered therapy.

When I married my wife Mary, the only thing I ever insisted on was that she was to never to bring anything by Liz Claiborne into our house or it was going in the trash. Bless her heart, she never has.

New Orleans is a different kind of town. For one thing, almost all business is conducted via the conduit of alcohol. At Snobs and virtually every other salon I worked at, we not only served wine to our clients, but were expected to drink along with them, to be sociable.

Not a problem there.

Like just about everybody I knew at the time, I was heavily into coke. I'd done drugs ever since the Navy, where I'd smoked my first joint, and there was a period before I was busted where I was running heroin, along with anything else I could get my hands on.

Coke was the best, though. Most people don't remember

this, but at that time—late seventies, early eighties—magazines and newspapers came out weekly with articles "proving" that cocaine wasn't addictive. Physicians stated categorically that one might "become addicted psychologically," but that there was nothing in cocaine's properties that would "physically addict" you. That's why it made such inroads so quickly into a heretofore non-drug segment of American society—professional people. Folks like lawyers and doctors and executives. Housewives and salesmen. Everybody. The media had proclaimed it a "safe" drug. I swear I'm not making this up. Look back at the journalism of the time.

It was such a socially-accepted drug that you could go virtually nowhere in public without seeing someone snorting out in the open. We'd go into New Orleans' best restaurants and people would be laying lines out on the table as they awaited their Oysters Bienville. You couldn't get near a sink in any public bathroom without having to wait in line behind the tooters. Men and women both carried pocket mirrors and razor blades. Men's purses became a hot fashion item and the main purpose was to carry paraphernalia.

Tony, a guy who lived downstairs from my apartment, came up with some wicked, table-grade toot and invited me to be his partner in dealing it. Working at Snobs gave me access to some of the richest people in New Orleans. He provided the "product" and I sold it. After we stepped on it a couple of times, of course. I was selling at least ten grams a day, at a cost to us of about a third of what we sold it for. Tony was selling about half that amount, but we split everything down the middle. We couldn't buy it fast enough with all the buyers we had. By cutting it, with Italian baby laxative or powdered Vitamin E, we were making money hand over fist. We'd cut out two or three grams apiece of the good stuff for our own use before we doctored it. Not a day went by when I wasn't snorting at least two grams and on some days as much as five.

Once in a while, I'd run it, but putting it in my arm scared me. It was *too* good that way.

Things were going so good that something had to go wrong. And it did.

One Sunday, Tony came barging into my apartment, all fired up. The guy supplying him had just sold him product that was almost pharmaceutical quality. We were going to make a killing on this stuff.

We went down to Snobs and began cutting it. Cutting it and doing it. We got so high and used up so much that I got worried that our customers would know right away it was weak shit. We must have stepped on it at least fifteen or sixteen times. What had started out as primo coke was pretty much all baby laxative and Vitamin E by now.

"We might as well throw this crap away," I said, when I realized what we'd done. The last hit had done nothing but burn the shit out of my nose. I could've gotten a better high snorting aspirin.

"Naw," Tony said. "Throw away money? No way. Here's what we'll do."

Tony's genius idea was to sell this batch to some guys who lived in our apartment complex. Six Mexicans, who worked on a Shell off-shore oil rig had gone together and rented an apartment in one of their names for a party crib when they came to shore. Two of the guys used it for their regular apartment when they weren't out in the Gulf, and the other four were married and just used it to party down in.

"We'll get rid of all this stuff to those bozos," he said. "Wait until they been partying awhile and then sell it to them. They'll be so high they won't know the difference."

A bad, bad idea, I thought, and said so, but Tony wouldn't listen to reason and just dump the stuff.

Sure enough, it was just like he predicted. All the guys were in town and partying. Tony and I sat down by the pool, drinking beers and waiting until they were good and high. That wasn't hard to determine. The complex we lived in was populated mostly by hustlers and prostitutes and other fun types. There were parties going on continually, day and night. Most of the residents kept their doors open and at any given time there might be four or five parties going on. Stereos blasting, people laughing and yelling and having a good time. These guys had one of the corner apartments on the second floor, just catty-corner from mine.

When night came, Tony decided it was time.

We went on up with our stash and sure enough; they were definitely in the market for some coke. We'd sold to them before, lots of times, so they didn't even question the quality. We made the sale, a grand for twelve grams, already in individual packets. Tony left about five minutes later. He'd collected the money and stuck it in his pocket. I didn't ask for my share then, figuring we'd divvy up later. I should have left when he did, but I was half in the bag myself, from drinking and tooting all day and I decided to stay and party with the Mexicans. A bunch of women kept coming and going and I had my eye on a cute little redhead who started flirting with me.

Things were rolling along smoothly and I was lying on one of the beds with this chick, both of us groping each other, when Mamie, a fat prostitute from downstairs, came up and joined the party. Mamie had to go at least 250 pounds and I never understood how she got customers. She was a nasty bitch. She had the apartment directly across from my top one, only at the lower level, and some days you could actually smell her clear upstairs when she lay out by the pool. I mean, she was nasty! She never lacked for johns, though. Every day there'd be four or five guys knocking on her door and leaving half an hour or an hour later. Sometimes, she'd leave her door open and you'd hear her in there, pretend-screaming in the throes of passion. Some of these guys were good-looking too; you wondered why they'd go to somebody like her. It's not like pussy was hard to get! In New Orleans? Right.

Anyway, Mamie trotted her fat ass up and joined the party.

Besides being fat and ugly and just generally nasty, she had a big mouth. This screeching voice you could hear a block away. Not to mention, she was a tight ass. That's what fucked me up.

She decided she wanted some coke too, but she wasn't going to fork over a hundred of her hard-earned bucks for a gram. She wheedled and whined until one of the guys sold her ten bucks worth. Ten bucks worth of coke won't get anyone high—snorting, that is—but ten bucks of coke could get you off pretty nicely if you ran it. And that's what she planned to do.

She whipped out her rig and started to mix in her spoon. The problem was, it wouldn't dissolve. The stuff just kept floating around on top of the water when she tried to cook it. A sure tip-off that it wasn't coke.

Mamie was no dummy, at least not with drugs. As soon as she saw what was going on—or *not* going on—in her spoon, she started screeching and squalling that she'd been robbed, that this shit was all cut. Cheap-ass bitch! If she'd kept her mouth shut, I'da given her a gram of the good stuff. It was too late, though.

The party stopped immediately. Everybody sobered up on the spot. My six Latino friends hustled everybody out of the apartment pronto—including my new girlfriend, who looked at the "dead man" she'd just been feeling up—and closed the door.

I was in some deep do-do.

They came and gathered around me where I sat on the bed. Two sat down on either side and the biggest guy, a bad piece of business named Tony, too, pulled out a knife and started tossing it from hand to hand, like he'd seen in some kung fu movie or some such shit. If I hadn't been so scared, I would have laughed.

"Our money," he said. "Give us our money back and we won't kill you. Maybe."

That posed a slight problem. I didn't have the money. The other Tony, my friend and partner, did. I explained that to them, knowing this was not what they wanted to hear.

Somehow, I convinced them to let me go and I'd find Tony and get their money back. They convinced *me* that if I didn't get it by the next morning, I wouldn't have any more use for oxygen.

I couldn't find Tony. He didn't come back to his apartment that night, nor the next morning. In fact, he didn't show up for four days. Had himself one hell of a party on *our* money.

I didn't have the luxury of waiting the four days for him to return. In fact, I didn't know then if he was ever coming back. The next day, Monday, I went down to the bank and drew out every cent I had and got a loan from a girl I was dating for the two hundred or so I was short. I'd been making good money— no, *great* money—both at work and in dealing—but I'd spent it as fast as I could make it, so I was basically tapped out.

And rent was due.

I was dead broke. At least, I was still alive. My Mexican compadres had taken my money, sullenly, and hadn't wasted me, but there was no love lost between us after that. I studiously avoided them and their part of the complex.

Payday was a week and a half off and rent was due on Tuesday. And there was no way I was going to come up with it. I kept putting the apartment manager off when he came around, but I knew that couldn't last forever. The complex was full of deadbeats and they didn't fuck around. About a week was all you could successfully slow-walk them. After that, a cop showed up and tossed your ass in the street. Usually, they kept your belongings. That was what was facing me. Out in the street with the clothes on my back…if I was lucky. If they came and evicted me in the middle of the night, I might be lucky to have on my skivvies.

Tony finally showed up on Thursday. When I came home from work, there he was, sitting out by the pool in a lounge chair, a six-pack in a cooler beside him. He didn't have a clue what had gone down. I filled him in, ASAP.

"No problem, partner," he said. "Except that I spent all the money. I got in this craps game." This kinda got my dander up and he could see that.

It seems there was another problem. The guy who had been supplying us had gotten his butt busted, it turned out. One of the reasons Tony had been out of sight the past few days.

"He should get out on bail any minute now," he said. His scheme was to cop more product on credit with the guy—I had a hard time swallowing that, but what else could I do?—and then sell it quickly. That would allow him to pay me my share that he'd spent and I'd be all right.

"Don't worry, man," he said. "I'll have it tomorrow."

Uh-huh.

The guy didn't get bailed out. Tony didn't seem to have a Plan B.

On Friday, I came home and there he was, stretched out in a lounge chair, toking on a beer. My patience was wearing thin.

On Saturday, I could see him lying out by the pool, drinking beer. I kept getting madder and madder.

Along about four in the afternoon, I walked down. Tony hadn't moved from his spot all day except to go to the john and get more beer.

I walked over to where he was stretched out.

"You got my money, Tony?" I said. I was as calm as you could get. Acted like I was asking him the weather forecast.

He looked up at me and grinned his "aw shucks" grin.

"Ah, man, don't worry. I'm working on it."

"Sorry, Tony," I said, my voice even. I unbuckled my belt. It had this big-ass heavy belt buckle. I wrapped the belt a couple of times around my fist. "I want my money. Now. You got it?"

"Man, Les," he said, sitting up, eyeing the belt in my hand. "Tomorrow. I promise I'll have it tomorrow."

"Tony," I said. "I hate to do this."

I hauled off and whipped him right in the chops with the belt buckle. I hit him so hard he fell off the lounge chair onto the concrete by the side of the pool. I came back the other way and slashed him on the other side of his head. Quick, like a cat, he came up as I was getting ready to nail him again. I punched him with my left and he charged me like a football player and tackled me. He was sitting on me in a second, holding my arms down. Not hard for Tony. He was about half again as big as I was and no visible fat.

I wasn't too calm by this point. Even though he had me securely pinned, I was screaming at him.

"You motherfucking cocksucker! I'm gonna kill you." Which was a rather foolish thing to be screaming, seeing as how he had me pretty easily down and under control.

"Les! Les!" he said. "I don't want to hurt you, man. If I let you up, will you be cool?"

"No," I screamed. "Fuck you, Tony. You let me up and I'll fuck you up."

He must have thought I was kidding. There was no question he could whip me and he and I both knew it. I was just a bit insane, however. He sighed and got up. I scrambled up and hit him again. Again, he charged me and pinned me a second time. My head was over the edge of the pool.

"Man! You can't whip me, man," he said. "I don't want to hurt you, Les."

"Then get me my money," I screamed back. "I ain't got a mommy or daddy to bail my ass out here. I don't have the rent money, I'm on the street."

"Give me until tomorrow," he said.

"Okay," I said, finally, and he let me up, backing up just in case I wanted to start up again.

I went back up to my apartment and cleaned up the blood. My back was all bruised and scratched and bleeding from the concrete where he'd pinned me. As soon as I was cleaned up, I went down and knocked on his door. When he opened it, I said, "Tomorrow, Tony. Tomorrow, or we're going to do this all over again. We're going to do this until you get it right."

Sunday morning, I got up and went outside on the walkway

and looked down at the pool. Sure enough, Tony was sitting in a lounge chair, sucking down a beer and reading the funnies. He glanced up and saw me and just went back to reading his paper. I walked back inside my apartment, calm on the outside, seething inside. I got dressed and picked up a straight razor.

At that moment, Pam walked in. She looked at me standing there with the straight edge in my hand and she must have seen something in my eyes, 'cause her own widened like pie plates, and she said, "What's going on, Les?"

"See that guy sitting downstairs?" I said. She nodded. "I'm going to kill him." And I was. I'd blanked everything out of my mind. If I got thrown out of my apartment, I was dead anyway. I'd have to rob something to stay alive and I figured since I was going to end up in jail anyway, I might as well be there for something that would make me feel better. Like cutting Tony's fucking throat.

I pushed by her and went out. I walked around to the stairs and went down. As I came off the last step, Tony saw what I had in my hand and he got up.

"What the fuck!" he said, backing away as I advanced.

"You got my money, Tony?"

"Aw, man, no. Not yet." He kept backing and I kept walking toward him.

"Then I gotta do this, man." I ran toward him and swiped at him with the razor and he ducked and ran over behind one of the poles that held up the second floor walkway. At the same moment, Pam started screaming from upstairs and people started popping out of doorways.

I ran after Tony and caught him the tiniest bit across his back as he ran. He got behind another pole and he looked as scared as anybody I've ever seen.

All of a sudden, Pam came flying from out of nowhere, yelling, crying and screaming, all at the same time. Trying to grab at my arm. All I had on my mind was I was going to cut this motherfucker into little pieces. I was totally focused on my goal. I shoved Pam away and ran after Tony again, blood in my eyes. He sprinted for his apartment and got inside, slamming the door before I could reach him. I went over and pulled up his lounge chair and parked my ass right outside his door, reaching in his cooler and grabbing one of his beers.

Pam came over and sat down on the concrete beside me.

"What in God's name's going on?" she said.

I was slowly coming back to reality. I explained the situation.

"You can't kill the guy," she said. "You'll end up in Angola. You don't want to end up in Angola, baby," she said, crying the whole time.

Tony opened his door a crack and peeped out. I got up, razor in hand.

"No! Wait, Les! I'll have your money."

"When?" I said, standing there, imagining how it would feel when my razor bit into his neck.

"Today," he said. "Tonight. I'll get it from my brother."

"No, Tony," I said. "I'm going to go down to The Godfather and have a couple of beers. When I get back, you better have my money. Or I'm going to kill you or you kill me. Whatever."

I turned and Pam started to say something and the look in my eyes must have said something to her because she didn't utter a peep. I folded the razor and slipped it down into my sock and walked away. I walked the two blocks to The Godfather, sat at the bar and ordered a beer. I was just about done with the second, when Tony walked in and over to me. His face was white.

"Here," he said, and thrust an envelope at me and walked back the way he'd come, out the door.

I opened it up and there was my share.

I don't know how he came up with it since we never talked again after that. Both he and I moved out of the complex a couple of weeks later. With what was left after I paid the rent and my next paycheck, I was able to get a better apartment with a guy who'd just moved into the complex. Mark Toal.

That's when Pam decided she'd fallen in love and all that shit started with her moving to California and talking me into joining her.

A few weeks before I moved west, Mark Toal moved into my apartment complex and we became fast friends immediately. He had just moved down from Washington, D.C. where his father was the head of some government agency. Poor little rich boy, but I really liked him. He was kind of a flake, probably why his dad had asked him to relocate and also the reason why he and I hit it off so well.

He'd gotten a job as a waiter at Confetti's, a really cool nightclub that had just opened in Fat City. When you walked into Confetti's, they handed you a pewter mug with champagne. Hot rock was shaking the mirrors and windows and the whole atmosphere was electric. They had these little stairways here and there that led to small platforms at the top where gorgeous, scantily-clad dancers gyrated to the music, a la the old *Laugh-In* TV show. The joint was open twenty-four hours a day, seven days a week.

Confetti's really made an effort to entertain the troops. Each of the three shifts had an assistant manager whose only job was to walk around and check to see if the action was dying down. If it was, several of the waiters and waitresses would suddenly charge out and put on sophisticated dance routines to pulsing, vibrating rock music. To get a job there as a waiter, waitress or bartender, Mark told me you went through three auditions and had to be able to sing and dance. The employees were all instructed that if they saw somebody standing by themselves and not seeming to be having fun, they were to go up and get them to dance with them.

It was the hottest place in town. Every Thursday was Ladies Night. When a female entered the door, she was given a Confetti's plastic cup or a pewter mug, and all she had to do was give it to a bartender and the bartender would fill it with whatever she was drinking. All night long.

At midnight, they rolled out this humongous steam table, a chef in dress whites presiding over a lavish spread. Every hour on the hour, until eight in the morning, they changed the food. And it wasn't any Swedish meatball crap. They served Oysters Rockefeller, Oysters Bienville, rare roast beef, crawfish etouffee, crawfish bisque...all gourmet dishes. And it was all free, just for being there and buying a drink.

That was their lagniappe. Lagniappe is a New Orleans tradition and it's a French word that means "something extra." Most businesses provided a lagniappe of some form or other. For instance, if you were down in the Quarter and walked into a gift shop, they might have plates of praline candy at the counter. You just helped yourself.

Many of the bars and nightclubs had more lavish forms of lagniappe. Usually, it would consist of a free meal. Again, not some steam table Swedish meatballs. At the Oriental Triangle on Jefferson Highway, their lagniappe was bulgogi, every Friday night. A joint on Veterans Highway served homemade seven-layer lasagna on Thursdays. Bart's, out on the lakefront, brought in a chef to serve rare roast beef and all the fixings on Sunday afternoons. Bart's was one of the two clubs in New Orleans—4141 Club was the other one—that regularly made Playboy's Top Ten Nightclubs in the U.S. list. At 4141, on Wednesdays, they had all the raw oysters and hot sauce you could eat for their lagniappe.

There were dozens and dozens of places that served complete meals for their weekly lagniappe. It was all free. All you had to do was go there and buy a drink and eat as much as you wanted. And it wasn't some cheesy chips and dip kind of crap like you might get in other cities. They were always superb, gourmet meals. If you knew where to go, you could eat at a different club every day of the week for free.

Anyway, Mark was working as a waiter/entertainer at Confetti's and that became my regular hangout. I'd be there half an hour after I got off work and usually didn't crash until the wee hours of the morning.

In New Orleans, the lifestyle of the young party animal is that you get off work at say four or five, go home and sleep until about midnight and then go out and party until it's time to go to work. You'd rush home, shower, shit and shave, and go back to your job. Every day of the week. New Orleans parties every single day of the year, amazing to newcomers who are used to partying only on weekends.

And nobody goes out much before one in the morning, except for the tourists who are used to a different schedule. Around 2:00 a.m., when the tourists are packing it in, the real party animals come out and the serious fun begins.

I've never needed more than three or four hours of sleep a night, and at that time, I could go days without much sleep at all. I was doing stupendous amounts of coke and drinking virtually every hour of the day and didn't sleep much more than an hour here, couple hours there.

One time, Tulane University conducted a study to see how much drinking actually went on in New Orleans businesses. They set up a station in the CBD—Central Business District—downtown and gave everybody that came by a breathalyzer. At ten in the morning on a weekday. Eighty-three percent were over the legal driving alcohol limit. You were just expected to drink with your customers, no matter what business or trade you were in. It's the normal way of life in the Big Easy. Carrie Nation would've stroked out after ten minutes of walking around town and observing the animal life. Novelist Ellen Gilchrist said it best when she said to survive in New Orleans one needed large amounts of sugar and alcohol.

As I needed less sleep than most, I had a different routine. As soon as I got off work, I headed home, slept until about 8:00 or 9:00 p.m., got dressed and hit the bricks.

I'd head to Confetti's or some other club and start in on the tourists. Not too many locals were out at that hour, but the visitors came out early. By the time the local citizens came out to play, I'd usually have already bagged a tourist. Kind of a tune-up for the real party pros. More than once, I'd talk to some tourist chick from Buffalo or Des Moines, go out in the parking lot, get a blow job or a quick fuck, head back in and pick up another one and do the same. There were just thousands and thousands of girls, itching to get picked up and laid. It's the atmosphere, something in the air.

I kept a kind of "log" of my sexual activities then, and in a little over a three-year period went to bed with over five hundred different women. Not a single dog in the bunch, either. It's difficult to remember a day when I didn't get laid. There weren't many at all.

Mark and I decided to get an apartment together—with the shit that had gone down with Tony I was ready to be out of Drug Central—and for the three or four months we shared a crib, we had a blast. He was as whacko as I was.

The place we got an apartment was a classy complex where a lot of the Saints players lived. Kenny Stabler was playing out the string as the Saints' quarterback and he had an apartment two doors down from ours. He had a palatial home in Gulf Shores, but needed a place for after the home games and some of the practices when he didn't want to drive clear to Mississippi.

Stabler was quite the party animal. I thought I was King Cock, laying at least a different girl pretty much every day and often more than one, but Stabler beat that all to hell. Hell of a nice guy, too. A man's man. He was living the American dream for sure. When they coined the term "party animal" it was Kenny they had in mind. I understand he's settled down quite a bit these days. I'm glad. He was a terrific guy.

One Saturday night, I went down to Confetti's around 1:00 a.m. and Stabler hit the door about the same time. Every time I went into the john there he was, doing lines. We both left the club at the same time, around six a.m. Sunday morning. The pigskin maestro wasn't hung over—he was stoned and high. The Saints had a home game that day. I had to do the cheerleaders' hair with the rest of the Snobs cast, but I could hardly move, my head was throbbing so hard from the night before. Stabler was in even worse shape than I was—*had* to be—but all he did was go out and throw about four-five touchdown passes. Between series, when the defense was on the field, he'd come over to the sidelines, flop down, and they'd hit him with the oxygen. He made Bobby Layne look like a Cub Scout.

Kenny had the women. Lots and lots of women. Anyone he wanted, practically, would jump in bed with him. It caught up with him though. One of the many ladies he was squiring around town, was a former Miss Alabama and a second or third runner-up in the Miss America contest. A seriously good-looking babe. He'd been seeing her a couple of years or more and finally she laid down an ultimatum to Kenny. Marry me or I'm out of here is what she allegedly said to him. So...he married her. Who wouldn't?

At the wedding reception, I approached Kenny and jokingly asked if I could have his old little black book.

"Dude," he said, "I don't have *one* book. I've got six and they're not 'little.' And, don't you know a good quarterback always keeps a backup plan? I'm holding onto them."

A couple of months later, one of my clients was late for her haircut appointment. Shea Hill, wife of the Saints' quarterbacks coach, King Hill. When she finally arrived, breathless, she told me why she was late.

It seems that King was supposed to be home to watch the kids while she went to Snobs, but King was called to the hospital with the rest of the Saints' coaching staff and administrators. As it turned out, Stabler's new wife was in the hospital, in bad shape. The story Shea related was that Kenny had been thumping on her noggin at home and she made a break for the car, only Kenny got just behind her, shoved her over and began driving all over town, continuing to blast her with his fist. He'd ended up hitting her so hard she flew out of the car and sustained some serious injuries.

The staff had been called in to close ranks for the press, which had gotten wind of the incident. The party line they came out with was that Kenny had simply been driving too fast and she fell out accidentally when the car went around a curve. That was the story that showed up in the press. Shortly after that, the new missus Stabler was the new ex-missus quarterback bon vivant.

This all happened about the time there was a national furor that some reporter from *Sports Illustrated* was at the center of. He went to Gulf Shores to investigate the rumors of Kenny's cocaine use. Hell, hang around Confetti's, that rumor'd get confirmed PDQ. While there, the local gendarmes found a large quantity of coke in the glove compartment of the reporter's car and he was arrested. He screamed to high heaven, claiming that either Stabler or some of his simpatico compadres had set him up. I don't remember what the outcome of all that was. Seems like I remember the charges were eventually dropped or he got probation or something and that was the end of it, exposé article and all.

The crew at Snobs was also the "official" hairstylists for the Heartbreakers, the cheerleaders for the New Orleans Breakers, the USFL football team. One of the girls Anthony had hired, Donna, was what we called a "star-fucker" and she had affairs with several of the players. She'd screw anyone who could prove he'd had his name in the paper. For anything. One such affair turned out pretty funny. He was a player for the Breakers, a former Tulane All-American lineman. She'd spent a fortune on this guy's Christmas present, on a bunch of gold chains and stuff and was planning on spending Christmas Day with him. It was all she talked about for days. After we came back to work after the holiday, I walked in and she had steam coming out of her ears she was so mad. Seems the player, a big star, had also given her a Christmas present. Only he hadn't spent quite as much on Donna's. She showed me what he'd given her. It was a black and white glossy of him, the same ones the team handed out to fans by the hundreds. It wasn't even personally signed by him, but they'd used the stamp of his signature. Hadn't cost him a dime. It wasn't even in a frame. She was smoking.

What she hadn't known until then was that this guy was also "dating" a thirteen-year-old cousin of one of my customers who'd told me about it. He liked 'em young. I'd known about it for weeks and figured that would be a good time to tell her. That really set her off!

Donna's biggest "conquest" was heavyweight boxer Gerry Cooney. He even took her up to Canada with him to his training complex as he was getting ready for his heavyweight title shot with Joe Frazier. She spent two weeks up there, helping him "train." Frazier knocked him out in the second or third round, from what I remember. Cooney took someone else with him to his next training camp.

Donna was all right, though. She just had this "star" thing going, but other than that she was a really nice person. She ended up working as a makeup artist for the New Orleans Film Commission and worked on a bunch of movies. I imagine she really stepped up her star fucking then...

That was our new apartment complex though. A laugh a night.

Mark had this suit of armor like the knights of old used to wear. Really heavy stuff. He also had an iron mask. We'd get a couple of ladies over and talk them into foursomes and then one of us would disappear into the other bedroom, shuck our clothes and don the armor and mask. Whoever wore it that night would come back out and screw in full King Arthur regalia. We started getting into a costume "thing." There are costume shops all over the place in New Orleans. Where other towns have gas stations or Starbucks on every corner, New Orleans has costume stores. Folks would costume at the drop of a hat, not just for Mardi Gras and Halloween.

We started collecting various costumes and wearing them when we brought girls over. They loved it. We had executioners hoods, monster masks, famous people masks. One night, one of us would be Nixon and the other would be Kennedy or Lyndon Johnson. We had masks for our dates, and it was hilarious to look over and see Dicky Nixon putting the wood to Jacqueline Kennedy. Or, Martin Luther King, Jr. getting blown by the Easter Bunny.

It was while I was sharing the apartment with Mark that I finally snagged a date with Brooke. Brooke was the marketing manager for the hottest rock station in New Orleans. Well, we didn't actually have a "date," not by the cornbelt definition. You know, where you call up and ask a girl to go somewhere, dinner, a movie, whatever. I'd had very few of those kinds of "dates." Actually...zero. Usually, you'd chat somebody up at a bar or club and end up awhile later in the sack at either your apartment or hers. Or up against a building or in the back seat of a car. That was a date. This was New Orleans.

I saw Brooke out at some club and went over and began talking. An hour later, we were walking into my apartment and shucking our clothes on the way to the bedroom. Brooke was absolutely a ten. Smart *and* good-looking. We boffed each other a couple more times that week and then she asked me if I wanted to go to Dallas with her. Michael Jackson was just starting his comeback Victory Tour then and the station was flying Brooke and one of the D.J.'s to Dallas for Jackson's concert. Brooke could take someone with her and the station would pop for his expenses.

At the concert, we were sitting in choice third row seats and Brooke was staring at something behind the stage through a pair of opera glasses she'd brought. There was a lattice-work set up all around where the Jackson Five were playing their guitars and cranking out their hits.

"Look at this shit," she said, handing me the glasses.

"What am I looking for?" I said.

"You'll see," she said.

I looked and sure enough, I saw instantly what she was talking about. Behind the stage were five guys playing guitars! You couldn't see it without the glasses as the lattice-work hid it. I looked at the stage and saw that the Jackson boys didn't even have cords on their electric guitars. The guys hidden behind the stage were playing the music and the Jacksons were pretending to play. What was weirder yet was that the guys behind the stage doing the real playing were all white.

That evening, the D.J.—I can't remember his name—called from Michael Jackson's suite and asked us if we wanted to come over and meet Michael at a party he was having. I wanted to go, but Brooke said she was too tired. So, I missed my chance to meet Michael Jackson in person.

While she had the disc jockey on the phone, Brooke told him what we'd seen at the concert. The D.J. said he'd ask Michael about it, but that since he didn't see it himself, he couldn't report on it on his show.

On the plane back, he said Michael had admitted that they had, indeed, hired five musicians, and that, indeed, they were all white. He said his brothers hadn't performed in so long they were rusty and that's why they'd brought studio guys in. He still didn't report it on the air.

Another funny thing happened while Mark and I were roommates. One night, I walked into a nightclub and saw a beautiful girl sitting by herself at a table, the kind of babe you'd donate a kidney just to get in her pants. I went over and started rapping to her and we ended up going back to my apartment and in bed. Just before we made love, she handed me a condom. This was long before the AIDs era and I'd never worn such a thing, but what the hell—anything for science.

I needed to use it, she said, because she had been living with her boyfriend for about ten years and he'd had himself fixed. She said if she came up pregnant he'd kill her, knowing it wasn't his.

"And he'll kill you, too," she added. "He's a cop and he'd shoot you and get away with it. He's crazy." That was more than enough motivation to strap on the rubber. It turned out this was the first time she'd strayed.

The only problem was, I couldn't get it on. I tried every way I could, but it just wasn't big enough. This isn't bragging, just the facts.

"Look," I said, after struggling with the damn thing for a couple of minutes. "This just won't go on. Do you have a bigger one?"

"One size fits all," she said, but it didn't. It might have fit all the second-stringers she knew, but it didn't fit me. With her help, we finally got it on, but it didn't reach the full length of Mr. Happy and was cutting me in half. Not the most conducive thing to keeping interested in the proceedings. I got it on, up to maybe four-five inches from the base of Dr. Feelgood, but it just wouldn't go any farther. It was painful. Finally, I grabbed it and with both hands began to pull it apart in an attempt to stretch it, trying to break it where it was cutting in. The damn thing stretched about eight-nine inches and then it slipped out of my hand and snapped back around Mr. (Un)Happy. Wow! That hurt! I pulled it again and this time it broke. I didn't see any reason to tell her I only had half a rubber on and went ahead and inserted Tab A into Slot B and we fucked.

Oh, I forgot to say that when the rubber snapped against my johnson, it turned the whole thing as black as a steel-belted radial. Black! The whole thing. It looked diseased. Mr. Happy's a tough cookie, and he finished his work, but it sure looked nasty afterward. Inwardly, I groaned. I was going to take out a girl the next day that I'd been trying to get next to for a while. She was going to take one look at my equipment and run screaming I figured. As it turned out, it stayed black for almost a month before it slowly began to regain its natural pink complexion. Every time I got laid during that time, I had to go through this long explanation of what had happened. At first, I didn't think it was quite as funny as most of them did, but I began to see the humor in it. I never used another condom after that, though. That was my one and only experience with a rubber.

That wasn't the end of the story. When we'd finished, the condom was nowhere to be found. She went into a major panic. We tore the bed apart, looking for it, but no rubber in the sheets or on the floor beside it. She went into the bathroom and tried to check inside herself but didn't have any luck. She called me in to do a search and rescue and sat on the stool with her legs spread while I dug around in there, but I couldn't find the sucker either.

She was in a serious panic by this time.

"If we don't find it, it might be in me. Way up there."

That was my guess, too.

"And if it's in me, that means you came in me and I could get pregnant."

That was serious shit and got my attention. I was remembering what she'd told me about her whacko cop boyfriend. Besides the gun she'd mentioned he had muscles big as taxes or at least the paperwork from a Hollywood divorce and had some kind of black belt in Oriental death.

"Call a hospital," she said. "See what they say to do."

"Okay," I said, only we didn't have a phone in the apartment. There was one outside, by the parking lot. We trucked out to the phone, and she sat on the hood of a car while I dialed the East Jefferson Hospital. It was about three in the morning.

"Hello," I said, when a woman answered. "I've got an emergency and I need to speak to a doctor."

When the doctor came to the phone—you could hear the sleep in his voice—I said, "Doc, I've got a problem here. I think I've got a rubber stuck up inside this girl."

He hung up. Hung up on my ass!

I called back and got the doctor back on. "Don't hang up, Doctor," I said, hurriedly. "This isn't a joke. I really did get a rubber stuck up inside a girl. She's worried that she might get pregnant."

He must have bought the seriousness in my voice because he stayed on the line.

"Did you ejaculate?" he said.

"Yes," I confessed.

"Well, then," he said, chuckling, "you bet your sweet bippy she could get pregnant." He thought it was all pretty humorous with his *Laugh In* line.

The upshot was, he said to bring her on down and they could find it if it was shoved up inside and they had something to kill the sperm to keep her from getting pregnant.

I volunteered to go with her, but she was really nice about everything once she was sure it could be taken care of. She said she'd go herself. Send me the bill, I told her as she left, but she never did.

We went out one other time after that, and I assured her I could withdraw before I came inside her and that went much better. When she left that time, Mr. One-Eye was still his natural color. Shortly after that, I joined Pam in California so I don't know if she ever had any more misadventures with condoms. Hope not. Those are just one miserable invention, in my opinion. Very dangerous to your health. Mr. Happy just curls up at the very mention of latex and stays indoors.

The few seconds it stayed on when I first started screwing convinced me condoms were useless even if the other hadn't happened. You absolutely can't feel a thing. That old saying about taking a shower with a raincoat on is a perfect description of the experience.

It was during all these shenanigans that Pam was calling every night and I finally decided it was time to leave New Orleans.

She sent me the money for airfare and I ditched my Monte Carlo by the side of the road and hopped on a jet for LAX.

I probably should have stayed in New Orleans.

California didn't work out all that well.

XI
CALIFORNIA

I got off the plane at LAX and caught a shuttle flight to John Wayne Airport in Orange County. Pam was waiting for me when I deplaned. She looked hot. Acted hot, too. She was all over me at the airport. I thought for a minute we were going to do it in the airport parking lot, but it turned out she had to get back to work as soon as she got me settled in at Jack Kelly's house.

I was prepared to be intimidated when I walked into their huge-ass house in Huntington Beach. After all, this was not only the mayor of Huntington Beach, but a famous actor. But, he was a nice as could be. His wife, too. I forget her name, but she was a sweet, sweet woman.

Jack Kelly liked his booze. He was a real trencherman. Popped down about a fifth of good scotch a day and ate half a steer at supper. He'd gained a bit of weight since his *Maverick* days. "Portly" would be a mild description.

During our stay with the Kelly's, they filmed a special twenty-fifth anniversary show of *Maverick*. Jack lost sixty or seventy pounds for it, but you still wouldn't have called him svelte. I'm sure the horse he rode on during the filming didn't. Someone told me they had to use a hoist to get him on his horse.

Pam and I had an upstairs bedroom, overlooking the pool. That was the biggest damn pool I'd ever seen in my life. You coulda floated the U.S. Enterprise in it and still had room for the Olympic synchronized swim team.

Adrenaline Junkie

That was also the biggest damn house I think I'd ever been in. I never counted them, but there must have been seven, eight or more bedrooms.

When I first got there, I looked around and said, "Where's the smog?" Never having been to the left coast, all I had to go on was all the propaganda I'd always heard about California. The air looked fine to me. The Kelly's just laughed. "You'll see," they said, shaking their heads the way folks do when they know something you don't.

About three weeks later, I discovered smog. It had been there all the time. Every morning, I'd back out of their driveway onto the street, cranking the car to the left, then head off to wherever I was going. One morning, I went through the same routine...and there were these mountains directly in front of me. And they looked like they were about twenty miles away. Actually, they were farther, but they looked that close, seeing them for the first time.

I ran back inside.

"Where'd those mountains come from?" I shouted at Mrs. Kelly, who was washing the breakfast dishes.

She came out, wiping her hands on her apron.

"We must have had a Santa Ana," she said, chuckling. A Santa Ana, she explained, was a wind that comes down out of the Santa Ana mountains—those peaks I had just seen for the first time—and blows all the smog out to sea. For three weeks—and probably a few million years—those mountains had been right there in front of me, unseen.

"I guess you do have smog," I said.

"I guess we do," she said and smiled.

I missed a couple of other things about California those first days as well.

Pam's fidelity, for instance.

Mrs. Kelly's brother would blow in from time to time, from some computer sales job he had in northern California. He'd stay a couple of days and then go back home. When I met him, he seemed friendly enough, but there was something about the way Pam acted around him that didn't seem right. My antenna must have been extended completely, because I asked her about it right away.

"Oh, no. Jim?" she said, her eyes wide in amazement that I could ever consider such a thing. "Jim's just a good friend. He's not even my type."

Six months later, I was to discover that "good friend Jim" had been nailing Pam on a regular basis, up until and including the day I arrived.

Things were going pretty good for the first month or so. Pam had a good job grooming dogs at Mrs. Kelly's pet store and I landed a job with the Joico beauty product company as a salesman. I'd drive to dozens of hair salons in Orange and Los Angeles Counties and take orders for products. It was a pud job. Go in, schmooze with the stylists, give them samples of our products and write up orders. I figured I'd work that gig until I could snag my California's barber's license.

I'd always heard that L.A. drivers were the worst in the world and that it was a nightmare to get around. Nothing could have been further from the truth. California drivers were too slow, if anything, and they had these Thomas maps you bought all over, showing all the freeways. It was a snap to get around. New Orleans' drivers were a thousand times worse. Most Californians were sober whereas in New Orleans you were a weirdo if you weren't high and drunk by ten in the morning. In California, you couldn't drive badly if you wanted to. There were cops everywhere.

I never saw so many cops in all my life. It was like a military zone or like the governor had declared martial law. It took me months to be able to get to sleep at night. As soon as the sun went down, these helicopters started buzzing the houses. "HB1" and "HB2" they called them. Huntington Beach One and Huntington Beach...well, you get it. They were there to look for prowlers in the neighborhoods. I could see right away that California wasn't the state to be an outlaw in. There were two cops for every citizen, it seemed.

I even got a ticket for jaywalking! I crossed PCH to get to the beach and a cop came over and stopped me. It seems you have to go to an official crossing.

"But," I said to the storm trooper, "there wasn't a car on the road."

Didn't matter. The law is the law. I'd never fucking heard of getting a ticket for jaywalking. I always thought that was one of those blue laws or something, back in the Stone Age or in Pennsylvania.

Speaking of the beach, did I ever get a surprise there. The first day I went—Pam was at work—I'm trotting down to the sand in my Speedos, and this movie star in training who was sidelining it as a lifeguard, came running up and asked if I had any booze in the cooler I was carrying.

"Well...yeah," I said, thinking what a dumb question to ask. "This is a beach, isn't it?"

Turns out that you can't drink beer on the public beaches in California. There was a real fear that somebody might have some fun. Besides, drinking sometimes leads to fist fights and things like that, and I figure they didn't want the boys in blue to be spending time on minor stuff like that when they were needed to fight all the jaywalking criminals.

Sorry, if I sound like I wasn't impressed by California. I wasn't. It was definitely not the "party state" I'd always been led to believe it was. Californians need to go to New Orleans to find out what partying is. The beaches were so quiet that you could hear a cricket peeing on cotton.

I saw the first day where all these myths about California beaches come from. There was some film crew filming some beach movie or TV episode and these guys were walking up and down the beach, approaching the odd person here and there like myself, asking if we wanted to be part of the crowd scene. They were paying something like twenty bucks or something. I turned it down, but they were filming close to me and I saw instantly why folks in Indiana think California beaches are such a hot time. There were maybe thirty people total on the entire beach as far as you could see in either direction. They hired all of them except me and some guy sleeping who wouldn't wake up when they approached him (smart guy!) and they had these crazy party zanies all crowded together along with the cast to make it look like the entire beach scene was wall-to-wall party animals. Outside of this group, there wasn't a soul on the sand except for me and the napper. I caught the show about a year later and they'd dubbed in what I assume was stock footage that made it look like the beach was crawling with people. So much for truth in advertising...

And, if you haven't been there, don't believe all that malarkey about California beaches. Outsiders think that everybody wears those rubber suits because most folks are surfers. Ha! You have to get a thermal outfit on just to go in the water. It's the coldest water I ever felt in my life.

The first day, I go running down to the water and dive in. California, right? It's hot there all the time—another fallacy. Ergo, the water's warm, right? Wrong. In August, it's about the same temperature as it is in Lake Michigan on Christmas Eve.

As soon as I came up from my virgin dive into the Pacific, I started yelling for one of those guys on jaywalk patrol. I figured they had to know CPR, and I just knew my heart had seized up. My balls had gone into full retreat and were somewhere up close to my Adam's apple. It's cold, Jack! That was the one and only time I ever put so much as a toe into the water. Actually, that just about ended my beach days. You couldn't go in the water and you couldn't drink, so what were you supposed to do? Look at the two-pieces? Yeah, right. This was the home base for feminists. Don't get caught looking or they'll haul you into court and have you castrated. Some fun.

The scenery isn't quite as lush as they'd have you think, either. All I'd ever seen of California before this was in movies and TV shows. In real life, much of California is pretty trashy. You'd look up on a hillside and the houses were packed together tighter than a nun's pussy. Expensive houses, too, only the price of your mansion obviously didn't include any land. Your yard was mostly taken up with your privacy fence.

Lush and green? You've heard California was verdant? Forget that business. There'd be a patch of grass here, then a stretch of brown stuff, then another patch of green. The beachfront was cool looking, but what beachfront isn't? Show me an ugly beachfront and I'll show you a successful Army of Engineers project.

And the food. Now, I'd just blown in from New Orleans, which only happens to have the best food in the universe...and my spaceship lands in California. By the time a week had gone by, I would have killed for something with grease in it. Or meat. Californians are all ruminants. They eat grass. Everything is made of exotic blends of grass. *Everything.* Can anybody please tell me what a soyburger is? I don't understand what the point of a long, healthy life is if you can't enjoy at least some of it.

You have to go to Mexico to find food with any flavor in it. 'Course, you might get your gringo throat cut, but it's almost worth it if they let you have a last meal.

And Mexicans! Illegal aliens is what I'm referring to. They have this big deal in the media all the time about what a terrible thing it is with all these wetbacks flooding the state. Give me a break, California. The state would collapse into anarchy if it wasn't for the folks coming north.

You'd drive in the neighborhoods in the early morning and see dozens and dozens of Mexican people in front of a gas station. There'd be a long line of pickups and limos picking them up in ones and twos and half-dozens. They were hiring them to clean their houses, work their fields, pick their sugar cane, or whatever they grow in California. Soyburgers, I guess. Each little neighborhood has its weekly newspaper and if you followed the paper, about every three months the letters to the editor would start complaining about all the Mexicans hanging out at Ray's Texaco. Then, the editor would print this scathing editorial, decrying the ruination of the neighborhood because of the visitors from the south. Pretty soon, the Jaywalker Tactical Crime Squad would show up, roust a bunch of them and the next day they'd be gone. Only they'd be at Jimmy's Sunoco, a block up, for the next three revolutions of the moon. This would go on, over and over.

The truth is, the state would go bankrupt if they ever did get rid of the illegal aliens. For one thing, they do the jobs nobody else in their right mind would want and for next to nothing in wages.

When I first started working at Joico, I walked into the plant where they made the shampoos and stuff—all decked out in a suit. When the brown-skinned guys and gals saw a stranger enter the workspace in a tie, they all ran for the back door. The boss ran after them to tell them I wasn't the Border Patrol or whoever sends them back. I ended up visiting just about all the professional shampoo manufacturers—Redken, all the biggies—and as soon as I walked into the plant area, everything stopped until they figured out I wasn't there to corral the illegal aliens.

You want to have some fun? Go to California, put on a suit, go into any classy restaurant and walk into the kitchen. Lunch is over. The help just left.

The first few weeks in California were kind of fun. Cat wasn't around threatening my ass and the weather was nice except for the beach with all the ice bergs floating around in it. The job with Joico was panning out well and Pam was screwing my brains out.

There was one odd thing. When Pam picked me up at John Wayne Airport she was driving this old beater.

"You won't believe how I got this car," she said.

Her story was that she'd run into this old hippie who happened to be a *rich,* old hippie at this stage of his life. Pam's octogenarian ex-flower child owned a car wash and a car rental agency. Most of the cars were beaters like the Nova she was driving.

"I met him in a bar when I first got here," she explained. "I was dead broke and he felt sorry for me. He's loaning me the car until I get on my feet. He's the nicest old man, Les."

She had to "check in" with him from time to time, she said. So he wouldn't think she'd stolen the car. So, every week, we'd drive over to his car wash and she'd go in and chat with him a bit. Let him know she still wasn't on her feet and then he'd let her keep the car another week.

"I just have to schmooze with him a little," she said. "The guy thinks of me as his daughter." I really must have been an idiot to believe this crap, especially when she made me duck down under the dash when we pulled into his lot and stay hidden while she went in for her weekly "schmoozing" session. She said if the guy thought she had a boyfriend, he'd take the car back, figuring she could afford to buy her own, so I needed to keep out of sight. Neither of us had much money and couldn't afford to buy a car, even a junker, so I went along with the program. What a chump I was!

I'd be out in the car, curled up in a ball on the floor, while she trotted in and spent half an hour, forty-five minutes with the guy. Our regular weekly schedule.

We were barely making it, but since we didn't have to pay rent at the Kelly's we were starting to save a little bit toward our own apartment. Things were looking up.

Then, the boom was lowered. I came home and Pam was face down on the bed, bawling her eyes out.

"We've got to leave," she said. She had our suitcases out and piles of our clothes all over the place.

"What the fuck?" I said. "What's going on?"

"Mrs. Kelly just fired me," she sobbed. "She's kicking us out of the house, too."

Her story was that some money came up missing at the pet store and Pam had been accused of stealing it.

"Did you?" I asked.

Of course not, she exclaimed, indignantly, like what kind of boyfriend would ask something like that. It was this other girl that worked there, she said, who was the thief. Pam had been set up, she said, but there was nothing she could do about it. The other girl had worked there longer and Mrs. Kelly refused to believe that she could do such a thing. I was livid. How dare she accuse my girlfriend of such a thing!

No one was home at the time, so I helped Pam finish packing and we left. She had a girlfriend she'd already called, an old friend of Pam's from New Orleans who lived in Sherman Oaks, who would let us stay with her until we found our own place.

We got to Sherman Oaks and unpacked and sat around the living room with Sherry and her two little kids, drinking beer, smoking weed and dissing the Kellys. The higher I got, the madder I became. Finally, I grabbed Pam and told her we were going to go see Mrs. Kelly. She wasn't going to get away with calling my sweetie a thief.

Pam was extremely reluctant to go, but I was going with or without her. She climbed in the car and all the way over tried to convince me to just forget it, let it lie. Not Sir Galahad Edgerton. No, sir! Nobody was going to insult my girlfriend.

When we got there, Mrs. Kelly came out just as we pulled up. I was totally blitzed by this time. I got right up in her face. How dare she accuse Pam of something like this, I wanted to know. Pam was the most honest person in the world. Mrs. Kelly tried to reason with me. She kept saying they had proof, but I knew that was a lie. Pam had explained to me how her coworker had framed her.

In the middle of all this, Jack Kelly came out of the house. Things got real ugly, then. I wanted to fight him. For my girl's honor. It was fortunate for me that he was sane enough to ignore my insults and drunken ravings. He was one big dude. I'm sure he would have wiped me out with ease if he'd deigned to mix it up. I mean, this is a guy who used to do his own stunts on *Maverick*! He just said he was calling the cops and went back in the house. Pam and Mrs. Kelly grabbed me and pulled me back to the car.

Pam wasn't able to get another dog grooming job right away, so she took a job in a boiler room phone sex operation. That bothered me at first, but after I got a look at the setup, it was mostly funny. There were seven people in this little room, with a bank of phones that rang continually. Guys calling a 900 number to get their rocks off. What was hilarious about the whole thing was that five of the seven people answering the phones and giving out the hot phone sex...were guys! That's right, phone sex dudes. Gay guys, who sounded more feminine and sexy than either Pam or the other girl who worked there.

It was a stitch to listen to these guys work. They'd all the time put a caller on a speaker phone when the others weren't "working" and in seconds the whole place would be in stitches. This horny old fart, calling from Bum Fuck, Idaho, would be panting and groaning on the phone while he talked to "Bridgette" who was really Sam the Swish. Everybody in the room would have red faces from trying to keep our giggles down, so the client wouldn't hear us. It was an amazing thing to witness.

Most of Pam's coworkers had been doing phone sex gigs for a long time and all of them said that wherever they had worked it had always been predominantly gay men manning the phones. They had that female voice down cold. Breathless and sultry. It was hysterical. Most such operations were reluctant to hire women. The men did it much better and enjoyed it more.

The outfit Pam worked for ran these late-night TV spots with these luscious-looking models urging men to call them. It was a riot to picture these poor slobs dialing the 900 number, a mental picture of "Suzette LaCoquette" from the TV or newspaper ad imprinted on their brains, while drooling over the

Princess Slimline to a guy with a bigger schlong than theirs.

I've got an idea for a comedy TV series based on this. If there are any agents reading this, have your people call my people.

After about a month of this, Pam found a job at a dog grooming place on PCH in Costa Mesa and quit the phone sex job.

That's when our troubles really began. A lady had just opened up the shop for an investment and Pam was her only groomer. As it was brand-new, there wasn't much business. Make that "no" business. That would have been okay since I was making decent money with Joico, but about a week after she landed the job, three things happened in a twenty-four-hour period that put us on our rear.

Pam's car was stolen. At least that's what I thought had happened. It turned out later that the owner himself had come by and repossessed it. Pam hadn't shown up at his place the week before. I also didn't find this out until much later. A day after this happened, her friend Sherry kicked us out. She said Pam had stolen some money she kept on her dresser. Once again, Pam vehemently denied the theft, and once again, I believed her.

This was serious shit, this time. No car and no place to stay.

Somehow, Pam convinced Sherry to do us one last favor and drive us over to the dog grooming shop. We decided to crash there that night and figure out what to do the next day.

I'd been using the car to make my calls for Joico. I thought I'd rent a car with the bit we had saved, but they wouldn't rent one to me without a credit card, which neither of us happened to be in possession of. Without a car, I couldn't perform my duties for Joico, so I ended up losing the job. Not only that, but most of my worldly possessions of any value were in the car and so I lost those as well. Years ago, when I had the salon in Warsaw, Indiana, Isolde had given me a numbered Ertè print and that was in the car as well. When Ertè died, a few years later, I really got sick, thinking how much the print was probably worth. Isolde had also given me an antique Russian pony full-length fur coat which was worth a lot of money which was also in the car.

I wasn't too worried at the time, figuring I'd land something else soon, but the very next morning after I'd been given my walking papers from Joico, I woke up in intense agony.

The grooming salon Pam was running was a converted garage, next to a Bob's Big Boy. At night, we'd pull down these huge bags of dog food they sold, down on the concrete floor and use them for a mattress. I must have twisted something sleeping like that, because I woke up with a severe pinched nerve in my back. I've never felt pain that intense.

There was no way I could work. My left arm was essentially useless. Besides the pain, it left my arm so weak, I couldn't lift it or even make a fist. It got so that I had to be up for two or three days in a row to get exhausted enough to fall asleep for an hour or two. And the pain just wouldn't go away, not even for a second or two.

We were almost broke and didn't have a stick of health insurance between us, so there was no way I could go to a doctor or get an operation or whatever was needed. I was basically a cripple. Pam was lucky enough to get two or three customers a week, barely enough for us to buy a few groceries.

Things got worse and worse as the weeks went by. There'd be days and days on end that no one at all showed up with their Pom and we were down to zilch. We started sneaking over to the Bob's Big Boy and glomming hamburgers and fries from the dumpster when they threw them out.

My arm was just plain killing me. Finally, I walked down to a chiropractor's office I'd seen a couple of blocks away and made an appointment. I gave a phony name to the receptionist since I knew I wouldn't be able to pay this guy. He took me back and put me on this table and took X-rays and then put various machines on my back while I lay on a table. He also "adjusted" me. Nothing relieved the pain. The doctor told me the X-rays revealed a number of problems. I had three vertebrae bent the wrong way and fused together, both rotator cups were torn, there were two arthritic bone spurs on my spine, and my spine was shot full of arthritis. Oh, yeah. I had a pinched nerve because one of my discs was degenerated. That's what was causing the pain. One of these days I'm going to get all that taken care of. I keep saying that...

I went back twice more to the good doctor, but then had to quit going as he was expecting payment. For the rest of the time we were in California there wasn't a single minute that I was free of pain. It got so that I half-seriously thought about having Pam amputate my arm. That had to be less pain than what I was going through. I'd always had a high threshold of pain, but this was intolerable. I'd sit and cry, it hurt so bad. It was relentless.

I suppose I could have gone to a hospital and they would have taken me as a charity case, but I'd rather have died than been on what my dad always called the "dole." Same way with welfare. No doubt, I could have collected that as well, but that was the same thing. Or Workman's Comp. We were just raised that no matter what, you didn't accept any handouts from the government. My father grew up during the Depression and his family never took a dime from anyone, even when they were starving and he passed this attitude down to me. And I agree with it. If my kids were involved, I'd apply for it though.

We decided we had to get out of California. If we could get to Indiana, I knew I could get a job there, plus I had friends who might be willing to help us. I couldn't get my California barber's license as it turned out, without going back to barber school for three hundred more hours. We couldn't even feed ourselves regularly, much less pay for more barber schooling. That hurt, especially since the leading salon in California, the Allan Edwards salons, had offered me a job once I got my license. I saw Jose Eber one time down at the sidewalk mall in Santa Monica and we'd known each other from when I was working as a platform artist for Clairol and he told me he'd hire me if I could get my license. Things might have turned out differently if I could have afforded to get it, but I couldn't.

Pam found a lifesaving ad in the newspaper. A car rental company wanted people to deliver cars to various parts of the country. They didn't pay you anything, but provided the car and gas. Lots of people used this as a cheap method of traveling.

We scrimped and saved every nickel we could get our hands on and in two weeks had accumulated about a hundred dollars. That week, we obtained virtually all of our meals from the dumpster. It wasn't the day on the beach some folks experience in sunny Costa Mesa.

At last, we had what we figured would be enough, and took a bus over to the rental agency, picked up the car—to be delivered in Chicago—signed the papers, picked up the gas money they gave us, and split for the Midwest.

We took the long way, down through Arizona, and drove straight through to Chicago, stopping only to piss and hit the McDonald's drive-thru's. We kept awake on speed and booze. When we got to Chicago, late on Saturday night, we discovered the address we were to deliver the car to was on the South Side. In a bad section of the South Side. Like there are good areas...

We turned the car in and caught a city bus back uptown. We were going to catch a Greyhound to South Bend. That was an exciting ride. Pam was six feet tall with flaming red hair, which I'd cut in kind of a punk "do" that sprouted upward from her scalp another foot at least. And we were the only honkeys on the bus, for blocks and blocks. Some fun!

We made it to the Greyhound station without any problems, unless you want to count six thousand glares and about fourteen come-ons to Pam by amorous young black men along the way who were itching to earn a tear-drop tatt for their cheek by eliminating the competition.

As soon as we hit South Bend, I called my daughters and told them I loved them, I was in town and would be over to see them as soon as I could. It had been almost two years since I'd seen them. There was a lot of guilt behind that call. I'd been able to send their mother very little in that time. In New Orleans, for most of the time I had barely enough to sustain myself and the few times I did start making serious money, I was too far gone on booze and drugs to be bothered sending money home. In California, there just hadn't been any to send.

That was all going to change now. Pam and I had decided to get married and settle down and I was going to start being a good father. Pam had been after me nonstop to get married and I kind of said okay...not really thinking it was going to happen. Mostly, I just wanted to get her off my ass. Besides, even if we did end up getting married, it wasn't something I saw at the time as being exactly a permanent situation...

The next call I made was to Michael Murray, the owner of Michael & Company, South Bend's premier hairstyling salon. My first really good job had been with Michael, years before, and we'd always remained friends. He came right over and picked us up, took us out for a meal.

I explained our predicament and he was first-class. He loaned us enough money to rent a trailer over in Elkhart and gave me a job in his Elkhart salon. He had three salons at the time, the other two in South Bend and Mishawaka. He loaned Pam a thousand dollars to put in a grooming salon. He called up his brother and his brother came over with an old beater he had and gave it to us.

That night, Pam and I slept in our own trailer, money in our jeans and a rosy future before us.

I went to work at the Elkhart salon and was eventually made manager in a couple of months. In six weeks, I was taking in more income than anyone else in the shop, even those who had been there a couple of years. If there's one thing I knew how to do, it's build a clientele quickly. In the right shop. And Michael's was the right shop. It had the best rep in the area and deservedly so. Michael's cutters just flat out-cut everybody else around and everybody knew it.

I also helped out Pam in her grooming salon. She was one of

the best in the country. At one time, she had been the groomer to dogs that won at the annual Westminster Dog Show. She'd quit working for those folks because, as she said, "When their dog loses, they always blame the groomer. It's never the damn dog's fault."

On our way to Indiana, somewhere in Arizona, Pam and I had gotten into a big-ass fight. Broke, tired, driving on no sleep and little food and eating speed and hitting on amyl nitrate, we were both a bit cranky. One thing led to another and then Pam let slip something I'm sure she was sorry for as soon as it was out of her mouth. She said something about Mrs. Kelly's brother being better in bed.

I had always suspected there was something there and besides the fact that it had severely wounded my ego, I was furious about her unfaithfulness. Immediately, upon uttering what she had about the guy, she took it back, said she was just trying to hurt me for whatever I'd said to her in the argument. I let it ride, but thought about what she'd said all the way back.

We found a spot we thought would be a good location for Pam's grooming salon in Gilmer Park on the south end of South Bend and went to work fixing it up. About half a mile south of the Shirley Motel where I'd been busted years before. Things were going well. I was seeing my girls, Britney and Sienna, and regretting every minute I'd spent away from them. Kids are so forgiving. You can shit all over them and they still love you. I hadn't meant to desert them, but that's the way it had turned out. When I left Indiana, it was to escape any reminder of Patty, not to leave them. Leaving the girls was the hardest thing I'd ever done. In the back of my mind, I was only going for maybe a year, to get over Patty, get her out of my head and heart and then I'd return.

I did believe my kids were doing all right without my help. The few times I called back, Sheila usually said they were making it all right.

At any rate, I was back in town and with the girls every chance I got. I had a real chance to redeem myself and start over with them.

Not me. Not Mr. Selfish. As soon as I could, I fucked it up again.

The thing with Pam and Mrs. Kelly's brother just ate at me. Finally, one day, I called the Kelly's and pretended that Pam and I had broken up.

"I just wanted to apologize," I told Mrs. Kelly, when she answered the phone. "Pam and I are history, but she told me she *had* stolen from you that time." Pam hadn't told me any such thing and we were far from broken up. We were living together and talking about getting married.

"I'm sorry I got in Jack's face that night," I went on.

"Oh, Les," Mrs. Kelly said. "We always liked you and knew it wasn't your fault. You didn't know. You were just sticking up for your girlfriend." With that, the dam was broken. Thinking that Pam and I were no longer together, she went on to tell me all kinds of interesting things.

It seems that Pam had regularly been screwing Mrs. Kelly's brother until I arrived. The whole time she was calling me nightly, begging me to leave and come to California to be with her—pledging her undying love—she was doing the horizontal bop with this guy. In fact, Mrs. Kelly said, the morning she was to pick me up at the airport, she had slept with him in what was to be our bed. As Pam was about ready to leave to pick me up, Mrs. Kelly asked her if she wasn't going to at least change the sheets and make up the bed she'd just gotten out of with her lover and Pam said naw, it wasn't any big deal.

It was all I could do to act composed as she laid out even more. It also seems that the "old hippie" who was so kind as to loan Pam one of his rental cars, hadn't done it out of the goodness of his heart. He'd made an arrangement with her to trade sex for the use of the car. When we'd go to his business, once a week, she was inside blowing this guy. All I could feel was an overwhelming sense of rage. I'd left a terrific job at Snobs to come to this bitch who pledged undying love...and she was screwing me every which way all the time.

I made up my mind to keep my cool. After learning what I had, it would be hard to even touch her or breathe the same air she did. But I didn't want the usual argument and then she'd leave scene. Not this time. Not after what she'd done. This time she was going to pay and she was going to remember my ass.

Except I couldn't keep my cool.

I picked her up from her grooming shop and barely talked all the way home. I was downright frosty. She knew I was mad about something.

As soon as we entered the trailer, I erupted. All the things Mrs. Kelly had told me came out. We had a regular donnybrook of an argument and then she picked up the phone and called her parents in New Orleans. I drove down to a bar and had a few drinks. And calmed down. This was just what I didn't want. This wasn't payback enough for what she'd done in my sick mind.

I went back and started copping major deuces. Told her I loved her and forgave her and that I wanted to start over. Get married. It worked.

She said I'd *have* to marry her because her parents were on their way, driving up to get her and she couldn't get in touch with them. If she made them leave without her, she'd be disowned and they'd never help her again. I put on the best acting job of my life, convinced her I really did love her.

Her dad and mom had jumped in the car the minute her dad got off work and drove straight through. They arrived at the trailer mid-morning of the next day. When they pulled up, Pam kissed me, tears in her eyes, and went out to the car. They talked about twenty minutes and then her dad tore out of the lot in reverse and left rubber as they departed.

She came in and said she was indeed, disowned. Her dad

had listened to her story and then said that if she didn't get in the car with them right then that she should never again call them for any reason. She told them she was marrying me, that we'd worked it all out. He just rolled up the window and screamed out of there.

The next day, we went to the Goshen courthouse and filled out the form for a marriage license. The waiting period was three days. At the end of the period, the plan was to go back to the courthouse and get married by one of the judges. During those three days, I acted like the lovelorn suitor, screwing her to death and showering her with affection.

On the morning of the day we were to be married, I dropped her off at work. She was going to close the shop at noon and we'd drive down and get hitched. As soon as I dropped her off, I drove to the bank and emptied out our accounts. We'd managed to save about a thousand bucks. After cleaning out every cent we had between us, I went to the trailer and packed all my stuff. I filled the car up, bought a six-pack and headed south to Fort Wayne. I didn't know what I was going to do, but I enjoyed myself tremendously on the ride. I kept picturing her face when I didn't show up right away and then imagined what she went through as it slowly dawned on her that I wasn't coming. When she finally got home to our trailer, I kept laughing out loud at what I figured her reaction would be. The same when she tried to take money out of the bank and found out the accounts had been closed.

It was the perfect payback. She was in a strange place; she'd broken forever her ties to her parents; and, she didn't have a dime to her name.

The way it turned out, all that happened pretty much the way I'd imagined it. She'd almost committed suicide once she realized her predicament. That had been my fondest hope. I hated the bitch for what she'd done. And she'd paid, in spades.

I ended up writing a short story about the whole episode, titled "Sheets" which I sold to a small lit mag in San Francisco called *The Typewriter*. It was also included in my short story collection, titled *Monday's Meal*. I wrote it as an abstract piece of writing, not as a traditional short story.

She did do something else I hadn't expected. During our time in Elkhart, she'd become friends with my ex-wife Sheila. Pam had always gone with me when I visited the girls and she and Sheila had hit it off immediately. As soon as she realized the spot she was in, she called Sheila, and Sheila came over and picked her up and took her home with her. The way it was later run down to me, Pam called her folks and told them what had happened and her mother convinced her father to send her airfare back to New Orleans. A few days later, Sheila drove her up to O'Hare Airport in Chicago and she caught a flight to New Orleans.

That was the end of it, I thought. I'd gotten my revenge and was tickled pink. I drove to Fort Wayne and stopped by to see an old friend, Jim Teusch, just to say hello. I didn't have any immediate plans, other than I thought I'd party a few days in Fort Wayne and then go back to New Orleans. Or Key West. I had a hankering for Florida as well. But I really didn't know what I was going to do.

Jim asked me how I was fixed for money. I was okay, I said, but could always use more. "Why don't you work for me for a while (at his salon, NuTech) and get a bigger stake," he said. He was one of the best friends I've ever had. It sounded like a good idea. I had no real plans anyway and could certainly use more money.

I got a cheap room at the Norton Motel a dump run by a family of Indians and figured I'd work a few weeks and then head south. Where, I didn't know, just south. I disliked Indiana in general and Fort Wayne in particular and didn't think I could stand it more than four or five weeks. The weather was too cold, there was nothing to do, and the food was horrible. A Hoosier's idea of a spice rack is a set of salt and pepper shakers.

I got in touch with Sheila and the girls a week later, told

them what I was up to. I'd been paying my support while I was in Elkhart and seeing the girls often and wanted them to know I'd continue to do so. I wasn't going to leave them in the lurch again, no matter what else I did. That's when I found out what had happened to Pam. Sheila must have given Pam my new phone number in one of their conversations, because a few days later I started to get phone calls at the shop from her. She said she forgave me. That she still loved me and if I wanted to get back together she'd be willing. Amazing!

She began calling daily, just as she had when I'd been in New Orleans and she'd moved to California. She kept saying she couldn't get me out of her mind and that she still loved me and would do anything for me. Simply unbelievable.

After a month of this, she called one afternoon and said she was marrying a doctor who was loaded. I just laughed and she hung up, mad that I hadn't come unglued. The next day, she called back and said she was going to marry the guy, but that if I ever came back she still loved me and would do anything I wanted with her. After that, I refused her calls and she finally quit calling.

I was a week away from leaving town, when the most momentous event of my life happened. I'd decided to return to New Orleans. I was going to pay back Anthony for the money he'd loaned me for the Monte Carlo and see if he'd hire me back. I figured the stuff with Cat had blown over by then and I was itching to get back to the action in the Big Easy. Fort Wayne was driving me crazy. The pace was so slow as to be nonexistent. It was just like when I'd gotten out of the service and went nuts from the boredom level and ended up beginning my life of crime. I didn't want that to happen again.

I ran out of gas on the way to work. That simple little twist of fate completely changed my life forever. I was on State Street, just a few blocks from NuTech when the car sputtered and died. I was also half a block from a shop I used to work at, a place called Professional Village.

I needed to get to work in fifteen minutes and I figured there should be someone at Professional Village I still knew, who might give me a ride to work. After I got off, I'd come back and get my car.

Sure enough, I knew several of the people gathered around the desk when I walked in and one of them was Mary Goff. Mary had been working at the Hall's Restaurant as a waitress when I worked at Professional Village and then took a job as a receptionist with us just before I left to open Prime Time Hair Salon. I hadn't been around in years and she was now their top stylist. The owners had helped her through beauty school and hired her when she graduated. Mary had a cancellation and was happy to drive me down to Jim's.

I'd been married to Sheila when I worked there years before, and Mary had been one of the few girls I hadn't hit on. After she dropped me off, I started thinking about her. It was a Friday and I called her up and asked her out. She had other plans, she said, but she'd go out with me next week if I wanted. I wanted.

She told me later that she didn't really have any plans that night but she thought I was pretty cocky, calling her up at the last minute like that. It was a new experience for me. Making a date. I definitely knew I was in Ft. Wayne.

I didn't to New Orleans the following week. Instead, I stuck around and Mary and I started dating. A year later, I did get back to New Orleans...along with Mary, my new wife. My entire life changed from that day when she gave me that ride. No longer did I even have even the most fleeting of desires for another woman. Or for drugs, alcohol or any of the things from my former existence. My partying days were over. I'd found something better. Love. There wasn't a blank spot in my DNA after all.

We moved to New Orleans shortly after we got married. We found a duplex apartment on Burthe near the Camellia Grill and Mary got a job at David DeLong's salon a block away and I got a job at Busta's at the Fairmont down in the CBD. I rode the streetcar to and from work each day and it was wonderful.

We had a weird experience the first weekend we were in town. Just about broke, we decided to drive down to Grand Isle on the Gulf which I was familiar with—my Uncle Buddy before he passed away had a vacation home there and we used to visit all the time. Our plan was to do some crabbing and enjoy the sun and surf. It was a holiday weekend, Labor Day.

A block away from our apartment, I discovered I'd left my billfold at home. We were already running late, so I decided not to turn back. That turned out to be a big mistake.

On the way down is a town called Golden Meadow. There was a famous bakery there that I wanted to show Mary. When I was a kid, we used to visit it and they were famous all over the world—even shipping their goods to Paris. Golden Meadow also had another claim to fame. They were the site of a well-known speed trap. Since the oil bust a few years back, the town had fallen upon hard times and to make money the police department had set up a speed trap for unsuspecting tourists that had been publicized in New Orleans. A reporter had gone undercover and exposed the scam and we'd just seen the TV report. Just before the bakery, the speed limit was thirty-five mph which I was careful to observe, remembering the report. We went in. Mary was impressed and we bought some rolls and other things and then came out to our car.

We jumped in and again, I was mindful of the speed limit. What I didn't notice was a *new* speed limit sign just on the edge of the bakery property. That one lowered the limit to twenty mph. A block away down the road, there was an old clunker parked by the side of the road and an old guy in front of it on the road, waving his arms. Figuring he had car trouble, I pulled over to give him a hand.

As soon as I approached him, he pulled out a gun from behind his back and stated he was a cop and had me lie down on the road where he cuffed me. For speeding. Out of nowhere, another car, this time a clearly-marked patrol car, appeared. I was put in the back seat and the uniformed cop told Mary to follow us to the police station.

Some shit, huh?

When we got there, the police chief who turned out to be the old guy I'd stopped to help, told Mary my fine would be a hundred dollars for both the speeding ticket and the fact that I didn't have a driver's license on me and that I wouldn't be released until it was paid. We didn't have a credit card and didn't have enough money on us to pay the fine. We had a book of checks but they were from a Ft. Wayne bank and we hadn't yet had time to open a New Orleans' account and he wouldn't take an out-of-state check. He said Mary would have to find someone to cash a check.

Mary's face was absolutely white. She had no idea where we were and her sense of direction was...how do I say this?... flawed, so I wasn't sure she could even find her way back if she went very far. I think she was thinking the same thing.

She left and I'm sitting there on a chair as the chief began taking info from me. When he got his paperwork done, he told me to stand up and follow him back to the cells. Another cop came out from some room and asked the guy if he was going to shake me down.

"Nah," the guy said. "I don't think he's got a hand grenade on him, do you?" If I had, it would have been hard to hide. I was wearing a T-shirt and a pair of cutoffs and flip-flops. He turned to me and said, "You don't have a hand grenade on you, do you?" He was laughing.

"Not *this* time," I said. I wasn't smiling.

Neither was he. The guy came unglued and walked over and got me in a hold and the other cop came over and shook me down. "That isn't funny," the chief said. "Last week we arrested a guy and he *did* have a hand grenade on him."

They took me back to a holding cell and I sat there for three hours. Mary finally returned just when I'd about given up hope of ever seeing her again. She had the money and paid my fine and we left. Just turned around and went back home.

On the way she told me why it took so long. She'd had to drive around to a bunch of little towns around Golden Meadow to try and find a place to cash a check. Most places were closed because of the holiday and the few she found wouldn't cash a check from Indiana. Finally, when she'd just about given up, she said a manager at a supermarket had taken pity on her and cashed one for her. She might have been crying at that point, though she never admitted to that.

A week later, we had another "adventure." I snagged a job at Busta's at The Fairmont after going through a couple of interviews with him and submitting my resume. It was a great salon in a great hotel. The salon was just across the hall from the famous Sazerac bar and just down the block-long hall from the famous Blue Room. The rumor at the time was that Frank Sinatra kept a suite there with a year-long lease for $10,000 a night and rarely visited it.

There was a front-page news story about a murder trial involving furniture magnate Aaron Mintz who had discovered his dead wife one morning along with his mistress. It seemed clear it wasn't the suicide Mintz claimed since she was found with the gun in her hand...what made suicide clearly not the cause of her death was that the gun was found in her right hand and she was left-handed...and she'd shot through a pillow Mintz's legal team claimed she'd placed over her own head before pulling the trigger. I guess out of consideration that she wouldn't wake anyone...

Well, after I set up my tools and met some of the staff, a gorgeous young woman with long blonde hair swept into the salon, tossed the receptionist her fur coat and sat down in my chair.

"Hi, Les," she said.

I wondered how she knew my name and that got cleared up quickly. She was Ruth-Ann Munitis, the aforementioned Aaron Mintz's mistress. Ruth-Ann was also reputed to have been

Dutch Morial's mistress before hooking up with Mintz.

She started talking to me like I knew all of these things—which I didn't and only learned later. She told me she was taking over the salon from Busta and had read my resume and was going to need a salon manager and thought I had the kind of qualifications she would be looking for.

In a daze, I excused myself from her and went to the back room where Busta was and told him what she was saying. He clued me in with the short version. That she'd bailed him out a few months ago when he was heavily into debt for cocaine and gambling debts and had become his financial partner. Then, things started going south, he said. She began taking over more and more of the salon and the last straw was when she told him she wanted all the stylists to start wearing tuxedos when we worked. At that point, he tried to pull out of the partnership, but she wasn't standing for that and had her lawyers trying to take over and he had his lawyers fighting all that. Each night after the salon closed, he would take the appointment book and all the client records home with him so she couldn't steal those and lock him out.

It was just a total clusterfuck. And here I was, first day on the job, and right smack in the middle of it. He advised me to keep on her good side as she might win and I'd need a job.

I didn't know what to do. I went back to her and told her I needed time to get up to speed on everything so if she'd be so kind I'd appreciate it if she had someone else cut her hair.

That night, I told Mary all that was going on and she was in a daze. New Orleans was turning out to be very different from Ft. Wayne.

The upshot was, I kept on working for Busta for another few weeks. Ruth-Ann would waylay me when I left for the day and I kept putting her off for a decision. The decision wasn't hard—I mean this was the mistress of a mob-connected guy and it looked obvious she'd taken part in the murder of her boyfriend's wife. I could get a glimpse of my future with her and it didn't look rosy.

Finally, I had to quit. I hated to since I really liked Busta and the salon, but then Mintz got acquitted and Ruth Ann got even bolder and it was time to boogie on down the road. Turns out Mintz was mob-connected also, as a few years later he got convicted in a mob scheme to steal from the Las Vegas gambling company Bally's.

From there, I got a job at the Uptown Square salon and that had another twist to it. Then-governor Edward Edwards used to come to New Orleans periodically, and bring his wife. When he came, he'd rent two adjoining suites in a good hotel and he and his wife would bunk in one of them with the other suite reserved for one of his many mistresses. All of that was quite open. In fact, they did a local documentary on Edward's philandering and interviewed his wife who was blunt about it. Yes, she said, she was very aware that he kept mistresses and she was friends with almost all of them. It's just the "Louisiana way" she said and it was.

Well, I inadvertently got involved. It turns out one of Edwards' favorite girlfriends was a fellow stylist at Uptown Square. Whenever he and his wife came to town, he'd give her a call. When that happened, she'd just take the weekend off and the clients on her book would go to the junior stylist. Who was moi. In addition to my own clients, I had to take care of hers as well. I was humping my ass off to take care of a double load. Thanks, Guv…

Stuff like that kept happening and I'm pretty sure Mary was kind of freaked out at the kind of town New Orleans was proving to be. I loved it, but I was an adrenaline junkie. That didn't describe Mary so much…

We might have stuck it out, but Mary became pregnant and then miscarried and with everything that was going on she just missed her family and support system back in Ft. Wayne so we ended up moving back. And, have been here ever since.

A couple of years later, back in Indiana, Mary gave me the

ultimate gift of a baby boy. My son Mike. With two beautiful daughters, a beautiful wife who loved me in spite of my bad qualities, and a terrific son, the old Les died. It's taken awhile to rid myself of the last vestiges, but I'm just about there.

Life is good.

XII
AND NOW...

I hesitated a long time before I wrote this account of my life. Did I want my kids to know the kinds of activities I had been engaged in for most of it? At first, I didn't think so. Let the past be buried. But, I kept thinking about my own father. All my life he's been a mythic figure to me. Someone so elevated I've never felt I could measure up to him. I realized something that convinced me to go ahead and write about my "secret life." It dawned on me one day—with one of those rare flashes of insight that we only rarely receive—that if I had ever seen just one tiny crack in my dad's armor, if I had witnessed one moment of weakness, then I would have realized that he was only human and not a superman who was impossible to measure up to. I never saw that moment with my father. He was always this terrible, righteous, fierce man who never wavered in his strength, at least from my perspective. My purpose in writing this and exposing my many warts is that I want my children to know that I was weak many times, that I made bad decisions, that I was selfish. Not that I'm proud of any of that—I'm not—but I want them to know that I have crawled through the slime and emerged on the other side and that the most important thing in the world is the love of others, especially your family. I don't want my kids to see their father as a perfect man. Just a man, full of weaknesses and failures...but also a human being imbued with hope and dreams and more love for them than they can imagine. That I came to that awareness late is a hard fact, but it's also true that I came to it, however delayed it might have been. My hope is that my children will see that crime and violence are not glamorous in the least, but dirty and vile and corrupt, and that there is nothing redeeming about such a life.

From the earliest age, I knew what I wanted to be in life. A writer. Most of the things I ended up doing in life were done because of this desire. For over fifty years, I was convinced that the way one became a writer was to go out and have experiences and then write about them. A colossal mistake.

Late in life, I've found out there's a better way than the "Jack London" school of prose. Always, I thirsted after experiences, the weirder and more bizarre, the better. I collected experiences like other people collect baseball cards. In the process, I nearly lost my soul.

Ever since I was a little kid, I remember having this vision in my head that one day I'd be eighty or ninety years old, sitting in a wheelchair in a nursing home. At this point in my life, I knew that no amount of material possessions would matter. All I would have would be memories. And I wanted memories! God, I craved them. The way you got memories was to gather experiences. That was my whole credo. It didn't matter who I hurt, whose life I might ruin, what insane chances I took with my life or liberty, gathering experiences was worth everything. Those fools who adopted materialistic goals were just that in my mind—fools. Well, it turns out the fool was I, as Pogo might put it. I have met the enemy and he is me...

I was very, very lucky. Most of it was because I met a wonderful girl named Mary who made me see what I really was. One selfish excuse for a human being.

The part of my life that dates from when Mary and I met and were married, except for that brief bit in New Orleans, is going to untold in this account. All I will say is that that blank spot I always thought was in my DNA wasn't missing after all. I *was* capable of love. Falling in love with her saved my life and gave me a chance at redemption. And when our son Mikey Bud was born, that redemption was complete. My biggest regret is that I hadn't been the father to my daughters as I have been to Mike. My story hasn't ended perfectly but it has gotten to the point where it's very satisfying. I certainly didn't deserve for that to happen! Nothing I did deserved such a second chance. It was a gift, pure and simple.

There was a seminal moment in our early relationship that awakened me to what a wonderful, loving person Mary was. When we met, I was living in a dump of a motel room and the second time she visited it, she brought me a plant to, in her words, "To liven up the place. Make it more homey."

I had to go into the bathroom. I didn't want her to see the tears that filled my eyes. She was the first woman out of many, many hundreds I'd had visit any room I'd ever lived in that did something like that. I knew at that exact moment that I never wanted to be out of her life. And, I haven't been.

As I write this, she's downstairs bringing in her potted plants from the yard—the first freeze of the year was predicted on TV last night. She does the things that make a home a home and she does the things that make a relationship a relationship. Our very *family* is the result of Mary and it was so at the very beginning. For the first time in my life, I felt part of a couple whenever I was with her and even when we were apart, I felt in my bones that we were a couple.

Most people of my present acquaintance are going to be very shocked when they read these pages. A few know I had some "wild times" in my past, but I doubt if they knew the extent. And I've left out quite a few things. I mean, a person can only tell so much, right? And...there's that statute of limitations thing I've got to pay attention to. Because I've moved so much all of my life and never formed any relationships that lasted beyond a few short years, everyone in my life has a different picture of me. When I got out of the joint, for example, I did my best to hide my complete past from everyone. Originally, I'd titled this account *My Secret Life* because at the time I began writing this, scarcely any of my acquaintances knew of my criminal background. So, those folks know an entirely different guy than say the folks I knew in New Orleans. Or the folks I knew in high school. Or when I sold life insurance. Or was in prison. Or...you get the picture.

The thing is, while I was doing all this stuff—the criminal behavior, the women, the drinking, the drugs—I didn't think about it much. It was just what it was. My life at the time. I was just hell-raising and most folks I knew at the time didn't see anything wrong with what I was doing either. Hell, everyone else was doing the same things. The women I messed with, for the most part, were raising their own brand of hell themselves. My male friends were doing the same thing.

When I met Mary, something clicked. I don't know what it was and I can't explain it. Maybe it was the hand of God, I don't know. I do know that when we fell in love and married, for the first time in my life I didn't just talk about writing, but actually began to write. And get things published. This will be the twenty-first book published since I looked into her beautiful brown eyes and said "I do." There weren't any before her.

Thanks to Mary and my kids' love and support, I've also been able to complete my bachelor's degree and also earn a master's. An MFA in Writing. Hey, how 'bout that!

I can finally say I am a writer and I can finally say I have found love and have learned how to return love.

Thank you, Mary. Thank you giving me my life. Everything I ever dreamed of and more has come true.

It's real funny. All my life I said all I wanted to do was to accumulate experiences. What I really wanted was to find a way to gain control. Neither, I've discovered, is a quality way to spend the days of our existence, precious few that they are. Now, I have a different desire. All I want at this stage of my life is for my children and my wife to be happy in their lives...and I want desperately to be able to contribute in at least a small way to their joy.

Control is way overrated.
And how did I arrive at this insight?
By writing this book.

Allow me to share this with you. First, writers know this, but non-writer's may not be aware that all good writing is *rewriting*. That's how I came to understand my life, as you'll see presently.

In the first rough draft of this, I had written this paragraph in the Prologue and then decided to omit it:

I'm also not going to provide you with startling insights as to why I did some of the things I did. No, I'm just going to lay the elements of my existence on this planet out on the page, and at the end of it, if the accumulation of these artifacts lead you to make certain conclusions, then so be it.

I deleted it in the next and all succeeding drafts. Why? Because I realized that I *had* gained an insight into myself, first by writing it and then by reading it once finished with that first rough draft. I learned that gaining insights about oneself was perhaps the whole point of writing a memoir.

I looked over what I'd written and realized something I never had before. That while my life's adventures and misadventures had an element of interest to me and hopefully also to readers, the *form* of my life seemed episodic. This happened, then this, then this...ad infintem. And I instantly realized—like I admonish my creative writing students—that episodic stories aren't publishable, simply because they resemble a TV series mostly—the protagonist never changes. He's the same person at the end of each episode as he was at the beginning. Sam Malone in *Cheers* ends up the same womanizer he was at the beginning of the episode and the same as he will be at the beginning of the next. That's not a proper literary story model, either in fiction or in memoir. Works in television, but not for novels. But...I *had* evolved into a different person as a result of the things that had happened to me and the choices I made.

It was exciting to learn that, unlike Sam Malone, I was able to change and change for the better. No…it was better than exciting. It gave my life a value.

Two other things happened that impacted our relationship. I began receiving phone calls from Charles Manson.

There. I bet that got your attention, made you sit up, didn't it!

A few years into our marriage, a professor at the University of Toledo—Dr. Russell Riesling—was writing a book about the drug experiences of famous people during their youth. He had folks like Big Brother of Big Brother and the Holding Company and some other folks. For some weird reason, he had a chapter on me. I'd done drugs but definitely wasn't famous.

Anyway, Russ interviewed me for his book—which hasn't been published yet, alas—and we became friends. I sent him a copy of my story collection, *Monday's Meal*. About two weeks after I sent it, I got a phone call from him. Seems he'd been out to Corcoran Prison to visit with and interview Charles Manson—who also had a chapter—and during the visit, Charlie spotted the copy of *Monday's Meal* that Russ had with him. He asked if he could "borrow it" and Russ loaned it to him. A few days later, he called Russ and was really excited—according to Russ. He said he'd read the book and loved it and that I was "the real deal" meaning a real-life outlaw, ex-con. He asked Russ if he'd ask me if I'd mind if he called me. I told Russ, sure, and thus began a series of phone calls from him to me.

Now, when I was in prison, we weren't allowed to call folks. At all. One of the many things that have changed. Because of that, I wasn't aware that all such phone calls are made collect. At the end of the month, after which he called three or four times a week, I got the bill and it was astronomical. Mary had a cow and I told Charlie we needed to dial it back a bit. (Pun intended…)

Mostly, Charlie talked and I listened. He's not hard to figure out. He was a nutcase, pure and simple. Knew lots of guys like him in the joint who just weren't as famous. Just your basic punk. We swapped stories and he may have told me a few things he'd done that he hadn't been nailed on and I may have returned in kind, but I won't talk about that. Anyway, I kind of got tired of talking to him—it was same-o, same-o all the time—and was about to disassociate myself, when he told me his cellmate, Roger Smith, really wanted to talk to me. I said okay and thus began a series of phone calls with Roger.

Roger bills himself as the "most-stabbed inmate in U.S. history"—and he is. As of that time, he'd been shanked over three hundred separate times. He was Charlie's cellmate since both were in protective custody because there were hits out on both of them from just about everybody in Corcoran. Over the years, Roger had hired himself out as a hit man for every single gang in the joint and now all of them had a hit out on him. The reason he wanted to connect with me was that he thought I was a "great writer" (his words and they had little effect on me—I've been on the receiving end of a shuck job more than once…), and he wanted me to write his life story. According to Roger, he'd had his "come to Jesus" moment and wanted to right all the wrongs in his life. He said he wanted his life story out there to help keep young kids from following in his footsteps. He'd been locked up ever since he was a juvie and all that. Grew up in one joint or another.

I had to laugh when he told me he was "saved." He sounded contrite…but every other word out of his mouth with "fuck this" or "motherfucker this" and he didn't sound much like the converts I'd met down at the First Baptist…But, I've been inside with a lot of guys who had these jailhouse conversions and he wasn't unusual.

He told me Charlie was letting him use his personal secretary—some gal who lives in North or South Carolina who has all of Charlie's journals and communications and writings and such and who handles all his commercial business. He can't profit by books and interviews but he does take checks from the networks and publishers and the proceeds all go to charity.

Roger told me he'd kept journals from when he was a little tad tyro outlaw and they were with Charlie's secretary and he said he'd have her send them to me—from what he said, a LOT of journals—and that he'd answer any questions I asked.

I told him I was just too busy with my own work and really couldn't do this project, but he wouldn't take no for an answer. Called me incessantly, trying to persuade me to write his life history. Finally, one time, he said, "What's the real reason you don't want to write it, Les?"

I asked him if he wanted the real reason and he said yeah, so I told him. "Roger," I said, "you're like a serial killer. In fact, you *are* a serial killer. Three hundred hits, dude."

"Yeah," he said, "and why would that prevent you from writing my story?"

To which I answered that serial killers just flat-out bored me (and they do). I told him serial killers just keep doing the same exact thing, over and over and over, ad nauseum. After about the third one, they're just boring. And, I didn't want to tie up a year of my life on writing about some boring-ass serial killer.

There was a silence and then he exploded. Called me everything but a white man. Sounded kind of like he'd kind of backslid on the "saved" deal. Screamed that if he ever got out of Corcoran my house was the first place he was heading. I listened to him ranting and screaming at me and then laughed and said, "Roger?" He got quiet and said, "Yeah?" I said, "Roger, you're not ever getting out of there unless there's a major earthquake and that isn't likely. But, if somehow you do get out, I'm aware that you prefer using a shank on your hits and if you come to my house to nail me, I won't have a shank. It'll be something that makes a louder noise. So, it's been nice talking to you and have a nice life, loser."

And that's the last I've talked to either Roger or Charlie. But, for a while we were all jam.

Mary had listened to all our exchanges and just shook her head at the guy.

And then, a couple of weeks later, we were lying in bed, watching MSNBC during one of their episodes inside various American prisons. They just happened to have my "alma mater" on, Pendleton. As it happened, I recognized one of the inmates.

"That's James!" I exclaimed. "He's in the barber school." The inmate I'd recognized had been there on many visits. He should have been—he was doing a life sentence. I couldn't wait to go back down in a few months and tell him I'd seen him on TV—that I guessed now he was a big television star. I suppose you could say, "starring in a reality show."

I went on as the show progressed, pointing out various places such as the chow hall, the quad, the exercise yard. Relating old anecdotes—about the time I was eating supper and the inmate cook came up and buried his meat cleaver in another inmate's stomach and I lost my focus and bit down on a rock, breaking my back tooth.

"You know," she said. "I know you were there and did all that stuff, but I just can't picture you as that guy. Just like that stuff with Charlie Manson. I heard you talking to him and that other guy, but you weren't anything like them."

"Thank you," I said. I hesitated a moment, then said, "It's your fault, you know."

She smiled, kissed my forehead like I was a little boy like she does sometimes, and said, "Goodnight, honey."

She fell asleep quickly and I just stared at her face that was as beautiful as the first time I'd ever seen her. My pulse always quickens.

I do that often.

I guess I'm still an adrenaline junkie. I just have a different source of supply these days.

-30-

XIII
THE FINAL CHAPTER

Perhaps you noticed the "30" at the end of the previous chapter. Those of you who are journalists or writers are aware that's the mark you put at the end of a manuscript. Only...as it turns out, that wasn't the end. I've left it there as a marker.

The pages before that 30 are the pages I wrote and intended as my memoir up until I met Mary. I've planned another one covering the almost thirty years since. Lots of stuff has happened in that period as well that further changed my life significantly.

But, something suddenly happened in the recent past that has a bearing on everything in these preceding pages. Something that's the single biggest emotional event in my life and that impacts what I wrote before here.

It's funny how life works. Not at all like we often expect it to or plan for it to. What's that saying? "Man plans and God laughs?" Something like that. Well, I imagine this is a serious rib-tickler for Him and is bringing tears to His eyes with gut-splitting guffaws if that saying is accurate.

I finally found out the truth about my father.

I was finally able to afford to pay for a DNA test for both me and my sister Ann, who was the one who suggested we do it.

When the results came back, my entire world shifted on its axis. Even though I suspected Edgy wasn't my father, to learn definitively that he wasn't shocked me to my core.

I won't go into all that happened from that point except for the bare facts. Mary rode with me up to my mother's home in

South Bend and I presented her with the DNA evidence. Don't laugh but she wasn't sure what DNA was. Remember, she didn't participate in anything in the outside world. No radio, no TV, no newspapers. No communications at all from outside her religious world.

At first, she tried to deny it and when she saw that wasn't working, began to fabricate her story.

In some ways, it was the darkest hour of my life, and in other ways, the most liberating news I'd ever received.

It was liberating in that everything in my childhood and relationship with my father and mother made sense. It wasn't me that had been at fault. I hadn't been a bad kid at all. I didn't deserve the abuse I'd received at both their hands.

It was the darkest because I realized I was sixty-eight years old and didn't know who my father was.

All kinds of thoughts came at me. She'd known I wasn't his kid, but when I was born she named me after him. What kind of person does that to her infant child? When I was born, Edgy was in England with the 8th Army Air Corps. He'd wanted to name me George if I was a boy. The story I'd always heard was that he was mad she'd named me after him because he didn't like his name himself and didn't want to wish the name on a boy. My name is Leslie Harold Edgerton, Jr. I hated it before I learned I wasn't even his biological son. I endured all kinds of grief during childhood for the name Leslie. I lived that life Johnny Cash sang about in "A Boy Named Sue!" I don't know what to do at this point. To change it—which is what I want to do more than anything—means untold complexities.

What also angers me is that I named my youngest daughter after him—we named her Sienna "Leslie"—and I named my son after him. Edgy always went by the nickname "Bud" and I was always "Butch" at home. When Mike was born, Mary and I were looking for a middle name and on a whim I suggested we name him after "Dad" and name him Michael "Bud." After Mike learned what the truth was he wanted to change both his last name and especially, his middle name. Again, an act that would mean untold complexities. What she did doesn't only impact me, it impacts others as well, in small and in large ways. My daughter Britney has Graves' Disease, among other ailments, and it would be a huge benefit for her health to know her real grandfather's medical history.

When I confronted my mom, at first I just handed her the report. It was written in small print and she said she couldn't read it. I started to grab it to read it and instead I did what I didn't want to do. I lost it. "It says Edgy (what she always called him) wasn't my father." I stood up and I was beyond angry. I was in a murderous mood. "I want to know who my real father is." Her eyes widened and she looked like a trapped animal. "He *was* your real—"

I could literally see her mind working frantically to come up with a good story. "Stop it!" I said. "The DNA report says he wasn't. DNA doesn't lie. He wasn't my father. All I want from you is the name of my real father."

Her response was, "I've been forgiven for that."

"Forgiven?" I said. "By whom?"

"By God," she said. "He forgave me a long time ago. I'm absolved of that sin. Yes, your biological father was someone else, but I confessed to God and He forgave me."

"I want to know how that forgiveness thing works," I said. "Since up until this minute, you were still lying to me about who my father was."

Indeed, two days earlier, she had phoned me and asked if I'd seen the news about the child who fell down a well in Midland, Texas. I hadn't, and she told me why she was asking. She said Midland was near where I was born and where my "dad" and she were married, and it had brought up memories and she just wanted me to know she was thinking about me being born.

Two days before! Still embellishing the lie she had delivered to me all of my life.

I went on. "So, how does that work, that forgiveness thing? Since you've maintained that lie to me all of my life up to this moment, does that mean that every single night you bring this sin to God and He forgives you each day? Is your idea of God and forgiveness that there's no atonement involved? That He gave you a blanket pardon that allows you to go on lying to me the rest of my life? That's how that works?"

She struggled to talk but just had no answer for that.

I won't give you a play-by-play of our entire conversation. I kept demanding to know the name of my real father and all she could come up with was that she'd tried to forget his name ever since then and all she could remember was what she thought was his first name—Gail. Or, Gayle or Gale—I don't know. She didn't spell it. Later, she came up with yet another spelling—Gel.

I told her she was a liar. Nobody forgets something like that. She just didn't want me to try to find him if he was still alive or any surviving relatives of his because then the truth would really come out. I was screaming at her at this point—I completely lost it. I told her she was dead to me, that she was only a mother because of the accident of birth and that she was never to come to our house or call me or be in my life in any way from then on. That all I wanted from her was the name of my father. She kept saying she didn't know and everyone was dead now and she had no way of finding out. I wouldn't buy it. I don't care how you find out, I said; just do it. When you do, write me and tell me who he was. Don't call. I never want to hear your voice again. You're dead to me.

At this point, I was screaming and Mary came in and told me to calm down. By now, my mother had gained enough time to begin fabricating a story, which she proceeded to lay on me. She said my real father had "forced himself on her." Not raped, but forced himself on her. Later, Mary said she noted the odd way she'd phrased it. She then went on to say something equally odd. That she didn't want to marry "a guy like that" when she found out she was pregnant (implying she'd had a choice—that he'd asked her or indicated he would). That she met Edgy and he was "everything she'd ever wanted in a man" and she decided she wanted to marry him so told him it was his child in her belly.

She said she lied to Edgy that it was his child so that he would marry her, and that years later, she confessed to him and he forgave her also. Which I knew was an outright lie from what my Aunt Lila had told me just the night before. Ann had told me Aunt Lila might know something as she was a teenager when Edgy married my mother. Lila did indeed know something. She said she remembered it as clear as yesterday. It seems Edgy had broken his leg and the Army Air Corps had sent him home—to South Bend—to recuperate. He'd been home several months when my mother contacted him and told him she was pregnant and that she wanted to get married. Aunt Lila said she was standing in the kitchen when he got the news and his dad was there and Edgy said to him that it wasn't possible that he was the father—the time frame didn't work at all. A month or so later, he went back down to his post in Texas, he and Dorothy got married, and he got shipped off to England with the 8th Air Force and then I was born a few months later.

On the way home, I got a call from her and didn't answer it and she left a message. I wouldn't listen to it, but Mary did and said she'd said she was sorry. That she'd meant to tell me but just didn't. Now, she'd embellished her story to that she was "she was powerless and was forced to have sex" with this guy. And, in the next breath, reiterated that she decided she didn't want to marry this guy—again, indicating she had the option, which doesn't sound like rape or forced sex to me—and said again, that Edgy was "the perfect man in her eyes." Mary observed that she really didn't care about my feelings at all. That this was my real father she was making these claims about and that she didn't care at all how that might make me feel.

On the way home, Mary said she bet she'd upgrade her story to where she'd been raped once she had more time to think about it.

Sure enough, the next day, she phoned again and again I wouldn't answer and she left another message. This time, she upgraded her story just as Mary had predicted and now she'd been "raped." Again, what a mother!

And, Mary revealed to me that Dorothy had called her and talked to her. Mary said that during that conversation it suddenly became clear to her that she was a cold, calculating person and she suddenly realized she was lying. It was how she was talking and what she was saying.

Dorothy called my cell phone every day for about a week and a half, leaving messages that she loved me and that she should have told me but just didn't. Her story became more and more embellished. Eventually, she began to claim that she "could have gotten an abortion or put me up for adoption." Few holes in that...

First, even though there were "back-alley" abortions in 1943, they were relatively rare. I really don't believe an abortion was even a consideration for her. As far as "putting me up for adoption," I wish she had! But, again, I don't believe that was something she even considered at that time since she admitted she was trying to trick Edgy into believing I was his child and marrying her. If he hadn't married her, maybe so, but the fact is, he did, and so I don't believe either abortion or adoption was ever on the table.

Then, since I didn't want to ever hear her voice again, I sent her a typed letter which read:

> Dorothy,
>
> I'm asking again for you to send me the name of my real father. I do not believe that you don't know who it is. And, tell me everything you can about him. For sixty-eight years I've been misled as to who my real father is

and all I want is to know the truth before I die. My son and daughters also need to know. I would prefer you send this information to me in a letter. I really don't wish to talk to you. This is all I ask of you—the name of my real father.

Butch

Her reply was handwritten, and legible, except for a few words.

> The name of the man is Gehl. I don't remember his last name. A girlfriend of mine & I were out with him. He and I walked over a (unreadable word—looks like "swamp"). He (crossed-out word I can't read) advanced toward me & I cried out & he told me to be quiet. Then, with both of us standing he attacked me & did his act. Rape. Rape—I was not caring to be around him then,
>
> But, Butch, I didn't abort you. I didn't destroy you—I had you & I loved you—I still do. These are the facts.
>
> [Unsigned]

Soon after this happened, my brother John emailed me to tell me that Mary and I were no longer invited to his daughter's wedding. Then Ann contacted us to tell us not to come by or call any more. Got a similar message from Kathy. It seems Dorothy had told them about me yelling at her and that I wouldn't buy her stories. Ann was mad at me for letting her know it was her suggestion we get a DNA test. So, I'm estranged from them all and at this point, I'm fine with that. They are all genuine Edgertons and don't fall far from the tree, it appears.

Here's what I think happened, arrived at through various pieces of evidence.

When I was a kid, there was an entire picture album of Dorothy with dozens of photos of her in a revealing bathing suit lying by a swimming pool and in various evening gowns. She ended up destroying all of them. She'd tell stories about her days as a coed at Baylor University. She was a sorority girl and was voted the "sweetheart" of their brother fraternity. I suspect a coed being voted a fraternity sweetheart in those days was arrived at pretty much as it is today in some instances...

I suspect she was kind of a "roundheels." Plenty of evidence to support that. Sorority girl, voted "fraternity sweetheart," pinned to a rich boy. Also, Ann told me something that lends credence to that. She said that Grandma Louise had never raised her, but had sent her off to boarding schools, beginning in her teens. Ostensibly because Grandma was too busy running her business to take care of her at home. Ann brought this up before we became "estranged" as she thought it was why Dorothy created such a dysfunctional family—that she'd never had a model of a typical family to base her own upon. I suspect there was another reason Grandma sent her to boarding school. Many young girls at that time were disposed of by their parents for a different reason. Because they were wild and uncontrollable and sexually active. Everything I'd heard in my youth from Dorothy's stories at the time—which she later became silent on and claimed she "couldn't remember"—points to the fact that she was, indeed, promiscuous. Things make perfect sense if so.

In fact, one of the biggest holes in her story as Mary pointed out, was that she claimed to be this "virtuous" person who was—at first "forced" and then changed to being "raped—was that to be able to convince Edgy that I was his child, she would have had to have had sex with him during the same time period. That means there were at least two instances of her having sex; one with my real father and at least one with Edgy. I'd suspect the "twinkie" was also getting some...In fact, I suspect she was having sex with a number of people.

One of the things I keep thinking about is that in every early version of her "rape" story, she always says, "I decided I didn't want to marry him." (Meaning the guy who supposedly raped her.) Who would even say something like that about a guy who purportedly raped her? I don't think she's thought her story all the way through...

I think what really happened was that she was planning on marrying this guy she was pinned to but really wasn't in love with, and then the war hit and this dashing, handsome airman came along, and she was simply struck by his animal magnetism and decided he was the guy she really wanted. But, that there was a little problem...She was pregnant. Perhaps my real father didn't rape her or force her at all, but found out she was pregnant and didn't want to marry her at all. He may have even laughed at her predicament and in desperation, she went after Edgy, lying to him that he was the father. Maybe even seducing him if she wasn't too far along so she could lie to him a bit later on and trap him. Or, maybe he didn't even know she was pregnant.

Am I bitter? Well, until a better word comes along, that'll do just fine. Yes, I'm very bitter. I'm bitter over the fact that the man I thought was my father wasn't. That he would come into my bedroom when I was little and molest me. That he would bully me in various and diverse ways and without cessation. At the time, I was terrified of him and he took every opportunity to make sure I stayed that way. At the time, I didn't think Dorothy knew about his nocturnal visits, but I'm having second thoughts now. I think she knew and because exposing him would mean she'd lose him, she chose to look the other way. She did on all the other forms of abuse. I don't imagine she would react any differently to that particular form.

She's already shown me that I'm expendable to her. It was clear she'd convinced John, Kathy and Ann that she was the victim here and I was the "mean" guy in confronting her. It didn't take her a nanosecond to throw me under the bus with them. Why would I think she would have stopped Edgy? The answer is I don't think she would have at all. After all, what kind of mother sets siblings against each other?

Do I forgive Dorothy? Not yet I don't. Will I? Perhaps. I've got a philosophy I've tried to live my life by. *Don't let anyone rent space in your head.* At the moment, she's taken up residence and I want her out. It takes time, but I'm working on it.

Besides her lifetime lie to me about my father, there's the matter of who she is today. Not a very good person, despite all of her "God" talk.

Fresh in my memory is the weekend before I found out the results of the DNA test. We couldn't afford it, but Mary and I drove up to South Bend to Dorothy's house to take her out for her birthday. We don't eat at Red Lobster ourselves because we can't afford to, but that's where we took her. It's her favorite restaurant.

While there, I asked her if she'd been following the news about the earthquakes and tsunami in Japan where 20,000 Japanese had died. I didn't know if she had or not since she doesn't listen to the radio and doesn't have a television. As it turned out, she hadn't heard this news. Her response?

"Serves them right," she said. Mary looked at me and raised her eyebrows. I'd been down this road before with her, many times, and so I pimped her a bit. "Whadday mean, 'serves them right?'"

"God's just punishing the Japs for what they did to us in World War II."

She was dead serious. That's my mom...

We learned something later from Ann later that night when we stopped by her house on our way home. Ann asked us if she went to the bathroom. Well, yes, we said; she had. "She's putting her religious pamphlets in the restroom," Ann said. "She does it all the time."

(Note to self: Don't ever return to that Red Lobster...)

Right now, when I think about forgiveness, I remember that last family outing. A perfect and true memory of my mother.

I am grateful for one thing. That I'm not related to Edgy. The thing I most regret is that I'm related to Dorothy.

***

But, she did give me great material!

I'll keep working on that forgiveness thing. It would be easier if she'd tell me who my father is.

If you were reading this expecting some kind of Hollywood, Pollyannish kind of ending where I forgive my mother for lying to me my entire life, for raising me in a hell and never acknowledging it, for throwing me under the bus with my brother and sisters...sorry.

In fact, once I send this off to my publisher, I doubt if I'll ever think of her again. As my son Mike and I learned years ago, it doesn't pay to have anyone rent space in our heads.

And, she won't.

I'll always wish I knew who my real father was. I'll always wish I could just see a picture of him. To see if I looked like him.

But, I can live with that.

I'm free of Dorothy and Edgy. I turned out to be a pretty good person in spite of them and in spite of my own bad choices for which I only have myself to blame. No one needs to tell me I'm guilty of many sins and transgressions. Like my hero, Harry Crews, I plead guilty to all of them. Also, like Harry, I don't want justice even though that's what I deserve. I want *mercy*.

It took long time to learn this, but anything worthwhile takes time. I've got a great wife and a great son and two wonderful daughters and my relationships with each of them is good.

And it feels really, really wonderful.

And that's enough for me.

As it turns out, there's one more development to my story. Last year, when I was seventy-two and still trying to find out who my real father is or was...I found out!

I'd joined Ancestry Dot Com in an effort to discover any

DNA link that would tell me who my real dad was.

I got lucky. I happened upon a wonderful woman who is related to me on my mother's side. I'll just use her first name—Pam—as she may not want to be identified. Pam has done many searches for others before and she graciously volunteered to help me navigate through the maze of Ancestry Dot Com. Eventually, she found a man whom I'll also just use his first name—Jerry—who turned out to be a solid link to who my real father was.

Through Jerry's relentless digging and his and Pam's brilliant detective work, I now know who he was.

And, finding out who he was was one of the happiest days of my life. And, one of the saddest.

His name was Weldon Anthony Geldmacher. And...everybody referred to him by the nickname "Gel."

Happiest, because it turns out he was a truly wonderful man. Learning who he was and what kind of person he was, made my entire existence make sense. First, he was brilliant. He co-invented the computer languages Fortran and Cobalt. He was the head of a NASA space lab in Metairie, Louisiana, just a few blocks from where I used to live at the same time he was there. He had a loving wife, several children and grandchildren. He lived a successful life and left behind a loving family.

It was one of the saddest because I learned he'd passed away in 1996. And, was living within blocks of me in Metairie at the time I'd lived there. I may well have passed him on the street or even sat near him at a restaurant or on the streetcar. I'll never know. I'm just very, very sad that we never got to meet in person.

He was the father I should have had. In talking to his daughter—and, yes, I have a sister!—he was the kindest, gentlest, most caring man in the world. Nothing like the picture my birth mother had created. Not even close to her description of him and not capable of what she accused him of.

I lost all of those years when I could have known him because of a mother who I can only view as an evil, selfish creature, whose fabricated life was built at the expense of the truth she so often proclaimed she was all about. I can't help but wonder how my life would have turned out if she hadn't created this lie.

Can I ever forgive her? I don't think so. I just had a birthday last week and not so much as a phone call or birthday card from her. Which was okay with me.

In fact, life is okay with me now. I know who my real father was and even if it took an entire lifetime to discover the truth, it just makes it all that sweeter.

The truth is indeed, freeing.

Life is good.

ACKNOWLEDGMENTS

A special thank-you to Merle Drown, author of *Lighting the World*, *Plowing Up a Snake* and *The Suburbs of Heaven* and others, who provided invaluable edits. Also, many thanks to Eric Campbell and Chantelle Aimée Osman for their editing. Big thank-yous to Gail Provost and the late Bob Stewart, who each provided invaluable advice during the writing of this memoir.

Les Edgerton is an ex-con, matriculating at Pendleton Reformatory in the sixties for burglary. He was an outlaw for many years and was involved in shootouts, knifings, robberies, high-speed car chases, dealt and used drugs, was a pimp, worked for an escort service, starred in porn movies, was a gambler, served four years in the Navy, and had other misadventures. He's since taken a vow of poverty (became a writer) with twenty-one books in print. Work of his has been nominated for or won the Pushcart Prize, O. Henry Award, Edgar Allan Poe Award, Derringer Award, PEN/Faulkner Award, Jesse Jones Book Award, Spinetingler Magazine Award, among others. He holds a B.A. from I.U. and an MFA in Writing from Vermont College. He lives in Ft. Wayne, Indiana, where he immigrated to some years ago from the U.S. and is currently learning the language and customs there. He writes because he hates…a lot…and hard. Injustice and bullying are what he hates the most.

http://lesedgertononwriting.blogspot.com/

On the following pages are a few
more great titles from the
Down & Out Books publishing family.

For a complete list of books and to
sign up for our newsletter,
go to DownAndOutBooks.com.

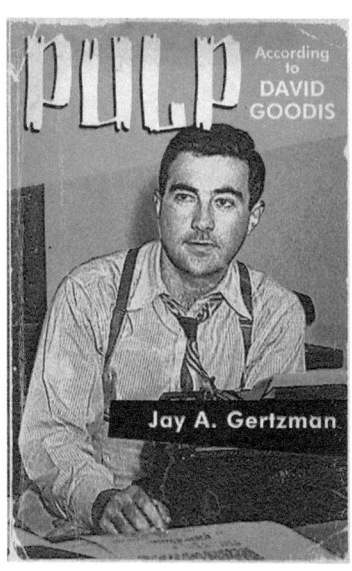

Pulp According to David Goodis
Jay A. Gertzman

Down & Out Books
October 2018
978-1-948235-36-5

David Goodis's novels mix realism, the disorienting, degeneration, and the dreamlike. Their narratives revolve around bottled up resentments, sexual fantasies (including incest), failure to combine trust with desire, and the trap of familial obligation. Goodis shows the way so-called escape literature with titles such as *The Moon in the Gutter* and *Street of No Return* can deal with personal suffering and hard-boiled nobility.

The One That Got Away
Joe Clifford

Down & Out Books
December 2018
978-1-948235-42-6

In the early 2000s, a string of abductions rocked the small upstate town of Reine, New York. Only one girl survived: Alex Salerno. The killer was sent away. Life returned to normal. No more girls would have to die.

Until another one did...

Gravy Train
Tess Makovesky

All Due Respect, an imprint of
Down & Out Books
November 2018
978-1-64396-006-7

When barmaid Sandra wins eighty grand on a betting scam she thinks she's got it made. But she's reckoned without an assortment of losers and criminals, including a mugger, a car thief and even her own step-uncle George.

As they hurtle towards a frantic showdown by the local canal, will Sandra see her ill-gotten gains again? Or will her precious gravy train come shuddering to a halt?

Slaughterhouse Blues
A Love & Bullets Hookup
Nick Kolakowski

Shotgun Honey, an imprint of
Down & Out Books
978-1-946502-40-7

Holed up in Havana, Bill and Fiona know the Mob is coming for them. But they're not prepared for who the Mob sends: a pair of assassins so utterly amoral and demented, their behavior pushes the boundaries of sanity. Seriously, what kind of killers pause in mid-hunt to discuss the finer points of thread count and luxury automobiles? If they want to survive, our fine young criminals can't retreat anymore: they'll need to pull off a massive (and massively weird) heist—and the loot has some very dark history…

www.ingramcontent.com/pod-product-compliance
Lightning Source LLC
Chambersburg PA
CBHW021428080526
44588CB00009B/462